An Introduction to Allocation Rules

Jens Leth Hougaard

An Introduction
to Allocation Rules

 Springer

Prof. Dr. Jens Leth Hougaard
Department of Food and Resource Economics
University of Copenhagen
Rolighedsvej 25
1958 Frederiksberg C
Denmark
jlh@foi.dk

ISBN 978-3-642-01827-5   e-ISBN 978-3-642-01828-2
DOI 10.1007/978-3-642-01828-2
Springer Dordrecht Heidelberg London New York

Library of Congress Control Number: 2009928107

Cover design: WMXDesign GmbH

Printed on acid-free paper

Springer is part of Springer Science+Business Media (www.springer.com)

To Pernille and Ida

Preface

This book contains a systematic analysis of allocation rules related to cost and surplus sharing problems. Broadly speaking, it examines various types of rules for allocating a common monetary value (cost) between individual members of a group (or network) when the characteristics of the problem are somehow objectively given. Without being an advanced text it offers a comprehensive mathematical analysis of a series of well-known allocation rules. The aim is to provide an overview and synthesis of current knowledge concerning cost and surplus sharing methods. The text is accompanied by a description of several practical cases and numerous examples designed to make the theoretical results easily comprehensible for both students and practitioners alike.

The book is based on a series of lectures given at the University of Copenhagen and Copenhagen Business School for graduate students joining the math/econ program.

I am indebted to numerous colleagues, conference participants and students who during the years have shaped my approach and interests through collaboration, comments and questions that were greatly inspiring. In particular, I would like to thank Hans Keiding, Maurice Koster, Tobias Markeprand, Juan D. Moreno-Ternero, Hervé Moulin, Bezalel Peleg, Lars Thorlund-Petersen, Jørgen Tind, Mich Tvede and Lars Peter Østerdal.

Contents

Chapter 1
Motivation and a Few Cases

1.1 Introduction

Consider two persons sharing a cab on the way home from a party. Typically, the one who gets off first either tries to avoid payment or pay some arbitrary amount (corresponding to whatever is left of cash) to the remaining passenger.

Now, analysing this scenario as a cost allocation problem between two agents it turn out that, despite the triviality of the situation, the problem is actually rather complex. In some sense it seems fair that the cost of the first part of the trip (that is, until the first person leaves the cab) should be shared by the two while the remaining cost should be covered solely by the remaining passenger. However, maybe the cab has to drive a longer route because the first passenger who gets off lives somewhat off the natural route going to the remaining passenger's destination and why should he pay for this? The remaining passenger may even reason as follows: the person who gets off first should have paid the first part of the trip by himself if they did not share the cab (his *stand-alone cost*) so in some sense this person must be willing to pay more than half of the amount – in fact, his stand-alone cost can be viewed as the upper limit of his willingness to pay. So clearly the situation is not simple at all although the persons involved of course are forced to find a fast and practical solution.

This book is about analysing such sharing problems in a systematic fashion. Broadly speaking, it examines various types of rules for allocating a common monetary value (cost) between individual members of a group (or network) when the characteristics of the problem are somehow objectively given. The monetary value (cost) must be allocated exactly, that is, with no profit or deficit (typically referred to as a requirement of budget-balance).

An allocation rule is a general allocation principle that is used with respect to an entire class of similarly structured allocation problems for which there is no objective way to attribute value (cost) to specific members.

J.L. Hougaard, *An Introduction to Allocation Rules*,
DOI 10.1007/978-3-642-01828-2_1, © Springer-Verlag Berlin Heidelberg 2009

Members should be thought of as the broadly defined economic notion of "an agent", typically ranging from individuals, firms and products to stated objectives.

Examples are many and a part from two persons sharing a cab they include creditors sharing the liquidation value of a bankrupt firm according to the size of their claims, farmers sharing the costs of irrigation, regions sharing a polluted river, a firm allocating joint costs on to its product profile, shipowner's sharing the scale economies of pooling their vessels, etc.

In order to ensure a systematic investigation the main approach is theoretical and builds on the methodology of modern economic theory contrary to being practically oriented with a direct relation to accounting practices.

As indicated by the cab sharing scenario above, the allocation problems that will be treated in the following are so common and such an integrated part of our daily lives that they have been present at all times and in all types of societies. Therefore, it is not surprising that we can find specific solutions to such problems among ancient writings like for example the almost 2,000 years old Babylonian Talmud, which contains early Jewish law and rabbinic discussions on ethics (we will return to the Talmud in Chap. 2 under rationing problems).

The question is therefore what seems to justify a theoretical treatment of such problems since they are quite fundamental and closely associated with specific practical problems concerning our daily lives. Why not just solve one problem at the time since their solutions seem arbitrary and often depend on rules of thumb or on the bargaining power of those involved? Just like in the case of sharing a cab where the outcome hardly is based on sophisticated considerations concerning the use of a proper and fair allocation rule but rather seems up to the generosity of person who gets off first.

1.2 Motivation

There are several ways to motivate a theoretical investigation of allocation rules, but here we shall focus on the following two: (1) An overall welfare economic argument for the need of fair allocation rules and, (2) A justification based on managerial arguments concerning the need for strategic information and "correct" incentives when designing allocation schemes on a company (organizational) level.

1.2.1 Fairness and Economic Efficiency

From an overall welfare economic point of view the main rationale for a theoretical investigation of allocation rules is related to the notions of

Fairness and *Efficiency*: Typically cooperation among agents is efficient at all levels in the economy due to various forms of synergies. Consequently, the organization of joint activities ought to sustain such cooperation in the long run.

Now, since all forms of cooperation will result in common benefits and burdens for those involved, the agents have to "agree" on some way of sharing these benefits and burdens. Clearly, if the actual allocation is conceived as unfair (or unjust) by some agents in the group these agents have an incentive to block the cooperation and thereby the group as a whole will suffer an efficiency loss.

This line of reasoning goes back a long way. At least implicitly it can be found among ideas concerning the state as an association by Aristotle (see Aristotle, "The Politics"). According to Aristotle, the (city-)state *polis* can be seen as the natural end-result of a process where individuals and groups of individuals gradually give up part of their freedom and self oriented interests in order to enter into various kinds of associations. The atom of *polis* is the household unit (*oikos*), which basically consists of the family. Within each *oikos* individuals will typically have opposing preferences and the power structure need not be the result of common agreement. For instance, in antiquity it was not unusual that slaves were part of the household. However, a good household is one where the "master" is fair and the benefits of cooperation is shared fairly among the members. It is tempting to interpret this as everyone being better off in the *oikos* than standing alone in terms of individual welfare.

Now, households group together in villages, which in the end group together and form *polis*. But even if every individual ought to appear equal in the association of the state through a democratic constitution (although democracy literally refers to rule of the poor majority), *polis* is full of inherent conflicts of interest between individuals as well as various coalitions. Thus, if *polis* is going to be a stable construction then everyone must feel that they are part of a just and fair association receiving fair shares of the benefits and burdens related to the creation of the state.

As such the overall issue of allocation goes far beyond the field of economics and concern also aspects of moral philosophy, law and political science. At a highly abstract level there are at least four widely discussed principles for fair allocation:

1. The proportionality principle by Aristotle:

   This, then, is what the just is – the proportional; the unjust is what violates the proportion . . . . . . For the justice which distributes common possessions is always in accordance with the kind of proportion mentioned above (for in the case also in which the distribution is made from the common funds of a partnership it will be according to the same ratio which the funds put into the business by the partners bear to one another); and the injustice opposed to this kind of justice is that which violates the proportion. (From Aristotle "Nicomachean Ethics" book V, 350 BCE)

Even though proportionality is used as a somewhat vague notion it seems rather straightforward to interpret this as proportionality relative to certain well defined parameters in practical cases, for instance, creditors claims when sharing the liquidation value of a bankrupt firm. As such the proportionality principle seems deeply rooted in western thinking. Perhaps the best way to realize this is by looking at alternative principles from different cultures as, e.g., the "contested garment" principle from the Jewish Talmud: Two women are fighting over some piece of fabric. One woman demand the entire piece while the other only demands half of it. Now, according to the proportionality principle a fair allocation can be implemented as two-thirds (to the one who demands the entire piece) and one-third (for the one demanding half of the piece) because in total 1.5 piece of fabric is demanded. However, according the Jewish rabbi referred to in the Talmud, the fair allocation should be three-fourths (to the one who demands the entire piece) and one-fourth (for the one demanding half of the piece). The rationale is as follows: Only half of the piece is contested and both women have an equal right to this half. Consequently the half is split in two equal pieces (yielding one-fourth of the piece for each). But the other half of the piece is not contested since only one of the women makes a claim for this. Hence this woman gets that half piece for herself, resulting in the allocation (three-fourths, one-fourth). (Note that while the proportionality principle is general the contested garment principle is not straightforward to extend to cases with more than two persons.)

2. The utilitarian principle by Bentham:

> "It is the greatest happiness of the greatest number that is the measure of right and wrong" (From Bentham "A Fragment on Government" 1776).

In terms of practical allocation this can be interpreted as goods should be allocated such that the total sum of the agents utilities from receiving their allocated share is maximized (although taken literally it is somewhat ambiguous what it means to maximize two things – happiness and the number of agents – at the same time). Moreover, the notion of happiness (or utility) is by itself ambiguous because there is no straightforward way of measurement and it is not even sure that it makes sense to compare the happiness of one agent with the happiness of another. Since the time of Bentham this has led to an ongoing discussion concerning the nature of utility and utilitarianism as an appropriate foundation for welfare theory, see, e.g., Roemer (1996).

3. The difference principle by Rawls:

> "Social and economic inequalities must be (a) to the greatest benefit of the least advantaged members of the society, and (b) attached to positions open to all". (From Rawls "A theory of Justice" 1971).

As such any deviation from the equal allocation can only be justified if it is to the advantage of the worst off individual in the group and consequently the difference principle is often considered as a maximin rule (also by

Rawls himself, see, e.g., Rawls 1974). The difference principle is argued to be the result of a rational collective decision made by a group of free and equal individuals. Equality is enforced through a "veil of ignorance", which is imagined to remove any trace of personal abilities, character and history of the individual. In effect, all individuals are hence transferred into the same being, i.e., an agent similar to what Adam Smith called "the impartial spectator" who is able to make decisions taking every agents interests into account. It is somewhat important to mention that Rawls only considered the allocation of so-called "primary social goods", which are goods that everybody are supposed to be able to evaluate in the same way like freedom, property rights, economic institutions, etc. But even though the difference principle is not directly meant to be implemented allocating normal commodities the contrast to utilitarian thinking is crystal clear and it is therefore not surprising that modern utilitarians like John Harsanyi has been among the greatest opponents to Rawls theory of justice (see, e.g., Harsanyi 1975).

4. The envy-free principle by Tinbergen: This notion was originally proposed in Tinbergen (1953) and related to particular allocations in Foley (1967). The idea is that allocations ought to be envy-free in the following sense: An allocation (of bundles of goods) is said to be envy-free if no agent prefers another agents' allocation to his own. This does not require interpersonal utility comparisons since each agent uses his own utility function to evaluate the other agents allocations. Note, that the word "envy", as used in common language, often refers to externalities in consumption (the utility of my own car decreases when my neighbour buys a new and more expensive model), but this is not the case here. Moreover, note that if only a single homogeneous good is being allocated (as in the case of cost sharing or bankruptcy problems where creditors share the liquidation value of a bankrupt firm) then an allocation is envy-free if and only if the total amount is equally divided.

Now, with the exception of the proportionality principle, which can be used more broadly, these general ideas of how to allocate fairly all require that agents have well defined preferences and that these are known to the analyst. The typical case, however, rather seems to be that an agents' preferences are unknown to the analyst (planner) as well as the other agents, and perhaps even to the agent himself. Moreover, in many of the situations considered in the following chapters it is even meaningless to talk about preferences in the first place: For example in case joint costs are allocated onto specific products or costs are allocated onto objects such as various purposes, objectives, etc. (see, e.g., the TVA case in Sect. 1.3.1). Clearly, it only makes sense to equip agents with a preference structure if the agents can be supposed to act strategically according to such preferences and in many cost (or surplus) sharing situations this will not be the case.

General principles, including those mentioned above, are therefore rarely operational (although intellectually appealing) and for most sharing problems as considered in the following, economists are typically forced to use more straightforward normative fairness requirements such as for example:

(a) Equal Treatment of Equals: If the relevant parameters describing the allocation problem are equal for two different agents then the resulting allocation should be the same. Clearly, if we violate this simple fairness requirement we deliberately discriminate between agents. If for some reason such a discrimination is justified we would typically be able to reformulate the allocation problem such that Equal Treatment of Equals can be met. For instance, if two municipalities engage in a joint project to the mutual benefit of their citizens and have to share the resulting common costs one reason to discriminate could be that one of the municipalities has more citizens than the other. In this sense the municipalities are not equal and treating them equally in terms of cost allocation might be seen as unfair. However, the cost model can easily be reformulated in terms of costs per citizen and in this case equal treatment seems a fair requirement.

(b) The Stand-alone Principle: The idea is here that no agent should be worse off joining a group than standing alone because standing alone is always a feasible option. Thus, when sharing the benefits and burdens of cooperation, agents allocations are naturally bounded by the result of their stand alone option. Say, for example, that a group of agents are sharing a common cost. Then, according to the stand-alone principle, no agent in the group can be forced to pay more than their cost of standing alone.

(c) Consistency: Consider the following extension of the contested garment principle from two to three agents, also from the Talmud:

> If a man who was married to three wives dies and the marriage contract of one was 100 zuz, of the other 200 zuz, and of the third 300 zuz and the estate is worth only 100 zuz the sum is divided equally. If the estate is worth 200 zuz the claimant of 100 zuz receives 50 zuz and the claimants of respectively 200 and 300 zuz get 75 zuz. If the estate is worth 300 zuz the claimant of 100 zuz receives 50 zuz and the claimant of the 200 zuz receives 100 zuz while the claimant of 300 zuz receives 150 zuz. Similarly, if three persons contributed to a joint fund and they made a loss or a profit they share in the same manner.

One way to verify that such an extension is in fact in line with the original allocation principle is to test whether the resulting allocation is Consistent in the sense that, if we take the (3-agent) problem and break it into (2-agent) subproblems using the same allocation principle as before with respect to the related reduced allocation problems then the resulting allocation should be the same for every agent in the subgroup as in the original problem. Note that this hinges on the formulation of the reduced allocation problem, which will be discussed in detail in the following chapters (particularly in Chap. 3).

These and several other requirements related to fairness in a broader sense will be used to characterize various allocation rules in the following chapters in order to present a detailed picture of how such rules perform in different allocation scenarios.

1.2.2 Management Decisions and Incentives

At organizational level, allocation problems typically concern either cost sharing issues or the allocation of rewards for those making an effort and taking risks within the organization.

Cost sharing issues crop up when costs need to be allocated over accounting periods or when common or overhead costs need to be attributed to different divisions (or other cost drivers) according to internal accounting schemes. Moreover, if production is characterized by economics of scope, there may also be a need for letting the resulting joint costs be attributed to specific products of the firms' output profile.

In the accounting literature it has been much debated whether or not it is rational for firms to allocate common and joint costs, see, e.g., Dopuch (1981) for a brief overview. Thomas (1969, 1974) represent one extreme in this debate arguing strongly against cost allocation. Yet, more recently there seems to be consensus among accounting experts that such cost allocations are useful to the company both in relation to the preparation of external financial reports and as important information with respect to company strategy and managerial decision making. For example, allocating costs can become a vital part of ongoing efforts to improve various operations and processes in the firm and may also help to identify the relative profitability of products.

Fact remains that the firms actually do make such allocations and therefore must find them useful with respect to various aspects of managing the company. But of course it is important how these common or joint costs actually are allocated as illustrated by the following example (mimicking a case discussed in Shank and Govindarajan 1993).

Example 1.1. A firm produces three products A, B and C involving a large element of overhead costs from activities concerning R&D, packing and receiving. In total there is an overhead of 1,000,000 euros where 500,000 is associated with the R&D department, 200,000 is associated with the packing department and 300,000 is associated with the receiving department.

Product A is produced in 10,000 units in one run and all units are shipped off in one shipment. Product B is produced in 15,000 units in three runs and these are shipped off in five shipments. Finally, product C is produced in 5,000 units in 10 runs and shipped off in 20 shipments.

Looking at production unit costs (in euros), i.e., the costs which can be directly attributed to the products, we have the following:

Unit costs	A	B	C
Materials	20	30	10
Set-up	0.02	0.04	0.44
Labour	10	6.67	5
Machine	17.5	23.33	35
In total	47.52	60.04	50.44

Recently the firm has experienced considerable price competition on product B from foreign competitors. Since the production facilities are modern and fully competitive the management consequently assumes that their foreign competitors are dumping their prices in order to establish themselves at the European market.

For product C the firm has experienced that they can raise their price without decreasing sales and, even more surprising, without introducing competition from other firms. The management assume that the product must satisfy some consumer need, which they were not aware off before.

Calculating the average unit cost for each product, the firm has traditionally allocated the overhead costs proportional to labour time. Since producing product A requires 0.5 h working time per unit, producing product B requires 0.33 h working time per unit and producing product C requires 0.25 h working time per unit the resulting weights are (0.44, 0.44, 0.12). Thus, the total overhead of 1,000,000 euro is shared as (44.44, 29.63, 22.22) euro per unit for products A,B and C respectively. Using this approach, the firms' total unit costs, profit margin, target price, actual sales price and realized profit margin is given in the table below:

Product	A	B	C
Total unit costs	91.96	89.67	72.26
Expected profit margin (%)	35	35	35
Target price	141.47	137.95	111.16
Sales price	141.47	125.50	123.70
Actual profit margin (%)	35	28.5	41.6

Allocating the common costs according to labour time hence provides an incentive to focus more on product C and move away from the main product B.

Now, instead of allocating costs according to labour time the management could also try to use an approach where common costs are related more directly to the activities by which they are caused (the main idea behind the notion of Activity Based Costing).

Looking at the receiving department (with its share of overhead at 300,000), costs ought to be related to the amount of work connected with receiving the products yielding the following weights on products (0.04, 0.15, 0.81).

Looking the packing department (with its overhead share of 200,000) they need to pack once for every shipment. This yields a set of weights on products (0.04, 0.19, 0.77).

Finally, looking at the R&D department (with its overhead share of 500,000) a subjective estimate of future activities concerning product A, B and C respectively results in the following weights (0.25, 0.35, 0.4).

Consequently, the picture of production costs changes radically allocating costs in accordance with activities as seen in table below:

Products	A	B	C
Total unit costs	62.02	77.23	169.84
Sales price	141.47	125.50	123.70
Actual profit margin (%)	56	38.5	−37.3

The first thing to notice is that product C originally was attributed too little unit cost. So from being the product with highest profit margin it actually now turns out to have a negative profit margin. Thus, it is not strange that other companies are not competing even though prices are raised slightly on this product. Likewise it is now clear why the foreign competitors are able to lower their price on product B since the profit margin here is higher than what the firm expected. Since the foreign competitors are not producing product C they got a better picture of B's true unit costs.   △

Even though it is important to allocate costs "correctly" as demonstrated by the example above, allocating costs in line with the activities from which they are derived (as in the spirit of Activity Based Costing, see, e.g., Kaplan and Bruns 1987) is not necessarily a goal by itself. There may be several other aspects, which needs to be taken into account when designing suitable allocation schemes.

The overall guideline for "good" design should be related to the firms' profitability in the long run as stated in Shubik (1962):

> A goal of good management should be to design a reward system for those who take risks in making decisions in such a manner that the rewards to the individual correlate positively with the worth of the decision to the organization. In many organizations cost accounting supplies much of the information used for control at several levels.

Here, of course, the word *individual* may be interpreted as any kind of agent able to make decisions influencing the profitability of the firm. It therefore becomes important to think in terms of incentives when designing specific allocation schemes. For instance, if the cost share of a given division increases as a result of this divisions efforts to save costs for the company as a whole, then the incentives of the cost sharing rule seem very unfortunate indeed.

Imagine, for example, a consultancy firm with a headquarter in one country and a branch in another country. Assume that both the manager of the headquarter and the branch manager are rewarded relative to the profit of their division. Now, when the branch demand staff services from the headquarter they pay a fixed internal rate per unit of working time. Say, this rate does not take staff overhead costs into account. Then the manager of the branch has no incentive for local expansion in terms of more personnel since by requiring staff services from the headquarter he avoids paying staff overhead costs and only pay for the effective working time. Clearly, this may be costly, not only for the manager of the headquarter, but also for the company as a whole since in the long run it may be cheaper to hire local staff and a large branch (in terms of staff) may represent a competitive advantage in the local market, etc.

Another example could concern firms' bonus schemes for employees. Typically, the firm wants to promote individual initiative and effort by rewarding this with some kind of bonus. However, the problem of designing such bonus schemes turns out to be rather delicate since it is important not to give too much incentive to overly individualistic behavior because employees often have to cooperate and assist each other in teams for the greater benefit of the firm. The problem is therefore to balance multiple and often opposing incentives when composing the right system of rewards.

In the present text this problem is approached by investigating various forms of monotonicity requirements with respect to cost shares: a somewhat primitive way to ensure right incentives is to require that cost shares should decrease (increase) as the result of decreasing (increasing) stand-alone costs of any agent or coalition of agents. Different types of such monotonicity conditions will be studied in detail in the chapters to follow (in particular in Chap. 3).

1.3 Some Practical Cases

To briefly introduce the types of problems considered in the following, this section will look at a few practical cases where the methodology has proved useful in solving actual economic problems arising from joint activities.

1.3.1 The Tennessee Valley Project

The Tennessee Valley Authority (TVA) case is a classic in the cost sharing literature, see, e.g., Young (1994) or Ransmeier (1942) for the original description.

During the 1930s the US government undertook a large redevelopment project for the Tennessee River Basin by building a series of multi-purpose reservoirs in order to (1) control flooding, (2) provide electric power and (3) improve navigation and recreation.

A dam can be build in different heights to accommodate different purposes. The costs estimated by TVA in relation to the fulfillment of various combinations of the purposes $\{1, 2, 3\}$ above, are given by:

Purpose	Cost (1,000 dollars)
{1}	163,520
{2}	140,826
{3}	250,096
{1,2}	301,607
{1,3}	378,821
{2,3}	367,370
{1,2,3}	412,584

It can be noticed that it is cheaper to fulfill several purposes at the same time rather than separately (i.e., costs are subadditive in purposes). For example, the costs of reaching a satisfactory level of flooding control and electric power simultaneously is \$301,607,000 while taken separately these costs amount to (\$163,520,000 + \$140,826, 000 =) \$304,346,000.

Now, referring to the Stand-alone principle the purposes 1,2 and 3 should not be charged more than at most \$163,520,000, \$140,826,000 and \$250,096,000 respectively since these costs represent the stand-alone options. Equivalently, none of the purposes ought to subsidize other purposes and hence should be charged at least their marginal cost, i.e., the cost of fulfilling all purposes minus the costs of fulfilling all purposes except for the one in question (that is, the additional costs of fulfilling this extra purpose). In the specific case of TVA marginal costs are given by:

Purpose	Marginal cost (1,000 dollars)
{1}	(412,584 − 367,370 =) 45,214
{2}	(412,584 − 378,821 =) 33,763
{3}	(412,584 − 301,607 =) 110,977
In total	189,954

Thus, according to the Stand-alone principle there is a natural range within which the cost shares must be located, i.e., between the marginal cost and the stand-alone cost. Knowing that the cost shares must result in budget-balance this gives rise to a set of possible allocations all respecting the Stand-alone principle. This set is also known as the *core* of the associated cost sharing problem. Further details will be postponed to Chap. 3.

In the TVA case, engineers and economists used the following approach called the Alternate-Cost-Avoided method (the ACA-method) building on marginal costs: The idea is that each purpose must pay its marginal cost. In this case total value collected will not be enough to cover all costs so the cost gap is then shared among the purposes in proportion to their marginal costs. Using the specific costs data of the TVA project the final allocation can be found as:

Purpose	Stand-alone − marginal cost		Cost share	
{1}	$(163{,}520 - 45{,}214 =)$	$118{,}306$	$45{,}214 + \frac{118{,}306}{364{,}488}(412{,}584 - 189{,}954) =$	$117{,}475.5$
{2}	$(140{,}826 - 33{,}763 =)$	$107{,}063$	$33{,}763 + \frac{107{,}063}{364{,}488}(412{,}584 - 189{,}954) =$	$99{,}152.3$
{3}	$(250{,}096 - 110{,}977 =)$	$139{,}119$	$110{,}977 + \frac{139{,}119}{364{,}488}(412{,}584 - 189{,}954) =$	$195{,}951.2$
In total		$364{,}488$		$412{,}584$

In this particular case it can be checked that the allocation of costs respects the Stand-alone principle (i.e., lies between the marginal cost and the stand-alone cost) but this is not a general property of the ACA-method as it can be demonstrated for more than four purposes (agents).

1.3.2 Farmer's Irrigation Costs

Another practical example is provided by the study of Aadland and Kolpin (1998), which considers cost sharing issues related to 25 irrigation ditches located in Montana, USA. The ditches are used to provide water to the farmers fields as well as livestock during the summer months. With the headgate located at the stream, water can be transferred from a stream in the main irrigation ditch passing through all the farmers fields. This ditch is therefore "common" among the farmers. From the main ditch individual farmers may then have their private ditches running through their own land. The farmers are responsible for their private ditches while the maintenance costs of the main ditch are subject to cost sharing among all the farmers. On average these costs are between $1,000 and $2,000 but may go as low as $0 and as high as $20,000 in certain years.

Two types of allocation rules seems to present themselves rather naturally in such a setting:

1. Farmers are located sequentially along the ditch borders therefore it seems that the maintenance costs of the segment of the ditch located at the headgate should be shared by all n farmers downstream while the costs of the following segment should only be shared among the $n - 1$ farmers downstream from there and so forth until cost associated with the last segment of the ditch is covered solely by the farmer furthest away from

the headgate. Now, costs associated with each segment can be established on per ranch (person), per water share or per acre basis as three natural choices.

2. Another way to consider the problem would simply be to share maintenance costs equally among all farmers along the ditch or in proportion to each ranchs' water share or size (measured in acres).

Rather interestingly, it turned out that these two types were exactly the types of rules used by the farmers located along the 25 main ditches. In fact, in 14 cases the farmers used the serial approach (7 on a per head basis, 3 on per water share basis, and 4 on per acre basis) while in 10 cases the farmers used variations of the average cost rule (1 on per head basis, 3 on per water share basis, and 6 on per acre basis). In 1 case, a combination of average and marginal cost sharing was used.

As an empirical fact, these solutions to the problem of sharing the maintenance costs have remained constant since the early 1900s. As such, both the serial and the average cost rule appear to give rise to allocations that must be conceived as being fair by all the agents involved. Such allocations therefore represent stable solutions in practice, at least in the context of sharing irrigation costs.

1.3.3 Regulating Public Monopolies

Over the last couple of decades Europe has witnessed a series of reforms from the European Commission aiming at introducing competition on markets that was previously covered by large public monopolies. For example, the market for postal services.

In general, this process moves slow and as recognized by ARCEP (Autorité de Regulation des Communication électroniques et des Postes – the French Regulatory Authority) France in one the countries where the market for postal services is most static (see `http://www.arcep.fr`).

The main idea behind market opening is to facilitate business adaptation and create economic effectiveness among the service providers; especially the Universal Service Provider (USO) like *La Poste* in France.

In the French case, reports had documented several imperfections such as (1) vague obligations on the incumbent whose cost and financing were all but transparent, (2) that tariffs were unrelated to costs leading to potential waste of resources, (3) that there was no incentives to economic efficiency, resulting in outdated industrial processes and (4) generally poor quality performances (see `http://www.arcep.fr`).

The role of ARCEP in this connection is to set up principles of cost accounting, which ensures separation and transparency of *La Poste*'s costs, as well as making annual audit of the compliance with these principles.

The cost standard used for the regulatory accounts aims at a full allocation of costs over products (in fact, less than 5% of *La Poste*'s total cost remain unattributed to products). The specific accounting method used is Activity Based Costing build around cost drivers related to all parts of the production process, that is; Counter (8% of costs), Collecting (7% of costs), Sorting (17% of costs), Transportation (8% of cost) and Delivery (51% of costs).

Consider, for instance, the most important cost driver in terms of percentage of costs, i.e., "Delivery". Here, a large part of the costs are fixed common costs mainly resulting from the carriers route time.

Allocating the common costs to products ARCEP requires that the applied allocation rule should not lead to cross-subsidies and should not assign cost shares to each product larger than the products stand-alone cost. Thus, ARCEP follows the Stand-alone principle as stated in Sect. 1.2.1.

Stand-alone costs are here interpreted as the costs incurred by the operator if each product (class of mail) were delivered separately: First class mail is delivered 6 days a week and therefore has a stand-alone cost of six times the cost of a daily delivery; Second class mail is delivered 3 days a week and therefore has a stand-alone cost of three times the cost of a daily delivery while; Third class mail is delivered once a week and therefore has a stand-alone cost of one daily delivery. Note that since the carrier can bring out 2' and 3' class mail as well when delivering 1' class mail then the stand-alone costs of any coalition of products become the maximum of the stand-alone costs of any single element of the coalition.

Moreover, as first class mail is quite expensive all fixed costs can be attributed to this product without violating the Stand-alone upper bound given by the stand-alone cost. Therefore, many rules will satisfy the Stand-alone principle and there is a need for additional requirements (in fact, any allocation resulting in shares between 50% and 100% for 1' class mail, 0% and 50% for 2' class and 0% and 17% for 3' class mail will satisfy the Stand-alone principle).

What ARCEP do is to estimate the economics of scope as the sum of the stand-alone costs minus the costs of delivering all three classes of mail. The cost shares related to each product is then computed as the stand-alone cost minus a share of the economies of scope proportional to the stand-alone cost. In effect, this implies that the total common cost is shared in proportion to the products stand-alone cost (a rule also known as the Moriarity rule in the accounting literature). It is easy to see that such a rule satisfies the Stand-alone principle.

Consequently, the resulting cost shares are given by (60%, 30%, 10%) for 1', 2' and 3' class mail respectively. This can be compared to *La Poste*'s own allocation of (80%, 15%, 5%) respectively. Hence, ARCEP requires that *La Poste* decrease its deficit on the first class mail while reducing the high profit margin on regular (second class) mail.

1.4 Limits of Scope

Although this book covers a wide range of allocation problems there are of course limitations of scope. To briefly mention just a few of the most important ones, the text does NOT consider:

- Allocation rules when goods are indivisible. For example, a couple sharing their kids in case of divorce. Clearly, in such cases we often need specific procedures like the kids being time-shared between the parents, a lottery or a priority list giving for example the mother priority. See, e.g., Young (1994) for a treatment of methods for allocating indivisible goods.
- Allocation of bundles of goods (even fully divisible) when preferences play a central role. For example, in case two heirs have to share three houses and 25 paintings. In case the goods are divisible we could, of course, assume that the problems can be solved separately (allocating one good at a time) but if agents have preferences over bundles of goods their conception of fairness may not correspond to the result of such separate procedures. See, e.g., Thomson (2008) for a recent survey of models dealing with fair allocation of bundles of goods.
- Allocation by voting. For example, voting over the partition of a piece of land. In such cases we cross the border of Social Choice theory, see, e.g., Moulin (1988) for a treatment of such procedures.
- Issues of bargaining related to allocation problems. For example, when countries bargain over emission cuts, fishing quota, mining rights, etc. The topic of bargaining is, e.g., covered in Osborne and Rubinstein (1990).
- "Cake-cutting" procedures. For example, the well-known process where two persons share a cake by letting one cut and the other choose first. See again Young (1994) or Brams and Taylor (1996).

Ending every chapter in the following, there will be a section named "Comments" pointing out some of the limitations as well as possible extensions of the issues analysed in the text.

References

Aadland D, Kolpin V (1998) Shared irrigation costs: an empirical and axiomatic analysis. Math Soc Sci 35:203–218.

Brams SJ, Taylor AD (1996) Fair division: from cake-cutting to dispute resolution. Cambridge University Press, Cambridge.

Dopuch N (1981) Some perspectives on cost allocation. In: Moriarity S (ed) Joint cost allocations. University of Oklahoma Press, Norman, OK.

Foley D (1967) Resource allocation and the public sector. Yale Econ Essays 7:45–98.

Harsanyi JC (1975) Nonlinear social welfare functions. Theory Decis 6:311–332.

Kaplan RS, Bruns W (1987) Accounting and management: a field study perspective. Harvard Business School Press, Boston, MA.

Moulin H (1988) Axioms of cooperative decision making. Cambridge University Press, Cambridge.

Osborne MJ, Rubinstein A (1990) Bargaining and markets. Academic, New York.

Ransmeier JS (1942) The Tennessee Valley Authority: a case study in the economics of multiple purpose stream planning. Vanderbilt University Press, Nashville, TN.

Rawls J (1974) Some reasons for the maximin criterion. Am Econ Rev 64:141–146.

Roemer JE (1996) Theories of distributive justice. Harvard University Press, Cambridge, MA.

Shank JK, Govindarajan V (1993) Strategic cost management. Free Press, New York.

Shubik M (1962), Incentives, decentralized control, the assignment of joint costs and internal pricing. Manage Sci 8:325–343.

Thomas AL (1969) The allocation problem in financial accounting. Stud Account Res 3. American Accounting Association.

Thomas AL (1974) The allocation problem: part two. Stud Account Res 9. American Accounting Association.

Thomson W (2008) Fair allocation rules. In: Arrow K, Sen A, Suzumura K (eds) Handbook of social choice and welfare. North-Holland, Amsterdam, (forthcoming).

Tinbergen J (1953) Redeljke Inkomensverdeling. N.V. DeGulden, Haarlem.

Young HP (1994) Equity. Princeton University Press, Princeton, NJ.

Chapter 2
Simple Sharing Problems

2.1 Introduction

Simple sharing problems involve a group of n agents indexed $j = 1, \ldots, n$. The term "agent" is here broadly interpreted as persons, firms, departments, branches, products, etc. Each agent is characterized by some one-dimensional factor $q_j \in \mathbf{R}_+$ such as demand, claim, "stand-alone" cost, effort, surplus, etc.

Basically, we shall distinguish between two types of situations: First, the case where agents characteristics $q = (q_1, \ldots, q_n)$ do not influence the costs (or value) which has to be shared, say, a fixed amount E. Second, the case where agents characteristics $q = (q_1, \ldots, q_n)$ influence the amount of costs (or value). To be more specific, we shall assume that q is a demand vector and that costs are given either as the costs associated with the total demand $Q = q_1 + \ldots + q_n$ or as the costs associated with the highest demand $\mathcal{Q} = \max_i \{q_i\}$. In both cases ($z = Q$ and $z = \mathcal{Q}$), cost will be modeled by a (one-dimensional) non-decreasing cost function $C : \mathbf{R}_+ \to \mathbf{R}_+$ (or the value modeled by a one-dimensional non-decreasing value function $V : \mathbf{R}_+ \to \mathbf{R}_+$).

The following scenarios may be imagined:

1. A firm goes bankrupt with liquidation value E. "Agents" may here represent n creditors each characterized by their verifiable claim q_j. Hence, characteristics are *not* linked directly to the size of E. If total debt exceeds the liquidation value the problem may equivalently be construed as that of sharing a loss between n claimants. Such bankruptcy problems are treated in Sect. 2.2, but given a fixed-price setting, any excess demand will cause similar problems to arise and they will generally be referred to as rationing problems.

2. A community of n households wants to be connected to a local power plant and has to share the costs of establishing a connection. Assume, for example, that the households are located as a chain and are characterized by their individual distance q_j from the plant. Clearly, characteristics influence the total costs in this situation: as it is economically rational to link all households to the same line rather than establishing separate

J.L. Hougaard, *An Introduction to Allocation Rules*,
DOI 10.1007/978-3-642-01828-2_2, © Springer-Verlag Berlin Heidelberg 2009

connections for each household the related cost function will be of the (decomposable) form $C(\max_j\{q_j\})$, since total costs will be determined by the most distant household. Alternatively, a decomposable cost function $C(\max_j\{q_j\})$ may be used to represent situations where a group of agents demand some amount of an excludable good which is consumed without rivalry (an excludable public good) and the total cost therefore is determined by the agent with the highest demand. Cost sharing rules that apply in such cases will be examined in Sect. 2.3.

3. Consider a firm where the total costs of operating a service department has to be allocated among n user departments or n products. That is, "agents" may refer to departments or products of the firm. If user departments are considered the characteristics q_j may simply be the amount of service demanded by department j which is, of course, directly related to the size of the total costs. If service can be considered as a homogeneous good, costs are generated by a (homogeneous) cost function $C(Q)$, where $Q = q_1 + \ldots + q_n$ is total demand. That is, $C(Q)$ has to be shared among the n user departments. Cost sharing rules that apply in such cases will be examined in Sect. 2.3. On the other hand, if index j refers to products the characteristics q_j may be the amount of working hours used to produce one unit of product j which is *not* linked directly to the size of total costs. Thus, total cost is regarded as a fixed amount E that has to be shared between products according to the characteristics vector q. Cost sharing rules that apply in such cases relate to the rules examined in Sect. 2.2.

In the present chapter we shall consider such simple sharing problems in further detail. First, the case of a fixed amount E will be analysed focusing on rationing problems and secondly, the case of a (one-dimensional) cost function will be analysed focussing on cost sharing problems.

2.2 Rationing Problems

As in (1) above, we consider a rationing problem where a given quantity $E \geq 0$ of money (or some other fully divisible good) has to be shared among n agents with non-negative *demands* $q = (q_1, \ldots, q_n)$ measured in monetary units (or in units of some other fully divisible good). Assume that E and q are measured in the same units and that individual demands are objectively determined, for example, as verifiable claims in case of bankruptcy problems. Moreover, assume for convenience that demands are increasingly ordered, i.e., $q_1 \leq \ldots \leq q_n$. Since the problem is that of rationing the *total demand* $Q = q_1 + \ldots + q_n$ exceeds the available quantity E, i.e., $Q \geq E \geq 0$.

Given a *rationing problem* (q, E), a *rationing rule* φ specifies a unique *vector of shares* $x = (x_1, \ldots, x_n) = \varphi(q, E)$ where $x_1 + \ldots + x_n = E$, and $0 \leq x_i \leq q_i$ for all $i = 1, \ldots, n$. The latter condition ensures that no agent gets a negative share or a share larger than what is demanded. Although this appears to be a rather natural constraint it actually excludes several well known sharing rules. Consider, for example the equal split rule where $x_j = E/n$ for all $j = 1, \ldots, n$ and the extreme priority rule where $x_j = E$ and $x_i = 0$ for $i \neq j$.

In the following we shall focus on rationing rules that are *order-preserving* in the sense that an agent with a higher demand than another agent will get both a larger share x_i and loss $q_i - x_i$, i.e.,

$$x_1 \leq \ldots \leq x_n, \quad \text{and} \quad q_1 - x_1 \leq \ldots \leq q_n - x_n, \tag{2.1}$$

and *resource monotonic* in the sense that the share of all agents, as given by $\varphi_i(q, E)$, $i = 1, \ldots, n$, is non-decreasing in the quantity $E \in [0, Q]$. Denote by $\mathcal{R}$ the set of order-preserving and resource monotonic rationing rules. Order-preservation and resource monotonicity seem to be natural requirements with respect to rationing rules. Note, for example, that the extreme priority rule violates order-preservation.

As mentioned in (1) above, any rationing problem (q, E) may be construed either directly as the problem of sharing the quantity E given demands q or indirectly as the problem of sharing the loss $Q - E$ given demands q. Thus, for any rationing rule φ there is a *dual rule* φ^* defined by

$$\varphi^*(q, E) = q - \varphi(q, Q - E). \tag{2.2}$$

If $\varphi = \varphi^*$ the rationing rule φ is called *self-dual*, i.e., the resulting shares will be the same whether focus is on gains or losses.

Remark 2.1. Although we use the set-up of rationing it can be noted that in terms of *cost sharing* the model may be given the following interpretation: $C \geq 0$ is a fixed common cost that has to be shared among n agents (communities, institutions, departments, etc.) with non-negative *stand-alone costs* $c = (c_1, \ldots, c_n)$. Cooperation is assumed to be profitable in the sense that $0 \leq C \leq \sum_j c_j$. Given a cost sharing problem (c, C) a cost sharing rule φ specifies a unique vector of cost shares $x = \varphi(c, C)$ where $\sum_j x_j = C$ and $0 \leq x_j \leq c_j$. Here the latter condition appears to be a natural condition of individual rationality since no agent wants to participate in a joint project if it results in a share of the common cost that exceeds the agents stand-alone cost. $\triangle$

2.2.1 Four Rationing Rules

Some rationing rules are particularly interesting due to their historical origins as well as wide applicability. Four such rules will now be further analysed. As we proceed we shall see that there are several good reasons for focussing on these particular rules.

Basically the rules relate to two different notions of fairness: *proportionality* and different versions of *equality*. The first three rules are:

- *The Proportional Rule φ^P* defined by shares

$$x_i^P = \frac{q_i}{Q} E, \quad i = 1, \ldots, n. \tag{2.3}$$

That is, E is shared in proportion to individual demands.
- *The Constrained Equal Gains Rule φ^{CEG}* defined by shares

$$x_i^{CEG} = \min\{q_i, \alpha\}, \quad i = 1, \ldots, n, \tag{2.4}$$

where α is chosen such that the shares add up to E. That is, E is shared equally provided that no one gets more than their individual demand.
- *The Constrained Equal Loss Rule φ^{CEL}* defined by shares

$$x_i^{CEL} = \max\{0, q_i - \beta\}, \quad i = 1, \ldots, n, \tag{2.5}$$

where β is chosen such that the shares add up to E. That is, the loss $Q - E$ is shared equally provided that no one gets a negative share.

Notice, that $\varphi^{CEG}(q, E) = q - \varphi^{CEL}(q, Q - E)$ implying that φ^{CEG} is the dual rule of φ^{CEL}, i.e., $\varphi^{CEG*} = \varphi^{CEL}$. Moreover, since $\varphi^P(q, E) = q - \varphi^P(q, Q - E)$, the proportional rule is self-dual, i.e., $\varphi^{P*} = \varphi^P$.

The fourth rule (the Talmud rule) is an amalgam of the constrained equality rules. One line of motivation is the following: First, the rule ought to be self-dual as gains and losses should be treated equally. Second, half of the demand can be construed as a psychological watershed for the individual agents. If $x < q/2$ the agent focuses on whatever he can get ("Less than half is like nothing"). If $x > q/2$ the agent is close to fulfilment of the demand and therefore focuses on his loss ("More than half is like the whole"). Fairness now prescribes that all agents ought to be on the same side of the watershed and should be treated equally. Hence, if $0 \leq E \leq Q/2$, focus is on gains, which shall be shared equally provided that no one get shares larger than half their demand and if $Q/2 < E \leq Q$, focus is on losses, which shall be shared equally provided that no one get shares smaller than half their demand – that is:

- *The Talmud Rule φ^T* is defined by shares

$$x_i^T(q, E) = \begin{cases} \min\{q_i/2, \alpha\} & \text{if } 0 \leq E \leq Q/2 \\ \max\{q_i/2, q_i - \beta\} & \text{if } Q/2 < E \leq Q \end{cases} \tag{2.6}$$

where α and β are chosen such that the shares add up to E.

Now, using the definition of the Constrained Equal Gains rule and the Constrained Equal Loss rule we get that the Talmud rule φ^T is defined as

$$\varphi^T(q, E) = \begin{cases} \varphi^{CEG}(q/2, E) & \text{if } 0 \le E \le Q/2 \\ q/2 + \varphi^{CEL}(q/2, E - Q/2) & \text{if } Q/2 < E \le Q, \end{cases}$$

and consequently $\varphi^T(q, E) = q - \varphi^T(q, Q - E)$, i.e., the Talmud rule is self-dual. Further, note that $\varphi^T(q, Q/2) = \varphi^P(q, Q/2)$.

In the particular case of nested 2-agent problems, i.e., problems where $q_2 = E$ (q_2 being the highest demand) we can interpret the Talmud rule as the contested garment principle mentioned in Chap. 1. For example, if $E = 1$ and $q = (1/2, 1)$ we get that $Q/2 < E \le Q$ and thereby $\varphi^T(q, E) = q/2 + \varphi^{CEL}(1/4, 1/2, 1/4) = (1/4, 3/4)$, i.e., the contested half is shared equally and the uncontested half goes to the agent demanding the entire piece of garment. As such the above definition of the Talmud rule (introduced in Aumann and Maschler 1985) is a modern extension of the contested garment principle to a larger domain of rationing problems.

Now, considering all four rules we are able to state the following well-known proposition.

Proposition 2.1. *The four rationing rules, $\varphi^P, \varphi^{CEG}, \varphi^{CEL}$ and φ^T are order-preserving and resource monotonic.*

Example 2.1. Consider a bankruptcy problem where $n = 5$ agents with claims $q = (50, 100, 150, 200, 250)$ must share an estate of value $E = 510$. First, we get that proportional sharing results in the vector of shares

$$x^P = (34, 68, 102, 136, 170),$$

whereas constrained equal sharing of gains results in

$$x^{CEG} = (50, 100, 120, 120, 120).$$

Since the total claim is $Q = 750$, the total loss is $750 - 510 = 240$. Thus, constrained equal sharing of the loss results in

$$x^{CEL} = (2, 52, 102, 152, 202),$$

and as $E = 510 \ge 375 = Q/2$ we have that $\varphi^T(q, E) = q/2 + \varphi^{CEL}(q/2, E - Q/2)$ and thereby that shares according to the Talmud rule are given by

$$x^T = (25, 50, 95, 145, 195).$$

Now, let the worth of the estate decrease such that $E = 240 \le Q/2 = 375$. In this case we get:

$$x^P = (16, 32, 48, 64, 80),$$
$$x^{CEG} = (48, 48, 48, 48, 48),$$
$$x^{CEL} = (0, 0, 30, 80, 130),$$
$$x^T = (25, 50, 55, 55, 55).$$

By resource monotonicity all agents receive weakly smaller shares than before and clearly order-preservation is confirmed in both cases. Moreover, the results also confirm that φ^P and φ^T are self-dual rules whereas φ^{CEL} is the dual rule of φ^{CEG}. △

Note that among the four rules, only φ^P is well defined if E and q are measured in different units. In fact, in such a case the conditions $0 \leq x_i \leq q_i$ for all i become irrelevant.

Remark 2.2. Young (1987) defines an interesting family of rationing rules comprising the four rules above: Let $f(q, \lambda)$ be a real-valued function of scalar variables q and λ where $q > 0$ and $\lambda \in [a, b] \subseteq [-\infty, +\infty]$. For each x, f is assumed to be weakly monotone increasing and continuous in λ with $f(q, a) = 0$ and $f(q, b) = q$. Given f the rationing rule φ is said to be *parametric with representation* f if, for every problem (q, E) that $x = \varphi(q, E)$ if and only if there exists a λ such that for all i,

$$x_i = f(q_i, \lambda) \quad \text{and} \quad x_1 + \ldots + x_n = E.$$

Note that by the assumptions on f, $0 \leq x_i \leq q_i$. Moreover, note that the proportional rule is given by $x_i = \lambda q_i$, $0 \leq \lambda \leq 1$, where λ is chosen so that $x_1 + \ldots + x_n = E$; the constrained equal gains rule is given by $x_i = \min\{q_i, \lambda\}$, $0 \leq \lambda \leq \infty$, where λ is chosen so that $x_1 + \ldots + x_n = E$; and the constrained equal loss rule is given by $x_i = \max\{0, q_i - 1/\lambda\}$, $0 \leq \lambda \leq \infty$, where λ is chosen so that $x_1 + \ldots + x_n = E$. △

2.2.2 Inequality Comparisons

From Example 2.1 we see that the rules differ considerably with respect to how they distribute the shares. It seems that φ^{CEG} results in distributions with the smallest spread whereas φ^{CEL} results in shares with the largest spread. In case $E \leq Q/2$, shares given by the proportional rule seems more spread than shares given by the Talmud rule whereas when $E \geq Q/2$ it appears to be the other way around. In fact, such characterizations in terms of economic inequality comparisons can be formalized using the notion of *Lorenz-domination* (also known as majorization).

Formally, for two increasingly ordered n-vectors of real numbers $x = (x_1, \ldots, x_n)$ and $y = (y_1, \ldots, y_n)$, x is said to *Lorenz-dominate* y if:

(1) $x_1 + \ldots + x_k \geq y_1 + \ldots + y_k$, $k = 1, \ldots, n - 1$.
(2) $x_1 + \ldots + x_n = y_1 + \ldots + y_n$.

The partial ordering defined by (1) and (2) is written $x \succ_{LD} y$ and referred to as *Lorenz-domination* (note that $x \succ_{LD} x$ for any x), see, e.g., Marshall and Olkin (1979). In terms of economics, $x \succ_{LD} y$ can be interpreted as x being more equally distributed than y (less spread out).

Now, it turns out that the constrained equal gains rule φ^{CEG} is the unique Lorenz-maximising rationing rule and dually, that the constraint equal loss rule φ^{CEL} is the unique Lorenz-minimising rationing rule. In other words, there is no other rule that results in more equally distributed shares than the constraint equal gains rule and no other rule that results in less equally distributed shares than the constraint equal loss rule.

Theorem 2.1. *For any rationing rule φ and rationing problem (q, E),*

$$\varphi^{CEG}(q, E) \succ_{LD} \varphi(q, E) \succ_{LD} \varphi^{CEL}(q, E).$$

Proof. We argue that φ^{CEG} is the unique maximizer of $\succ_{LD}$ on the set of rationing methods and hence by Proposition 2.1, φ^{CEL} is the unique minimizer. Indeed, consider some arbitrary value E. By definition there exists a λ and a $k \in \{1, \ldots, n\}$ such that $x^{CEG} = (q_1, \ldots, q_k, \lambda, \ldots, \lambda)$. Now, suppose that there is some n-vector y originating from some allocation method where $x^{CEG} \not\succ_{LD} y$. Then there exists some smallest j where $k < j < n$ such that

$$\sum_{i=1}^{k} q_i + (j - k)\lambda = \sum_{i=1}^{j} x_i^{CEG} < \sum_{i=1}^{j} y_i,$$

and hence $y_j > \lambda$. However, since y is increasingly ordered it follows that $\sum_{i=1}^{n} x_i^{CEG} < \sum_{i=1}^{n} y_i = E$, a contradiction. □

In fact, for fixed E all four rules mentioned above are completely ordered by Lorenz-domination since for $0 \le E \le Q/2$ (or $Q/2 < E \le Q$), then $x^T \succ_{LD} x^P$ (or $x^P \succ_{LD} x^T$).

Theorem 2.1 indicates that it is possible to construct a finite sequence of inequality monotone transfers from x^{CEL} to x^{CEG}, in the sense that the vector of shares gradually becomes more and more equal in terms of Lorenz-domination. It is well-known that such transfers are possible (see Marshall and Olkin 1979) but generally there is no upper bound on the number of transfers required. However, as shown in Hougaard and Thorlund-Petersen (2002) one needs at most $n - 1$ transfers in order to go from x^{CEL} to x^{CEG} (and thereby x^T) as we shall demonstrate below. To be more specific, consider a sequence of transfers from "rich" to "poor" agents; first the agent with the largest share transfers value to all agents with smaller shares until his share is at the same level as that of the agent with the second largest share. Then the two agents with the highest value of shares transfer value to all agents with smaller shares until their share is at the same level as that of the agent with the third largest share, etc., i.e., $x^{CEL} + T\theta = x^{CEG}$ where T is an $n \times (n - 1)$ matrix

$$T = \begin{bmatrix} 1 & 1 & \cdots & n-1 \\ 1 & 1 & \cdots & -1 \\ \vdots & \vdots & \ddots & \vdots \\ 1 & \frac{-(n-2)}{2} & \cdots & -1 \\ -(n-1) & \frac{-(n-2)}{2} & \cdots & -1 \end{bmatrix},$$

and $\theta = (\theta_1, \ldots, \theta_{n-1})$.

Example 2.1 (continued). Let $n = 5$, $E = 510$ and $q = (50, 100, 150, 200, 250)$ as in Example 2.1 where $x^{CEL} = (2, 52, 102, 152, 202)$. Therefore the first sequence of transfers is given by $202 - 4\theta_1 = 152 + \theta_1 \Leftrightarrow \theta_1 = 10$ – that is, we go from x^{CEL} to the shares $x^1 = (12, 62, 112, 162, 162) \succ_{LD} x^{CEL}$. Next, we get that $162 - 1.5\theta_2 = 112 + \theta_2 \Leftrightarrow \theta_2 = 20$ – that is, we go from x^1 to the vector $x^2 = (32, 82, 132, 132, 132) \succ_{LD} x^1$. Finally, we solve $132 - 0.66\theta_3 = 82 + \theta_3 \Leftrightarrow \theta_3 = 30$ – that is, we go from x^2 to the vector $x^3 = (50, 100, 120, 120, 120) = x^{CEG} \succ_{LD} x^2$, in less than $4 (= n - 1)$ inequality monotone steps. $\triangle$

By Theorem 2.1 we can obtain a characterization of the Talmud rule in terms of Lorenz-domination.

Theorem 2.2 (Hougaard and Thorlund-Petersen 2002). *A rationing rule $\hat{\varphi}(q, E) \in \mathcal{R}$ is self-dual and satisfies $\hat{\varphi}(q, E) \succ_{LD} \varphi(q, E)$, for $0 \leq E \leq Q/2$, for any self-dual rule $\varphi \in \mathcal{R}$ if and only if $\hat{\varphi}(q, E) = \varphi^T(q, E)$.*

Proof. First, consider a self-dual rule $\hat{\varphi}(q, E) \in \mathcal{R}$. By self-duality

$$\hat{\varphi}(q, Q/2) = q/2,$$

and by resource monotonicity $\hat{\varphi}(q, E) \leq q/2$ for $0 \leq E \leq Q/2$. Now, by Theorem 2.1 the unique maximizer of $\succ_{LD}$ on the set of order-preserving rationing rules is φ^{CEG}. Hence, $\hat{\varphi}(q, E) = \varphi^{CEG}(q/2, E) = \varphi^T(q, E)$ for $0 \leq E \leq Q/2$.

Second, it follows from Theorem 2.1 and the definition of the Talmud rule that φ^T is self-dual and satisfies $\hat{\varphi}(q, E) \succ_{LD} \varphi(q, E)$, for $0 \leq E \leq Q/2$. $\square$

In other words, the Talmud rule is the unique order-preserving, resource monotonic and self-dual rule that maximises equality in gains or losses depending on E being smaller than or larger than half the total demand.

Now, it is natural to examine which rationing rules that preserve Lorenz-dominance in gains and in losses. We say that a rationing rule φ satisfies:

- *Lorenz-monotonicity in Gains:* If, for any E and $q' \succ_{LD} q$ that $\varphi(q', E) \succ_{LD} \varphi(q, E)$.
- *Lorenz-monotonicity in Losses:* If, for any E and $q' \succ_{LD} q$ that $q' - \varphi(q', E) \succ_{LD} q - \varphi(q, E)$.

Lorenz-monotonicity in gains ensures that shares become more equally distributed when the demands become more equally distributed. Likewise, Lorenz-monotonicity in losses ensures that the losses become more equally distributed when the demands become more equally distributed. The two concepts are related in the following way:

Proposition 2.2. *A rationing rule φ satisfies Lorenz-monotonicity in Gains if and only if its dual rule φ^* satisfies Lorenz-monotonicity in Losses.*

Proof. Let $q' \succ_{LD} q$. Recalling the definition of duality $\varphi^*(q, E) = q - \varphi(q, Q - E)$, and Lorenz-dominance, we get that for all $k = 1, \ldots, n$,

$$\sum_{i=1}^{k}(q_i' - [q_i' - \varphi_i(q', Q - E)]) \geq \sum_{i=1}^{k}(q_i - [q_i - \varphi_i(q, Q - E)]) \quad \Leftrightarrow$$

$$\sum_{i=1}^{k}\varphi_i(q', Q - E) \geq \sum_{i=1}^{k}\varphi_i(q, Q - E).$$

Hence, clearly if φ satisfies Lorenz-monotonicity in Gains then φ^* satisfies Lorenz-monotonicity in Losses and vice versa. $\square$

We are now able to show that:

Proposition 2.3. *The Proportional rule φ^P satisfies Lorenz-monotonicity in both gains and losses. The Constrained Equal Gains rule φ^{CEG} satisfies Lorenz-monotonicity in gains whereas the Constrained Equal Loss rule φ^{CEL} satisfies Lorenz-monotonicity in losses.*

Proof. It is straight forward to see that φ^P satisfies both Lorenz-monotonicity in Gains and in Losses. By Proposition 2.2, it suffices to show that φ^{CEG} satisfies Lorenz-monotonicity in Gains. Hence, consider φ^{CEG}, and let $q' \succ_{LD} q$. Let q and q' be strictly increasing in demands. Let E be fixed, then clearly, $\sum_{i=1}^{h} q_i' \geq \sum_{i=1}^{h} q_i$, for $h = 1, \ldots, n - 1$, implies that $\lambda(q') \leq \lambda(q)$ where $\lambda(q)$ is defined by $E = \sum_i \min\{q_i, \lambda(q)\}$.

Moreover, since $\succ_{LD}$ is a cone-ordering (see, e.g., Marshall and Olkin 1979) we may always replace q with a convex combination $\alpha q + (1 - \alpha)q'$ such that we obtain solutions $\varphi^{CEG}(q', E) = (q_1', \ldots, q_h', \lambda(q'), \ldots, \lambda(q'))$ and $\varphi^{CEG}(q, E) = (q_1, \ldots, q_{h+1}, \lambda(q), \ldots, \lambda(q))$.

Thus, assume w.l.o.g. that Lorenz-monotonicity in Gains is violated for index $h + 1$:

$$\sum_{i=1}^{h} q_i' + \lambda(q') < \sum_{i=1}^{h} q_i + q_{h+1} \quad \Leftrightarrow \quad \sum_{i=1}^{h} q_i' - \sum_{i=1}^{h} q_i < q_{h+1} - \lambda(q').$$

Now, since

$$E = \sum_{i=1}^{h} q_i' + (n - h)\lambda(q') = \sum_{i=1}^{h} q_i + q_{h+1} + (n - h - 1)\lambda(q)$$

we get that

$$\sum_{i=1}^{h} q_i' - \sum_{i=1}^{h} q_i = q_{h+1} + (n - h - 1)\lambda(q) - (n - h)\lambda(q') < q_{h+1} - \lambda(q')$$

$$\Leftrightarrow \lambda(q) < \lambda(q'),$$

a contradiction.   □

It is easy to verify that the constraint equal gains rule φ^{CEG} violates Lorenz-monotonicity in Losses and that the constraint equal loss rule φ^{CEL} violates Lorenz-monotonicity in Gains. Moreover, it follows that the Talmud rule φ^{T} violates Lorenz-monotonicity in Losses when $0 \leq E \leq Q/2$ and Lorenz-monotonicity in Gains when $Q/2 < E \leq Q$. Consequently, the Talmud rule satisfies neither forms of Lorenz-monotonicity in general.

The concepts of Lorenz-monotonicity in Gains and Losses will further analyzed in Sect. 2.2.4 in relation to the issue of manipulation of resulting cost shares.

2.2.3 Axiomatic Characterizations

As a first natural property it seems that the way E is allocated should only be determined by agents demands q and not by who the agents are. In other words, if two agents have identical demands then a rationing rule ought to assign identical shares to these agents, i.e., agents with equal demand should be treated equally. If equal treatment is violated we either deliberately discriminate between agents or we should be able to reformulate the problem such that equal treatment can be met.

Formally, a rationing rule φ satisfies:

- *Equal Treatment of Equals*: If $x = \varphi(q, E)$ and $q_i = q_j$ implies that $x_i = x_j$.

  Note that order-preservation implies Equal Treatment of Equals.

  Second, it seems that when a group of agents agree to use some allocation principle then this agreement should not be influenced by the number of agents in the group. In other words, rationing rules ought to be consistent in the sense that reallocating the sum of shares for any subgroup of agents between the agents themselves should leave their original shares unchanged. If some agents were to gain by applying a given rationing rule on a subset of the original population (including themselves) they would have strong incentives to block any enlargement of such a group. Thereby consistency is closely related to the concept of population monotonicity stating that the addition of new agents should affect all original agents in the same direction (either all gain or all loose). In fact, as demonstrated in Chun, resource monotonicity together with consistency implies population monotonicity.

Formally, a rationing rule φ is:

- *Consistent:* If for all q, that $x = \varphi(q, E)$ implies that for all $i \in S$, $x_i = \varphi_i((q_i)_{i \in S}, \sum_{i \in S} x_i)$ for all $S \subseteq \{1, \ldots, n\}$ $(S \neq \emptyset)$.

Note that a rationing rule φ is consistent if and only if its dual rule φ^* is consistent.

All four rules defined in Sect. 2.2.1 satisfy equal treatment of equals and consistency. In fact, together with continuity of φ, Equal Treatment of Equals and Consistency characterize the entire family of parametric sharing methods defined in Remark 2.2.

Theorem 2.3 (Young 1987). *A continuous rationing rule φ satisfies Equal Treatment of Equals and Consistency if and only if it is representable by a continuous parametric function.*

Proof (sketch). Let φ be continuous and satisfy equal treatment of equals and consistency. First it is shown (by contradiction) that then φ is also resource monotonic. Suppose that φ is *not* resource monotonic. Then by consistency there exists a pair $(x_1, x_2) = \varphi((q_1, q_2), x_1 + x_2)$ and $(\bar{x}_1, \bar{x}_2) = \varphi((q_1, q_2), \bar{x}_1 + \bar{x}_2)$, where $x_1 + x_2 < \bar{x}_1 + \bar{x}_2$ and $x_1 < \bar{x}_1$, $x_2 > \bar{x}_2$. Now, choose n such that $x_1 + n x_2 > \bar{x}_1 + n \bar{x}_2$, and consider demand profile $\tilde{q} = (q_1, q_2, \ldots, q_2)$ with n times q_2. For all $E \in [0, q_1 + n q_2]$ define

$$\alpha(E) = \varphi_1(\tilde{q}, E) + \varphi_2(\tilde{q}, E),$$

which is continuous in E and $\alpha(0) = 0$. Moreover, by equal treatment $\alpha(q_1 + n q_2) = q_1 + q_2$. By continuity there exists $\bar{E} \in [0, q_1 + n q_2]$ such that $\alpha(\bar{E}) = \bar{x}_1 + \bar{x}_2$. By consistency and equal treatment $\varphi(\tilde{q}, \bar{E}) = (\bar{x}_1, \bar{x}_2, \ldots, \bar{x}_2)$ with $\bar{E} = \bar{x}_1 + n \bar{x}_2$. Since $\alpha(0) = 0 \leq x_1 + x_2 \leq \alpha(\bar{E})$ continuity of α implies that there exists E such that $0 \leq E \leq \bar{E}$ and $\alpha(E) = x_1 + x_2$. By consistency and equal treatment $\varphi(\tilde{q}, E) = (x_1, x_2, \ldots, x_2)$ with $E = x_1 + n x_2$. By choice of n, $E = x_1 + n x_2 > \bar{x}_1 + n \bar{x}_2 = \bar{E}$ contradicting $E \leq \bar{E}$. We conclude that φ satisfies resource monotonicity.

Now suppose that φ satisfies *strict* resource monotonicity (only weak monotonicity was shown above) then the proof could continue like this: For every 2-agent problem and every $\lambda \in [0, 1]$ define $x_1 = f(q_1, \lambda)$ if and only if $(x_1, \lambda) = \varphi((q_1, 1), x_1 + \lambda)$. Continuity and strict monotonicity of φ imply that f is continuous and strictly monotonic in λ. Now, fix $x^* = \varphi(q, E^*)$ where $E^* \in [0, \sum_i q_i]$. Consider $(x, \lambda) = \varphi((q, 1), E)$ as E varies from 0 to $\sum_i q_i + 1$. By continuity there exists a $\bar{E}$ that renders agent 1 and 2 a total of $x_1^* + x_2^*$ which by consistency must be allocated as (x_1^*, x_2^*). Likewise there exists a $\bar{E}$ that renders agent 1 and 3 a total of $x_1^* + x_3^*$ that must be allocated as (x_1^*, x_3^*). As φ is strictly monotonic and agent 1 receives the same amount in both cases $\bar{E} = \tilde{E}$. Continuing this argument there is a value E^* and a value λ^* such that $\varphi((q, 1), E^*) = (x^*, \lambda^*)$. Consistency implies that $(x_i^*, \lambda^*) = \varphi((q_i, 1), x_i^* + \lambda^*)$ so by definition of f, $x_i^* = f(x_i, \lambda^*)$ for all i.

Conversely, suppose that $f(q_i, \lambda) = x_i$ for some λ and all i. The above argument implies that there exists a λ' such that $f(q_i, \lambda') = x_i'$ where $\sum_i x_i' = \sum_i x_i$. Since f is monotonic in λ, $x_i' = x_i$ for all i and f is a parametric representation of φ.

For the exact proof the reader is referred to Young (1987) which also demonstrates that, in fact, only pairwise consistency is needed in the sense that consistency only has to be satisfied for all coalitions of cardinality two.

□

Example 2.1 (continued). Consider the 5-agent problem of Example 2.1 with $q = (50, 100, 150, 200, 250)$ and $E = 510$. Here the Talmud rule resulted in the following allocation $x^T = (25, 50, 95, 145, 195)$. It is easily checked that for any subset of the agents, application of the Talmud rule results in consistency. For example the sub-problem of $q = (50, 100)$ and $E = 75$. Here $Q/2 = 75 = E$ and E is shared in proportion to demands or, interpreted along the lines of the contested garment principle; 50 is contested and hence shared equally whereas the residual of 25 is only claimed by agent 2 – hence the allocation becomes (25, 25+25). For any 2-agent rationing problem (q_1, q_2, E) the "contested-garment" principle can be defined (as in Aumann and Maschler 1985) by the shares,

$$x_1 = \frac{1}{2} \min\{q_1, E\} + \frac{1}{2} \max\{0, E - q_2\},$$

$$x_2 = \frac{1}{2} \min\{q_2, E\} + \frac{1}{2} \max\{0, E - q_1\}.$$

As shown in Aumann and Maschler the Talmud rule is the unique consistent extension of the contested garment principle.   △

In order to single out the rules of Sect. 2.2.1 further axioms are needed. For example an axiom of scale invariance to rule out any influence of the units of measurement. In case of a bankruptcy problem, for instance, it seems very natural to demand that the underlying allocation principle should be independent of whether we measure in Danish kroner, dollars or euro's.

Formally, a rationing rule φ satisfies:

- *Scale Invariance:* If for all (q, E) and $\lambda \in \mathbf{R}_+$,

$$\varphi(\lambda q, \lambda E) = \lambda \varphi(q, E).$$

Note that all four rules of Sect. 2.2.1 satisfy Scale Invariance.

The next two axioms may be interpreted along the following line: Assume that a group of agents have agreed to use a given rationing rule φ for some rationing problem (q, E'). However, it turns out that the true value of the amount that has to be shared is $E < E'$. Then using φ we should be able to take the solution $\varphi(q, E')$ and solve the problem $(\varphi(q, E'), E)$ instead of (q, E) – called Upper Composition. On the other hand, if $E > E'$ we should be able to determine $\varphi(q, E)$ by adding the solution of the problem $(q - \varphi(q, E'), E - E')$ to the solution $\varphi(q, E')$ – called Lower Composition.

Formally, a rationing rule φ satisfies:

- *Upper Composition:* If, for all (q, E) and $E' > E$,

$$\varphi(q, E) = \varphi(\varphi(q, E'), E).$$

- *Lower Composition:* If, for all (q, E) and $E' < E$,

$$\varphi(q, E) = \varphi(q, E') + \varphi(q - \varphi(q, E'), E - E').$$

Note that a rationing rule φ satisfies Lower Composition if and only if its dual rule φ^* satisfies Upper Composition. Moreover, note that the Proportional rule, the Constrained Equal Gains rule and the Constrained Equal Loss rule satisfy Upper and Lower Composition whereas the Talmud rule satisfies neither Upper nor Lower Composition.

Theorem 2.4 (Moulin 2000). *A rationing rule φ satisfies Equal Treatment of Equals, Consistency, Scale Invariance, Upper and Lower Composition if and only if $\varphi \in \{\varphi^P, \varphi^{CEG}, \varphi^{CEL}\}$.*

It has already been noted that all three rules $\{\varphi^P, \varphi^{CEG}, \varphi^{CEL}\}$ satisfy the axioms. To prove the converse, the reader is referred to the elaborate proof in Moulin (2000) or the alternative proof in Thomson (2006).

Finally, there are several alternative characterizations of the individual rules; a recent survey can be found in Thomson (2003).

2.2.4 Manipulation

When rationing rules are implemented in practice they may give rise to strategic reactions among the agents involved. In other words, agents (or some coalition of agents) may be able to manipulate the result of given rules to their own advantage. Since each individual demand q_i is considered to be verifiable, manipulation is not possible via strategic choice of q_i. Hence, manipulation can appear either by merging or splitting individual demands or by reallocating demand between groups of agents. Notice that by merging or splitting demands the dimension of the rationing problem is changed whereas by reallocation the dimension remains fixed.

Rationing rules are non-manipulable by merging and splitting if it is disadvantageous for any coalition of agents to merge and split their demands in the sense that the resulting aggregated or disaggregated shares are smaller than the shares resulting from the original problem of dimension n. That is, rationing rules φ must satisfy:

- *No Advantageous Merging:* Let E be given and let q' be determined by aggregating the demand of a subset M of the n agents, i.e., $q' = (\sum_{j \in M} q_j, (q_i)_{i \in N \setminus M})$ for $M \subset N = \{1, \ldots, n\}$. For all such coalitions $M \subset N$, $\varphi_M(q', E) \le \sum_{j \in M} \varphi_j(q, E)$.

and

- *No Advantageous Splitting:* Let E be given and let $\hat{q}$ be determined by splitting the demand of agent j into s separate demands $(q_{ji})_{i=1}^s$ where $\sum_{i=1}^s q_{ji} = q_j$ – that is, $\hat{q} = ((q_{ji})_{i=1}^s, (q_l)_{l \in N \setminus j})$. For all such disaggregated demands $(q_{ji})_{i=1}^s$, $\sum_{i=1}^s \varphi_{ji}(\hat{q}, E) \le \varphi_j(q, E)$.

Theorem 2.5 (Banker 1981; De Frutos 1999). *The proportional rule φ^P is the only rationing rule that satisfies both No Advantageous Merging and No Advantageous Splitting.*

Proof. It is easy to verify that φ^P satisfies No Advantageous Merging and Splitting. To prove the converse, let for given q, $q' = (q_i, Q - q_i)$ be the demand of an arbitrary agent i and coalition $M = N \setminus i$. First, note that No Advantageous Merging and Splitting implies that $\sum_{j \in M} \varphi_j(q, E) = \varphi_M(q', E)$ and by budget balance $\varphi_i(q, E) = \varphi_i(q', E)$. Secondly, note that No Advantageous Merging and Splitting implies Equal Treatment of Equals: Suppose not. Then there exists a pair (i, j) with $q_i = q_j = \bar{q}$ where $\varphi_i(q, E) > \varphi_j(q, E)$. By the above argument $\varphi_i((\bar{q}, Q - \bar{q}), E) > \varphi_j((\bar{q}, Q - \bar{q}), E)$. Now, let agent i split the demand into two equal amounts. Then

$$\varphi_i((\bar{q}, Q - \bar{q}), E) = \varphi_{i'}((\bar{q}/2, \bar{q}/2, Q - \bar{q}), E) + \varphi_{i''}((\bar{q}/2, \bar{q}/2, Q - \bar{q}), E)$$
$$> \varphi_j((\bar{q}, Q - \bar{q}), E),$$

that is, agent j has incentive to split his demand – a contradiction.

To finish the proof, note that for any vector $q \in \mathbf{R}^n$, every element can be written as

$$q_i = \frac{a_i}{p} Q,$$

where $p > 0$ and a_i is non-negative number such that $a_1 + \ldots + a_n = p$. Now, let p agents each demand Q/p. Then Equal Treatment of Equals and budget balance implies that each of the p agents receives the share E/p. Moreover, as $\varphi_i = \varphi_{i'} + \varphi_{i''}$ when $q_i = q_{i'} + q_{i''}$ then by sequential merging or splitting of the demand of the p agents, coalitions i receive

$$\varphi_i = a_i \frac{E}{p} = \frac{q_i}{Q} E, \quad i = 1, \ldots, n.$$

$\square$

Example 2.2 (continued). Consider the 5-agent problem of Example 2.1 with $q = (50, 100, 150, 200, 250)$ and $E = 510$. Here the Talmud rule resulted in the following allocation $\varphi^T(q, E) = (25, 50, 95, 145, 195)$. Now, assume that agent 1 and 2 merge such that $q_{\{1,2\}} = q_1 + q_2 = 150$. In this case the rationing problem is reduced to a 4-agent problem where $\varphi^T((150, 150, 200, 250), 510) = (90, 90, 140, 190)$ making it advantageous for agent 1 and 2 to merge as $\varphi_1^T(q, E) + \varphi_2^T(q, E) = 75 < 90$. Now, consider the problem (q, E) where $E = 240$. Here, $\varphi^T(q, E) = (25, 50, 55, 55, 55)$. Let agent 3 split his demand $q_3 = 150$ into $q_{3'} = 50$ and $q_{3''} = 100$. In this case the problem is extended to a 6-agent problem $((50, 50, 100, 100, 200, 250), 240)$ where $\varphi^T((50, 50, 100, 100, 200, 250), 240) = (25, 25, 47.5, 47.5, 47.5, 47.5)$ making it advantageous for agent 3 to split his demand as $\varphi_3^T(q, E) = 55 < 25 + 47.5 = 72.5$. Hence, the Talmud rule can be manipulated both by merging and by splitting. This is a consequence of the fact that the Constrained Equal Gains rule can be manipulated by splitting and that the Constrained Equal Loss rule can be manipulated by merging as clarified in Remark 2.3.   △

Remark 2.3. Recall the definition of parametric rules with representation f in Remark 2.2. The representation f is said to be superadditive (subadditive) in demand if for all λ and all $q_i, q_i' \in \mathbf{R}_+$ that $f(q_i + q_i', \lambda) \geq (\leq) f(q_i, \lambda) + f(q_i', \lambda)$. In Ju (2003), it is shown that a parametric rule satisfies No Advantageous Merging if and only if the representation f is subadditive in q_i for each value of λ. Likewise a parametric rule satisfies No Advantageous Splitting if and only if the representation f is superadditive in q_i for each value of λ. As the Constrained Equal Gains rule has parametric representation $f(q_i, \lambda) = \min\{q_i, \lambda\}$, f is concave and hence subadditive in q_i, i.e., satisfies non-manipulability by merging. As the Constrained Equal Loss rule has parametric representation $f(q_i, \lambda) = \max\{0, q_i - 1/\lambda\}$, f is convex and hence superadditive in q_i, i.e., satisfies non-manipulability by splitting. Finally, note that the proportional rule has representation $f(q_i, \lambda) = \lambda q_i$ that is linear and hence both sub- and superadditive in q_i, i.e., satisfies non-manipulability by both merging and splitting. (On the other hand note, that there may be functions f that are sub- resp. superadditive and *not* concave resp. convex.)   △

As mentioned above, there is another way to manipulate the resulting shares and that is by reallocating demand between groups of agents keeping the number of agents fixed. If such manipulation shall be prevented no coalition of agents shall be able to increase their total share by reshuffling their individual demands – that is, the rationing rule φ must satisfy:

- *No Advantageous Reallocation:* Let E be given. Then for every $S \subset N$ and $q, q' \in \mathbf{R}_+^n$, if $\sum_{i \in S} q_i = \sum_{i \in S} q_i'$ and $q_j = q_j'$ for all $j \in N \setminus S$, it implies that $\sum_{i \in S} \varphi_i(q, E) = \sum_{i \in S} \varphi_i(q', E)$.

Note that No Advantageous Reallocation is only meaningful in case $|N| \geq 3$. It is clear that the proportional rule φ^P satisfies No Advantageous Reallocation. The other three rules, however, do not as demonstrated by the following example.

Example 2.1 (continued). Consider the 5-agent problem of Example 2.1 with $q = (50, 100, 150, 200, 250)$ and $E = 510$. Here the Constrained Equal Gains rule resulted in the following allocation

$$\varphi^{CEG}(q, E) = (50, 100, 120, 120, 120).$$

Assume now that agent 1, 2 and 3 form a coalition where they average their demands such that the reallocated demand vector becomes

$$q' = (100, 100, 100, 200, 250).$$

Using the Constrained Equal Gains rule we get that

$$\varphi^{CEG}(q', E) = (100, 100, 100, 105, 105)$$

making it advantageous for agent 1, 2 and 3 to perform their averaging operation. Likewise, consider the Constrained Equal Loss rule that resulted in the following allocation $\varphi^{CEL}(q, L) = (2, 52, 102, 152, 202)$. If the agents 1,2 and 3 now spread their demands such that the new demand vector becomes $q'' = (0, 100, 200, 200, 250)$, we get that $\varphi^{CEL}(q'', E) = (0, 40, 140, 140, 190)$ making it advantageous for agents 1,2 and 3 to reallocate as in q''. Since both the Constrained Equal Gains rule and the Constrained Equal Loss rule fail to satisfy No Advantageous Reallocation so does the Talmud rule by definition. $\triangle$

By Proposition 2.3 and order-preservation, it can generally be concluded that the Constraint Equal Gains rule can be manipulated by all lower coalitions $\{1, \ldots, k\}$ averaging their demands (as $q' \succ_{LD} q$ implies that $\sum_{i=1}^{k} \varphi_i^{CEG}(q', E) \geq \sum_{i=1}^{k} \varphi_i^{CEG}(q, E)$ for $k = 1, \ldots n - 1$.). Likewise, it can generally be concluded that the Constraint Equal Loss rule can be manipulated by all lower coalitions $\{1, \ldots, k\}$ spreading their demands (as $q' \succ_{LD} q$ implies that $\sum_{i=1}^{k}(q'_i - \varphi_i^{CEG}(q', E)) \geq \sum_{i=1}^{k}(q_i - \varphi_i^{CEG}(q, E))$ for $k = 1, \ldots n - 1$.).

In fact, it can be shown that the Proportional rule is the only rule that cannot be manipulated by reallocation of demands.

Theorem 2.6 (Moulin 1987). *The proportional rule φ^P is the only rationing rule that satisfies No Advantageous Reallocation.*

Proof (sketch). From Chun (1988) it is known that all rules that satisfy No Advantageous Reallocation (plus a weak continuity and symmetry property) are of the following form for all $i = 1, \ldots, n$,

$$\varphi_i(q, E) = \frac{q_i}{Q} E - \frac{1}{Q}[nq_i - Q]g(Q, E),$$

where $g : \mathbf{R}^2 \to \mathbf{R}$ is a continuous function. Since we require that a rationing rule must satisfy $0 \leq \varphi_i(q, E) \leq q_i$ for all i, we have that $g(Q, E) = 0$. □

Note that the equal split rule (which is not a rationing rule as defined above since E/n may exceed q_i for some i), satisfies No Advantageous Reallocation ($g(Q, E) = E/n$) but is manipulable by splitting. Likewise, equal split of the loss (that may result in negative shares) satisfies No Advantageous Reallocation ($g(Q, E) = (E - Q)/n$) but is manipulable by merging.

To demonstrate that there is a close connection between No-advantageous Reallocation and Lorenz-monotonicity, as defined in Sect. 2.2.2, we reconsider the Lorenz-monotonicity properties in light of manipulation. Indeed, due to order-preservation the Lorenz-monotonicity properties may be construed as follows: Suppose that some lower coalition of agents (ordered by the size of their demands) equalize their demands resulting in a new vector of demands that Lorenz-dominates the original demand vector. In this case, Lorenz-monotonicity in gains requires that such a reallocation is not disadvantageous for this lower coalition. Consequently, if a rationing method satisfies Lorenz-monotonicity in gains then it cannot be manipulated be any lower coalition spreading their demands (without changing the rank of agents according to demand). Likewise, Lorenz-monotonicity in losses concerns a spread of demands; If a rationing method satisfies Lorenz-monotonicity in losses then its resulting vector of shares cannot be manipulated by any lower coalition equalizing their demands.

Thus, if a rationing method satisfies Lorenz-monotonicity in both gains and losses it cannot be manipulated by any lower coalition of agents spreading or equalizing their demands. In fact, we are able to provide the following alternative characterization of the proportional rule based on Lorenz-monotonicity.

Theorem 2.7 (Hougaard and Østerdal 2005). *The Proportional rule φ^P is the only continuous and order-preserving rationing rule that satisfies Lorenz-monotonicity in both gains and losses.*

Note that Lorenz-monotonicity in Gains and Losses together are weaker than No-Advantageous Reallocation (on the other hand, Moulin's characterization – as in Theorem 2.6 – is not limited to order-preserving rules). In Proposition 2.3 it is shown that the Proportional Rule satisfies Lorenz-monotonicity in both gains and losses. For a proof of the converse claim the reader is referred to Hougaard and Østerdal (2005).

2.2.5 *Comments*

Before turning towards cost sharing with a common cost function as in scenarios (2) and (3) in Sect. 2.1, a few final comments concerning the rationing model will be made.

First, even though all claims are verifiable not all claims may be viewed as equal from the outset. For example, in cases concerning bankruptcy of firms Danish law states that in principle all claimants are equal and that the estate should be allocated according to the proportional rationing rule. However, some groups of claimants are favored: In case of unpaid salaries, employees have a so-called privileged claim that will be covered (or partly covered according to the size of the estate) before other claimants get their share of the estate. As such, agents may be ranked according to some prespecified list of priority and their claims handled accordingly. From a theoretical point of view there is an interesting generalization of the contested garment principle based on random priorities (O'Neill 1982): In particular if there are two agents, shares corresponding to the use of the contested garment principle can be found as the average of the shares in two situations – one where agent 1 has priority over 2 and one where 2 has priority over 1. In general, there are $n!$ possible orderings of n agents. For each such ordering let agents receive as much of their demand as possible, that is if $E > q_1$ then $x_1 = q_1$ and if $E - x_1 > q_2$ then $x_2 = q_2$, etc. Now, the random priority rule assigns shares which are then defined as the average over all such orderings for each agent. In general, concerning models of priority, each agent is described not only by their demand (or claim), but by a combination of their demand and type. Another well known type is "time of arrival" – here a rule could be the familiar "first to arrive on the spot is the first to be served" rule which clearly violates order-preservation in terms of demand. For further discussion of priority rules see, e.g., Moulin (2000, 2002).

Secondly, as noticed by Young (1987, 1988) the entire rationing model may alternatively be construed as a taxation problem where the sum of taxes $x_1 + \ldots + x_n$ must equal a given revenue constraint E and q_i is the pre-tax income of agent i (post-tax incomes are hence given by $q_i - x_i$). Thus, the above results have a "dual" interpretation with respect to the taxation model (q, E). For example, in Theorem 2.7 it was demonstrated that the proportional rationing rule was the only (order-preserving) rule that satisfied both Lorenz-monotonicity in Gains and Losses. In terms of the taxation model this result reads: Proportional taxation – called a flat tax – is the only taxation rule that preserves equality in the sense that if pre-tax incomes become more equally distributed then both taxes and post-tax incomes become more equally distributed. Note that in case of taxation it could naturally be argued that the post-tax income of the agent i should be *independent* of the other agents pre-tax incomes q_{-i}. The distributional aspects of taxation rules with respect to such a taxation model is, for example, examined in Moyes (1989, 1994).

2.3 Cost Sharing with Joint Cost Function

Suppose that n agents are engaged in a joint project. Let $N = \{1, \ldots, n\}$ denote the set of agents. Moreover, let $q = (q_1, \ldots, q_n)$ be a vector of non-negative demands $q_i \in \mathbf{R}_+$ of each agent i for some homogeneous good (hence demand is not necessarily measured in monetary units). Assume for simplicity that these demands are increasingly ordered $q_1 \leq \ldots \leq q_n$. Since the demand of each agent refer to the same (homogeneous) good we shall focus on two particular cases: one where the joint cost is a function of total demand $Q = q_1 + \ldots + q_n$ (homogeneous cost functions), and one where the joint cost is a function of maximal demand $\mathcal{Q} = \max_i\{q_i\} = q_n$ (decomposable cost functions), see, e.g., scenarios (2) and (3) of the Introduction.

For fixed N, let (q, C) be a *cost sharing problem* where $C : \mathbf{R}_+ \to \mathbf{R}_+$ is a (one-dimensional) non-decreasing cost function with $C(0) = 0$ and denote by $\mathcal{D}$ the set of such cost sharing problems. For a given cost sharing problem $(q, C) \in \mathcal{D}$, a *cost sharing rule* ϕ specifies a unique vector of cost shares $x = (x_1, \ldots, x_n) = \phi(q, C)$ where the cost shares x_i add up to the total costs $C(Q)$ or $C(\mathcal{Q})$.

In practice, the cost function may be construed either as the costs of production or as a pricing scheme faced by the agents. In the latter case this pricing scheme can be used directly. In the former case, the cost function can be estimated using registered cost data.

Remark 2.4. Although we shall use the framework of cost sharing it can be noted that in terms of sharing some worth (surplus sharing) the model may be given the following equivalent interpretation: suppose that agents $N = 1, \ldots, n$ are engaged in a joint project. Let $q = (q_1, \ldots, q_n)$ be a vector of homogeneous characteristics $q_j \in \mathbf{R}_+$, for example, individual working hours supplied for the joint project. If working hours supplied by different agents are considered as homogeneous we may focus on the total number of working hours supplied $Q = q_1 + \ldots + q_n$ and thereby on a one-dimensional non-decreasing value function $V : \mathbf{R}_+ \to \mathbf{R}_+$ with respect to Q. Hence, (q, V) is a surplus sharing problem and ϕ is a surplus sharing rule specifying a unique vector of surplus shares $y = (y_1, \ldots, y_n) = \phi(q, V)$ where $y_1 + \ldots + y_n = V(Q)$. $\triangle$

2.3.1 Rules Based on Equality and Proportionality

Within the framework of cost sharing problems $(q, C) \in \mathcal{D}$, the proportional rule of the rationing model is known as

- *The Average Cost Rule ϕ^{AC}*, defined by cost shares

$$x_i^{AC} = \frac{q_i}{Q}C(z), \quad i = 1, \ldots, n, \tag{2.7}$$

where $z = Q$ in case of homogeneous costs and $z = \mathcal{Q}$ in case of decomposable costs.

The name refers to the fact that all agents pay the average price, $C(z)/Q$ for all units demanded. Thus, ϕ^{AC} is order-preserving, i.e., $x_1^{AC} \leq \ldots \leq x_n^{AC}$ when $q_1 \leq \ldots \leq q_n$.

In case of homogeneous cost functions $C(Q)$, the connection with the proportional rule of the rationing model implies that the average cost rule can be characterized by the same properties as the proportional rationing rule. In particular, the result of the average cost rule cannot be manipulated by neither reallocation nor by merging or splitting of demands.[1] However, one further general characterization is interesting since it relates to a monotonicity property that may be viewed as extending the resource monotonicity property of the rationing model to the present framework. This monotonicity property is defined as follows:

- *Monotonicity:* Let $C_1, C_2 \in \mathcal{D}$ and let $C_1(z) \leq C_2(z)$ for all z. Then $\phi_i(q, C_1) \leq \phi_i(q, C_2)$ for all i and all q.

In other words, Monotonicity states that all agents should benefit from a new technology that reduces costs. Cost sharing rules satisfying Monotonicity hence ensures that all agents have incentive to innovate and use cost reducing technologies. Now, this property proves rather powerful since together with a natural property related to linear cost functions (Constant Returns) it actually characterizes the average cost rule. The property of Constant Returns states that if the cost function is linear in total demand then there is a natural cost share per unit demanded, i.e., the constant average cost. Formally

- *Constant Returns:* If $C(z) = \lambda z$ for all $\lambda \geq 0$ then $\phi_i(q, C) = \lambda q_i$ for all i.

Indeed,

Theorem 2.8 (Moulin and Shenker 1994). *The Average Cost Rule ϕ^{AC} is the only cost sharing rule that satisfies Monotonicity and Constant Returns.*

The formal proof may be found in Moulin and Shenker (1994). At first sight, this result seems somewhat surprising since if we stick to the idea that everybody should be held responsible for their own demand and not share according to some degree of egalitarianism (which is basically the message of Constant Returns) then we cannot guarantee that all agents would gain from a general cost reduction using any alternative to average cost sharing. But as we shall see, this is closely linked to the fact the average cost rule only relates to the total cost $C(Q)$ and not to other parts of the cost function.

---

[1] Clearly, the average cost rule can be manipulated in case of decomposable cost functions, however, it is questionable whether there exists situations where a decomposable cost function is a proper description of the cost structure and where it makes sense to talk about agents equalizing or splitting their demands.

Example 2.2. If the agents know how the total cost of the group will be shared, it is easy to imagine a variety of situations where it would be natural for them to act strategically in their choice of demand. However, if the cost function is concave and they share costs using the Average Cost rule, a Nash equilibrium in the induced cost sharing game may not exist.

Consider the following example[2] where two agents jointly buy long-distance calls from AT&T at a (concave) two-part tariff "the One Rate 7c Plus", i.e., total cost is given by the function $C(q_1 + q_2) = 0.07(q_1 + q_2) + 4.95$. Let the benefit $h(\cdot)$ from demanding quantity (minutes calling) q be given by,

$$h_1(q_1) = \begin{cases} 0.55q_1 & \text{if } q_1 \in [0, 10) \\ 0.12q_1 + 4.3 & \text{if } q_1 \in [10, 30) \\ 7.9 & \text{if } q_1 \in [30, \infty), \end{cases}$$

and

$$h_2(q_2) = \begin{cases} 0.17q_2 & \text{if } q_2 \in [0, 30) \\ 5.1 & \text{if} q_2 \in [30, \infty), \end{cases}$$

respectively. Hence, using the average cost rule ϕ^{AC} and maintaining the assumption that both agents have quasi-linear utility functions, i.e., $u_i(q_i, q_j) = h_i(q_i) - \phi_i^{AC}$, induces a cost sharing game with pay-off's given by,

$$u_1(q_1, q_2) = h_1(q_1) - 0.07q_1 - \frac{q_1}{q_1 + q_2} 4.95,$$

and

$$u_2(q_1, q_2) = h_2(q_2) - 0.07q_2 - \frac{q_2}{q_1 + q_2} 4.95.$$

Now, this results in the following "best reply" correspondences for agent 1 and 2 respectively,

$$q_1^*(q_2) = \begin{cases} 30 & \text{if } q_2 \in [0, 5.6] \\ 10 & \text{if } q_2 \in [5.6, 53.4] \\ 30 & \text{if } q_2 \in [53.4, \infty), \end{cases}$$

and

$$q_2^*(q_1) = \begin{cases} 0 & \text{if } q_1 \in [0, 19.5] \\ 30 & \text{if } q_1 \in [19.5, \infty). \end{cases}$$

Clearly, no equilibrium exists in this particular case since if agent 1 demands 10 then agent 2 will demand 0 and if agent 2 demands 0 then agent 1 will demand 30 – but if agent 1 demands 30 then agent 2 will demand 30 and in this case agent 1 will rather demand 10, etc.

---

[2] Kindly provided by Lars Thorlund-Petersen.

However, notice that if the agents announce their demand in a sequence and these announcements are observable by the other agents, then an equilibrium will exist. For example, let agent 1 determine his demand first and let this be observed by agent 2, who then determines his demand. In this case backward induction gives the (subgame-perfect) equilibrium $(q_1^* = 30, q_2^* = 30)$.

Moreover, implementation in Nash equilibrium is generally possible in case the cost function C is convex, see, e.g., Watts (1996). $\triangle$

Egalitarianism becomes a relevant alternative because, contrary to the scenario of the rationing model, the present framework does not initially exclude,

- *The Equal Split Rule, ϕ^E,* defined by cost shares,

$$x_i^E = \frac{C(z)}{n}, \quad i = 1, \ldots, n, \tag{2.8}$$

where $z = Q$ in case of homogeneous costs and $z = \mathcal{Q}$ in case of decomposable costs.

Clearly, the equal split rule ϕ^E is (trivially) order-preserving and satisfies Monotonicity but *not* Constant Returns.

Now, both the average cost rule and the equal split rule only relates to the total cost while the information contained by the rest of the cost function is "ignored". For example, it could be argued that the level of the stand-alone cost $C(q_i)$ for each agent i ought to influence the final allocation of costs. An immediate way to meet such a requirement could be to allocate costs in proportion to stand-alone costs instead of demands, i.e., to use cost shares,

$$x_i = \frac{C(q_i)}{\sum_{j \in N} C(q_j)} C(Q), \text{ for } i = 1, \ldots, n \tag{2.9}$$

(with the obvious changes for a decomposable cost function). Note that for homogeneous cost functions this version of proportional cost sharing satisfies Constant Returns but *not* Monotonicity. The problem with Monotonicity occurs because the rule exploits other parts of the cost function (the stand-alone costs) than just the total cost, while satisfying Constant Returns.

In the same spirit, cost could be allocated using constrained equal split

$$x_i^1 = \min \left\{ C(q_i), \frac{C(Q)}{n} \right\} \text{ for } i = 1, \ldots, n \tag{2.10}$$

and adding an equal share of any resulting deficit, i.e., $1/n[C(Q) - \sum_{j \in N} x_j^1]$ (with the obvious changes for a decomposable cost function). Note, that for homogeneous cost functions this version of egalitarianism satisfies neither Constant Returns nor Monotonicity. Further, note that, except for (2.9) with respect to a decomposable cost function, none of these suggestions guarantee individual rationality, i.e., that no agent pays more than his stand-alone cost.

In case of decomposable cost functions $C(\mathcal{Q})$, however, there is a more direct way to ensure individual rationality. For example, we may define the *restricted equal split rule* by cost shares,

$$x_i^{RE} = \min\{C(q_i), \alpha\}, \quad i = 1, \ldots, n, \tag{2.11}$$

where α is chosen such that the cost shares add up to total costs $C(\mathcal{Q})$. This rule captures the spirit of the constrained equal gains rule of the rationing model. We may further define the *restricted average cost rule* by the following cost sharing scheme: First, calculate shares

$$x_i^1 = \min\left\{C(q_i), \frac{q_i}{Q}C(\mathcal{Q})\right\}, \quad i = 1, \ldots, n. \tag{2.12}$$

If some agents are bounded by their stand-alone cost the remaining agents must further share $C(\mathcal{Q}) - \sum_{i=1}^{n} x_i^1$ in proportion to their demand and so forth until total costs are fully allocated.

However, knowledge of the entire cost function opens up for the definition of types of rules that has not been treated so far since costs related to any subset of agents can be assessed. As argued such information, if accessible, may influence the way that costs (or value) should be shared. In the following we consider cost sharing rules based on two main principles: the *serial principle* and the *incremental principle*.

2.3.2 Rules Based on the Serial Principle

The serial principle basically states that agents with equal demand must be treated equally and that, according to a given ordering of demands, an agent's cost share should not depend on the demand of agents that appear after him in the ordering. The spirit of the serial principle is perhaps most clearly illustrated in case of decomposable cost functions.

2.3.2.1 Serial Cost Sharing: Decomposable Costs

We start out by demonstrating that sharing costs equally or in proportion to individual demand q_i may, in case of a (non-decreasing) decomposable cost function $C(\mathcal{Q})$, lead to violation of the stand-alone cost principle as illustrated by the following simple example.

Example 2.3. Let three agents have demands $q = (q_1, q_2, q_3) = (1, 2, 3)$ with associated stand-alone costs $C(q_1) = 100$, $C(q_2) = 800$ and $C(q_3) = 900$.

Since the cost function is decomposable, the total cost of a joint project is $C(q_3) = 900$. Now, if the total cost is shared equally, all agents pay $x^E = 300$. If, instead we use average cost sharing we get:

$$x^{AC} = \left(\frac{1}{6}900, \frac{1}{3}900, \frac{1}{2}900\right) = (150, 300, 450).$$

Notice, that in both cases, agent 1 will end up paying more than the stand-alone cost of 100. Moreover, notice that both methods only use individual demands q and the total costs $C(q_3)$ as relevant information whereas the information contained by the remaining part of the cost function is ignored. $\triangle$

Although lack of individual rationality can be ensured using the restricted versions defined in (2.11) and (2.12), it seems natural to look for alternative cost sharing rules, where more of the information contained by the cost function is utilized. Indeed, one may suggest to use equal sharing but with respect to incremental costs, rather than total cost, following the serial principle.

Consider, for example, three agents with demands $q_1 \leq q_2 \leq q_3$, and total joint cost $C(q_3)$. If all agents had demanded q_1 the total cost of $C(q_1)$ should be split equally (according to "equal-treatment-of-equals"), i.e., all agents get cost share $1/3C(q_1)$. Now, the incremental cost in going from demand q_1 to q_2 should be split equally among agents 2 and 3 as they alone are responsible for this demand, i.e., both agents 2 and 3 further pay $1/2(C(q_2) - C(q_1))$. Finally, only agent 3 is responsible for the incremental demand going from q_2 to q_3 and should consequently cover the associated incremental costs alone, i.e., agent 3 further pays $C(q_3) - C(q_2)$. Thus, total cost is shared as

$$x_1 = \frac{C(q_1)}{3}, \quad x_2 = \frac{C(q_1)}{3} + \frac{C(q_2) - C(q_1)}{2},$$

$$x_3 = \frac{C(q_1)}{3} + \frac{C(q_2) - C(q_1)}{2} + C(q_3) - C(q_2).$$

As such, cost shares found using the serial principle can never exceed the stand-alone cost of any agent in case of decomposable cost functions.

In general, for a decomposable cost function we say that cost shares are associated with the *serial cost sharing rule* if they are determined as

$$x_j = \sum_{k=1}^{j} \frac{C(q_k) - C(q_{k-1})}{n - k + 1}, \quad j = 1, \ldots, n, \qquad (2.13)$$

where $x_0 = C(q_0) = 0$.

Example 2.3 (continued). Use of the serial cost sharing rule will, in the case of Example 2.2., result in cost shares $x_1 = 33.33$, $x_2 = 33.33 + 350 = 383.33$ and $x_3 = 33.33 + 350 + 100 = 483.33$. Clearly, no agent pays more than their stand-alone cost by this method. Of course, we could have used restricted versions of equal split and average cost sharing to ensure that no agent pays more than their stand-alone cost (i.e., comply with individual rationality). In case of restricted equality, this would result in cost shares $x_1^{RE} = 100$, $x_2^{RE} = x_3^{RE} = 100 + 300 = 400$ whereas in case of restricted average cost sharing, resulting cost shares are given by $x_1^{RAC} = 100$, $x_2^{RAC} = 300 + (2/5)50 = 320$ and $x_3^{RAC} = 450 + (3/5)50 = 480$. $\triangle$

2.3.2.2 Serial Cost Sharing: Homogeneous Costs

Consider now a (non-decreasing) homogeneous cost function $C(Q)$ and denote by $\hat{\mathcal{D}}$ and $\check{\mathcal{D}}$ the set of cost sharing problems with convex and concave homogeneous cost functions, respectively. Finally, denote by $\mathcal{D}^+ = \hat{\mathcal{D}} + \check{\mathcal{D}}$ the set of cost sharing problems where the homogeneous cost function equals a sum of a convex and a concave cost function.

The basic motivation behind serial cost sharing in case of homogeneous cost functions (as introduced in Shenker 1995 and Moulin and Shenker 1992) is given by the serial principle, i.e., agents with identical demand should be treated equally and no agent will be held responsible for the consumption of "greedier" agents even though they are associated with a joint project.

Consider, for example, three agents with individual demands $q_1 \leq q_2 \leq q_3$, and total cost $C(q_1 + q_2 + q_3)$. Cost shares according to serial cost sharing is found as follows: The agent with the smallest demand pays one-third (an equal share) of the total costs in case all agents had been as "modest" as agent 1 in their demands. The second agent further pays half (an equal share) of the incremental cost in going from a situation with total demand $3q_1$ to total demand $q_1 + 2q_2$ – that is, to a situation where agent 1 demands q_1 and the remaining agents are as "modest" as agent 2. Finally agent 3 further pays the incremental cost of going from a situation with total demand of $q_1 + 2q_2$ to a total demand of $q_1 + q_2 + q_3$. This leaves the agents with cost shares,

$$x_1^{IS} = \frac{1}{3}C(3q_1)$$

$$x_2^{IS} = \frac{1}{3}C(3q_1) + \frac{1}{2}(C(q_1 + 2q_2) - C(3q_1))$$

$$x_3^{IS} = \frac{1}{3}C(3q_1) + \frac{1}{2}(C(q_1 + 2q_2) - C(3q_1)) + C(q_1 + q_2 + q_3) - C(q_1 + 2q_2).$$

Clearly, $x_1^{IS} + x_2^{IS} + x_3^{IS} = C(q_1 + q_2 + q_3)$, and the cost share of agent i is independent of the demands of agents $j > i$.

Now, the serial rule has a natural mirror-image commencing with the agent having the largest demand instead of the agent having the smallest demand, as suggested in De Frutos (1998). Intuitively, no agent will be held responsible for the consumption of agents with smaller demands even though they are associated with a joint project. In this case the resulting cost shares will be,

$$x_3^{DS} = \frac{1}{3}C(3q_3)$$

$$x_2^{DS} = \frac{1}{3}C(3q_3) + \frac{1}{2}(C(q_3 + 2q_2) - C(3q_3))$$

$$x_1^{DS} = \frac{1}{3}C(3q_3) + \frac{1}{2}(C(q_3 + 2q_2) - C(3q_3)) + C(q_1 + q_2 + q_3) - C(q_3 + 2q_2).$$

Again, clearly $x_1^{DS} + x_2^{DS} + x_3^{DS} = C(q_1 + q_2 + q_3)$, and the cost share of agent i is independent of the demands of agents $j < i$. However, in this case agents are not guaranteed non-negative cost shares for problems in $\mathcal{D}$. In general, non-negative cost shares are only guaranteed for problems in $\check{\mathcal{D}}$, i.e., for concave cost functions.

Remark 2.5. The cost shares of serial cost sharing are characterized by some degree of independence of other agents demands. At first sight, this seems to be in line with straightforward ideas of fairness. However, if consumption of the produced good involves externalities such an independence may seem less appealing. For example, in case the cost function is related to a vaccination program, agents with zero demand pay zero but potentially benefit from the consumption of agents demanding the vaccine. Hence, the presence of externalities calls for the use of alternative rules or further knowledge about the agents individual utility functions. $\triangle$

2.3.2.3 Increasing, Decreasing and Mixed Serial Rules

In general, consider the case of n agents. Let the vector of demand q define intermediate production levels given by vectors $r \in \mathbf{R}^n$ and $s \in \mathbf{R}^n$ as,

$$\begin{bmatrix} r_1 \\ r_2 \\ r_3 \\ \vdots \\ r_n \end{bmatrix} = \begin{bmatrix} n & 0 & 0 & \ldots & 0 \\ 1 & n-1 & 0 & \ldots & 0 \\ 1 & 1 & n-2 & \ldots & 0 \\ \vdots & \vdots & \vdots & & \vdots \\ 1 & 1 & 1 & \ldots & 1 \end{bmatrix} \begin{bmatrix} q_1 \\ q_2 \\ q_3 \\ \vdots \\ q_n \end{bmatrix}.$$

$$\begin{bmatrix} s_1 \\ s_2 \\ s_3 \\ \vdots \\ s_n \end{bmatrix} = \begin{bmatrix} n & 0 & 0 & \ldots & 0 \\ 1 & n-1 & 0 & \ldots & 0 \\ 1 & 1 & n-2 & \ldots & 0 \\ \vdots & \vdots & \vdots & & \vdots \\ 1 & 1 & 1 & \ldots & 1 \end{bmatrix} \begin{bmatrix} q_n \\ q_{n-1} \\ q_{n-2} \\ \vdots \\ q_1 \end{bmatrix}.$$

Since demands are increasingly ordered we get that, $r_1 \leq \ldots \leq r_n = Q = s_n \leq \ldots \leq s_1$. Now, define the Increasing resp. Decreasing Serial Cost Sharing Rule as follows:

Increasing Serial Cost Sharing ϕ^{IS} is defined by cost shares

$$x_i^{IS} = \sum_{k=1}^{i} \frac{C(r_k) - C(r_{k-1})}{n+1-k}, \quad i = 1, \ldots, n, \tag{2.14}$$

where $r_0 = 0$ by definition.

Decreasing Serial Cost Sharing ϕ^{DS} is defined by cost shares

$$x_{n-j+1}^{DS} = \sum_{k=1}^{j} \frac{C(s_k) - C(s_{k-1})}{n+1-k}, \quad j = 1, \ldots, n, \tag{2.15}$$

where $s_0 = 0$ by definition.

Both rules are *order-preserving*, i.e.,

$$x_1^{IS} \leq \ldots \leq x_n^{IS} \quad \text{and} \quad x_1^{DS} \leq \ldots \leq x_n^{DS}.$$

Moreover, if C is linear $x^{IS} = x^{DS}$ and clearly both rules satisfy Constant Returns. Consequently, by Theorem 2.8, neither increasing nor decreasing serial cost sharing satisfy Monotonicity. (In particular, note that ϕ^{IS} does not satisfy Monotonicity on $\mathcal{D}$.)

It is possible to establish some bounds (in q_i) on the cost shares. If C is *convex* then cost shares resulting from increasing serial cost sharing are bounded from below by the stand-alone cost and from above by the unanimity cost, i.e., $C(q_i) \leq x_i^{IS} \leq C(nq_i)/n$. Cost shares resulting from decreasing serial cost sharing are bounded from above by the unanimity cost whereas there is no lower bound, i.e., $x_i^{DS} \leq C(nq_i)/n$. If C is *concave* then x^{IS} is bounded from below by the unanimity cost and from above by the stand-alone cost, i.e., $C(nq_i)/n \leq x_i^{IS} \leq C(q_i)$, whereas cost shares resulting from decreasing serial cost sharing are bounded from below by the unanimity cost, i.e., $C(nq_i)/n \leq x_i^{DS}$. Hence, the increasing serial cost sharing rule ϕ^{IS} has the following (universal) bounds on $\mathcal{D}$;

$$\frac{1}{n} C(q_i) \leq \phi^{IS}(q, C) \leq C(nq_i),$$

whereas the decreasing serial rule fails both these (universal) bounds (note that the average cost sharing rule ϕ^{AC} also fails both these universal bounds).

Thus, in general with homogeneous costs there is no guarantee that using a serial rule we obtain individual rationality. This may not be surprising for convex cost functions but even if the cost function C is concave some groups of agents may end up paying more than their stand alone cost using the decreasing serial rule. Hougaard and Thorlund-Petersen (2000) provide a set of sufficient conditions for the decreasing serial rule to satisfy the stand alone requirements for all coalitions in case of concave cost functions.

Example 2.4. Assume that a group of n agents make a joint decision of renting a copying machine at a fixed cost of β whereafter each copy taken has a constant marginal cost of α. That is, for a given total demand Q the (concave) cost function can be written as $C(Q) = \alpha Q + \beta$ with $C(0) = 0$. Now, it could be argued that the cost share of agent i ought to be determined by $x_i = \alpha q_i + \beta/n$ since all agents are supposed to share the fixed cost equally and pay the marginal cost of each copy demanded. This is, in fact, also the result of using both increasing and decreasing serial cost sharing if all demands are strictly positive. However, if some agent demands 0 then according to decreasing serial cost sharing he will still be forced to pay his equal share of the fixed cost whereas using increasing serial cost sharing agents with zero demand avoid payment. Moreover, since all agents pay an equal share of the fixed cost, both rules works to the relative advantage of agents with high demands in the sense that agent specific unit prices x_i/q_i are decreasing in i. For comparison, note that average cost sharing results in shares, $x_i^{AC} = \alpha q_i + q_i \beta/Q$, where the fixed cost is shared in proportion to demand (also ensuring that zero-demand avoid payment) and agent specific unit prices are the same for all agents. $\triangle$

It can be shown that if C is convex then the cost share of agent i using the increasing serial rule ϕ_i^{IS} is non-decreasing in the demand of agent j, q_j, for any $j \neq i$. If C is concave then the cost share of agent i using the increasing serial rule ϕ_i^{IS} (resp. the decreasing serial rule ϕ_i^{DS}) is non-increasing (resp. non-decreasing) in the demand of agent j, q_j, for any $j \neq i$.

In general, both rules have decreasing (resp. increasing) agent specific unit prices when the cost function is concave (resp. convex), i.e.,

$$\frac{x_1^{IS}}{q_1} \geq \ldots \geq \frac{x_n^{IS}}{q_n} \quad \text{and} \quad \frac{x_1^{DS}}{q_1} \geq \ldots \geq \frac{x_n^{DS}}{q_n},$$

for problems in $\check{D}$ and

$$\frac{x_1^{IS}}{q_1} \leq \ldots \leq \frac{x_n^{IS}}{q_n} \quad \text{and} \quad \frac{x_1^{DS}}{q_1} \leq \ldots \leq \frac{x_n^{DS}}{q_n},$$

for problems in $\hat{D}$. Thus, under concave cost functions (increasing returns in production) agents with modest demands are penalized whereas under convex cost functions (decreasing returns in production) agents with modest demands are favored by both rules.

Example 2.5. Assume that agents can choose their demand strategically and let costs be shared using Increasing Serial Cost Sharing ϕ^{IS}. For instance, assume that two departments demand some service in quantity q_i delivered at quadratic costs $C(q_1 + q_2) = (q_1 + q_2)^2$. Let both departments have linear utility in demand q_i and payment ϕ_i^{IS}, i.e., $u_i(q_i, \phi_i) = \alpha_i q_i - \phi_i^{IS}$, where $\alpha \in \mathbf{R}_{++}$. That is, dept. 1 chooses its demand for service q_1 by solving

$$\max_{q_1} \alpha_1 q_1 - 2q_1^2,$$

yielding $q_1^* = \alpha_1/4$. Note, that the optimal demand level of dept. 1 is independent of the demand of dept. 2 (since the cost share of dept. 1 does not depend on the demand of dept. 2). Dept. 2 chooses its demand for service by solving

$$\max_{q_2} \alpha_2 q_2 - \left[(q_1 + q_2)^2 - 2q_1^2\right],$$

and knowing that dept. 1 demands $q_1^* = \alpha_1/4$, we get that $q_2^* = (\alpha_2 - \alpha_1/2)/2$. Hence, in this case the cost sharing game induced by the increasing serial rule has got a unique Nash equilibrium in demands

$$(q_1^*, q_2^*) = \left(\frac{\alpha_1}{4}, \frac{2\alpha_2 - \alpha_1}{4}\right),$$

and total cost is shared as

$$(\phi_1^{IS}, \phi_2^{IS}) = \left(\frac{\alpha_1^2}{8}, \frac{2\alpha_2^2 - \alpha_1^2}{8}\right).$$

As indicated by the example, it turns out that (when the cost function is convex) the cost sharing game induced by ϕ^{IS} is dominance solvable and yields a unique (Strong) Nash equilibrium for any (convex and monotonic) preference profile, see Moulin and Shenker (1992). Recall, that in case of convex cost functions we disregard ϕ^{DS} as it may result in negative cost shares.

For comparison, assume that costs are shared using the Average Cost rule ϕ^{AC} instead. In this case it turns out to be important how we construe the process of announcing the demands (strategies). For instance, imagine that the departments simultaneously choose their level of demand. Then the corresponding induced (normal form) game has got at least one Nash equilibrium (Watts 1996): In the current example we get the unique equilibrium

$$(q_1^*, q_2^*) = \left(\frac{2\alpha_1 - \alpha_2}{3}, \frac{2\alpha_2 - \alpha_1}{3}\right).$$

However, if the departments make a sequential choice of demands making the induced cost sharing game dynamic (for example dept. 1 chooses first and that choice is observed by dept. 2, which then chooses) the resulting (subgame-perfect) Nash equilibrium becomes

$$(q_1^*, q_2^*) = \left(\frac{3\alpha_1 - 2\alpha_2}{4}, \frac{2\alpha_2 - \alpha_1}{2}\right).$$

For results on equilibrium existence in case of increasing returns (concave cost functions), see, e.g., Moulin (1996) concerning the Increasing Serial rule and De Frutos (1998) concerning Decreasing Serial rule.

A recent survey of main results concerning strategic games in cost sharing problems can be found in Koster (2009).   △

Now, consider problems in $\mathcal{D}^+$ where the cost function equals a sum of a convex and a concave function. Such functions often appear in managerial economics where they are used to model that returns to scale may vary with the size of production. Clearly, the increasing serial cost sharing rule can be used directly on this domain. However, alternative rules may be defined using a decomposition of the cost function into a convex and a concave component.

Let a *decomposition rule* be defined by a mapping $\Gamma : \mathcal{D}^+ \to \hat{\mathcal{D}} \times \check{\mathcal{D}}$ where $C = R + S$ for $\Gamma(C) = (R, S)$ and normalized by the requirement that the right derivative of R at $Q = 0$ equals zero. In particular, we shall focus on the so-called *complementary-slack* (CS) decomposition which maximizes the role of the concave component, see Thon and Thorlund-Petersen (1986). Formally, let Γ_{CS} denote the complementary-slack (CS) decomposition where $\lim\sup_{\epsilon \to 0} \Delta_\epsilon^2 R(Q) \Delta_\epsilon^2 S(Q) = 0$ and $R'(0) = 0$ with $\Delta_\epsilon^2 C(Q) = \epsilon^{-1}(C'(Q + \epsilon) - c'(Q))$ for $Q + \epsilon \geq 0$, $\epsilon \neq 0$ and C' being the right derivative. If C is twice continuously differentiable the conditions read $R''(Q)S''(Q) = 0$ and $R'(0) = 0$.

Example 2.6. In some cases there is a unique way to decompose a cost function into a convex and concave component. For example, consider the case where a good is sold at a price of \$1 per unit and a bundle of 10 goods is offered at a price of 80 cents per unit implying that the cost function is determined by

$$C(Q) = \begin{cases} Q & \text{if } Q < 8 \\ 8 & \text{if } 8 \leq Q < 10 \\ Q - 2 & \text{if } 10 \leq Q. \end{cases}$$

This cost function is uniquely decomposed into a sum of a convex and concave function as $C(Q) = R(Q) + S(Q) = \max\{0, Q - 10\} + \min\{Q, 8\}$. However, if a 10 cent excise tax is added then total costs equal $C(Q) + 0.1Q$ with CS-decomposition $\max\{0, Q - 10\} + \min\{1.1Q, 0.1Q + 8\}$ but this decomposition is not unique as, for example, another decomposition could be $\max\{0, 1.1Q - 11\} + \min\{1.1Q, 0.1Q + 8, 9\}$.   △

Using the CS-decomposition rule to decompose the cost function into a convex and a concave component, we are able to introduce a mixture of increasing and decreasing serial cost sharing as suggested in Hougaard and Thorlund-Petersen (2001). Here, it is argued that the spirit of increasing serial cost sharing seems to fit best with convex cost functions (as agents with smaller demands should not be penalized by the fact that agents with larger demands cause the common cost to escalate) whereas the spirit of decreasing serial cost sharing fits well with concave cost functions (as decreasing marginal costs should penalize agents with small demands). Hence, the cost share paid by agent i should be determined as a sum of i's cost shares related to using ϕ^{IS} on the convex part and ϕ^{DS} on the concave part of the CS-decomposition respectively:

Mixed Serial Cost Sharing ϕ^{MS} is defined for problems in $\mathcal{D}^+$ where C has CS-decomposition $C = R + S$ as

$$\phi^{MS}(q, C) = \phi^{IS}(q, R) + \phi^{DS}(q, S). \tag{2.16}$$

Clearly, if C is convex (resp. concave) then mixed serial cost sharing coincides with increasing (resp. decreasing) serial cost sharing. Hence, for any problem in $\mathcal{D}^+$, mixed serial cost sharing results in non-negative cost shares.

Example 2.7. Consider three agents ($n = 3$) with demands $q = (1, 3, 5)$ and cost function $C(Q) = Q^2 + 64\sqrt{Q}$ which is concave on $[0, 4)$ and convex on $(4, \infty)$. This cost function C can be decomposed into a convex function $R^*(Q) = Q^2$ and a concave function $S^*(Q) = 64\sqrt{Q}$. Using the principle of mixing the serial cost sharing rules with respect to such a decomposition results in the following cost shares:

	Agent 1	Agent 2	Agent 3	Sum
$R^*(Q)$	$x_1^{IS} = 3$	$x_2^{IS} = 23$	$x_3^{IS} = 55$	81
$S^*(Q)$	$x_1^{DS} = 44.6$	$x_2^{DS} = 63.8$	$x_3^{DS} = 82.6$	192
Sum	$x_1^{IS} + x_1^{DS} = 47.6$	$x_2^{IS} + x_2^{DS} = 87.8$	$x_3^{IS} + x_3^{DS} = 137.6$	273

Alternatively, consider the CS-decomposition $C = \tilde{R} + \tilde{S}$ where

$$\tilde{R}(Q) = \begin{cases} 0 & \text{if } Q \leq 4 \\ Q^2 + 64\sqrt{Q} - 24Q - 48 & \text{if } Q > 4, \end{cases}$$

and,

$$\tilde{S}(Q) = \begin{cases} Q^2 + 64\sqrt{Q} & \text{if } Q \leq 4 \\ 24Q + 48 & \text{if } Q > 4. \end{cases}$$

Notice that for $Q \neq 4$ we have $\tilde{R}''(Q)\tilde{S}''(Q) = 0$. Using the CS-decomposition and the mixed serial cost sharing rule we obtain the following cost shares:

	Agent 1	Agent 2	Agent 3	Sum
$\tilde{R}(Q)$	$x_1^{IS} = 0$	$x_2^{IS} = 1.2$	$x_3^{IS} = 7.8$	9
$\tilde{S}(Q)$	$x_1^{DS} = 40$	$x_2^{DS} = 88$	$x_3^{DS} = 136$	264
Sum	$x_1^{IS} + x_1^{DS} = 40$	$x_2^{IS} + x_2^{DS} = 89.2$	$x_3^{IS} + x_3^{DS} = 143.8$	273

Notice that there is a significant difference in the resulting cost shares depending on the particular way that the cost function is decomposed. In particular, it appears that the cost shares resulting from mixed serial cost sharing (and the CS-decomposition) are Lorenz-dominated by the cost shares related a mixture of ϕ^{IS} and ϕ^{DS} but related to the alternative decomposition. In fact, this is no coincidence as it will be demonstrated in Theorem 2.12. $\triangle$

2.3.2.4 Inequality Comparisons

Using the ordering of Lorenz-domination we can consider the relation between the serial rules and average cost sharing with respect to equality of the resulting cost shares. Such an ordering naturally depends on the specific domain of problems considered.

Proposition 2.4 (Hougaard and Thorlund-Petersen 2001). *For problems in $\hat{\mathcal{D}}$ (with convex cost functions) we have*

$$\phi^{AC} \succ_{LD} \phi^{IS} \succ_{LD} \phi^{DS}.$$

For problems in $\check{\mathcal{D}}$ (with concave cost functions) we have

$$\phi^{DS} \succ_{LD} \phi^{IS} \succ_{LD} \phi^{AC}.$$

Finally, for problems in $\mathcal{D}^+$ (with sums of convex and concave cost functions) we have

$$\phi^{MS} \succ_{LD} \phi^{IS} \, (\phi^{DS}).$$

Proof (sketch). First we note that $x_i^P = ACq_i$ where $AC = C(Q)/Q$. Hence by increasing (resp. decreasing) agent specific unit prices of ϕ^{IS} and ϕ^{DS} on $\hat{\mathcal{D}}$ (resp. $\check{\mathcal{D}}$,) we get that

$$\frac{x_1^{IS(DS)}}{x_1^{AC}} \leq \cdots \leq \frac{x_n^{IS(DS)}}{x_n^{AC}} \quad \left(\frac{x_1^{IS(DS)}}{x_1^{AC}} \geq \cdots \geq \frac{x_n^{IS(DS)}}{x_n^{AC}} \right).$$

Since, in general we have that if $u_1/v_1 \leq \cdots \leq u_n/v_n$ for $v_1 > 0$ then $v \succ_{LD} u$ (see, e.g., Marshall and Olkin 1979) we obtain the desired result with respect to the relation between the serial rules and average cost sharing. The relation between ϕ^{IS} and ϕ^{DS} follows from Lemma 4 in Hougaard and Thorlund-Petersen (2001). □

In other words, Proposition 2.4 states that for problems with convex cost functions the cost shares of average cost sharing are more equally distributed than the cost shares of increasing serial cost sharing which are more equally distributed than the cost shares of decreasing serial cost sharing. For problems with concave cost functions the cost shares of decreasing serial cost sharing are more equally distributed than the cost shares of increasing serial cost sharing which are more equally distributed than the cost shares of average cost sharing, and finally, for problems where the cost function is a sum of convex and concave cost functions the cost shares of mixed serial cost sharing are more equally distributed than the cost shares of both increasing and decreasing serial cost sharing.

2.3.2.5 Axiomatic Characterization

Characterizing cost sharing rules in general, the structural property of additivity has drawn much attention: if a cost function is a sum of two separate cost functions then finding cost shares with respect to this aggregate function is tantamount to adding up the cost shares with respect to each separate cost function. In other words, cost shares should not depend on the way that the costs are categorized. Formally:

- *Additivity:* Let C_1 and C_2 be two cost functions then $\phi(q, C_1 + C_2) = \phi(q, C_1) + \phi(q, C_2)$.

Additivity is satisfied by increasing as well as decreasing serial cost sharing (and the average cost rule) but *not* by mixed serial cost sharing. Now, it turns out that Additivity together with Constant Returns and one further property of limited consistency is sufficient to single out increasing serial cost sharing. This limited consistency property (called Free Lunch) states that if the cost of serving n replica of a given agent's demand is zero then this agent i pays zero and cost shares of the remaining agents, $\phi_{-i}^{N \setminus i}$, are found removing the "zero-cost agent" and sharing the cost in the reduced problem $(q_{-i}, \tilde{C})$ where $\tilde{C}(z) = C(z + q_i)$ for agents in the set $N \setminus i$. Formally:

- *Free-Lunch:* If $C(nq_i) = 0$ then $\phi_i(q, C) = 0$ and

$$\phi_{-i}(q, C) = \phi_{-i}^{N \setminus i}(q_{-i}, \tilde{C}).$$

Clearly, Free-Lunch is violated by both the average cost rule and decreasing (and thereby also mixed) serial cost sharing since basically it states that if an agent can satisfy his demand by the free goods available to the group then he need not participate in the cost sharing exercise.

Theorem 2.9 (Moulin and Shenker 1994). *A continuous cost sharing rule ϕ on $\mathcal{D}$ satisfies Order-preservation, Constant Returns, Additivity and Free-Lunch if and only if it is the Increasing Serial Cost Sharing Rule ϕ^{IS}.*

It has already been noticed that Increasing Serial Cost Sharing satisfies Order-preservation, Constant Returns, Additivity and Free-Lunch. To prove the converse the reader is referred to the proof in Moulin and Shenker (1994). On the restricted domain of convex cost functions $\hat{\mathcal{D}}$, Moulin and Shenker (1994) note that ϕ^{IS} can be characterized by an axiom called Unanimity (Upper) Bound (stating that the cost share of agent i cannot exceed i's unanimity cost $C(nq_i)/n$) together with Continuity, Additivity and Free Lunch.

Now, a natural mirror image of the above characterization of the increasing serial rule can be provided in case of the decreasing serial cost sharing rule ϕ^{DS}.

Consider cost functions of the type $\Delta^t(z) = \min\{z, t\}$ where $t \geq 0$. These functions will be called plateau cost functions in the following, i.e., functions where total costs equal total demand z up to some threshold t from where the total cost remains fixed.

In case of plateau cost functions, the agent with the highest demand (agent n) should pay t/n if the total demand exceeds t in case all agents demanded the same quantity as agent n. This seems reasonable considering that average costs are decreasing and the group as a whole benefits from a large total demand. Now, having settled the cost share of the agent with the highest demand, this agent may now be removed from the set of agents and the cost shares of the remaining agents can be specified by imposing the same cost sharing rule on a reduced cost function (along the lines of the Free Lunch axiom). To formally define this property of Plateau Consistency we shall make use of the following definitions: For $S \subset N$, q^S is the projection of q on $\mathbf{R}^S$. Moreover, let $\alpha \geq 0$ be a demand and let $\beta \in \mathbf{R}$ be a cost share and define $C_{\alpha,\beta}(z) = (C(z + \alpha) - \beta)_+$ for $z \geq 0$ with $C_{\alpha,\beta}(0) = 0$, where for $z \in \mathbf{R}$, $(z)_+ = \max\{0, z\}$.

- *Plateau Consistency:* Let $n \geq 2$ and $C(z) = \min\{z, t\}$ and $nq_n \geq t$. Then $\phi_n(N, C, q) = t/n$ and $\phi_i(N, C, q) = \phi_i(N\backslash\{n\}, C_{q_n,t/n}, q^{N\backslash\{n\}})$ for $i \neq n$.

It is easy to see that Plateau Consistency is violated by increasing serial cost sharing: For example, let $N = \{1, 2\}$, $C(z) = \min\{z, t\}$ and $q = (0, t)$. Then according to the increasing serial rule $\phi_1^{IS}(\{1, 2\}, C, q) = 0$ and $\phi_2^{IS}(\{1, 2\}, C, q) = t$. According to the decreasing serial rule $\phi_1^{DS}(\{1, 2\}, C, q) = \phi_2^{DS}(\{1, 2\}, C, q) = t/2$ in line with Plateau Consistency. Actually, the plateau cost functions are extreme examples of how the increasing and decreasing serial rules differ on concave cost functions as specified in Proposition 2.4.

Now, it turns out to be convenient to extend $\mathcal{D}$ to the domain of all non-decreasing cost functions $\tilde{\mathcal{D}}$ (note that $C(0) = 0$ is not required here) since handling fixed costs becomes relevant.

Hence, we will introduce two additional axioms: (1) Fixed Cost, which states that in a situation of a fixed cost all agents have to share this cost equally, and (2) Zero Cost, which states that if it is free to provide n times the demand of agent n (the agent with the highest demand) then no agent pays. Formally:

- *Fixed Cost:* Let $\alpha > 0$ and $C(z) = \alpha$ for $z \geq 0$. Then, $\phi_i(N, C, q) = \alpha/n$, for all $i \in N$.
- *Zero Cost:* If $C(nq_n) = 0$ then $\phi_i(N, C, q) = 0$, for all $i \in N$.

Note that Zero Cost is satisfied by increasing serial rule while Fixed Cost obviously is not. Furthermore, it can be noted that Zero Cost together with Additivity and Plateau Consistency implies (a weak form of) Constant Returns.

Theorem 2.10 (Hougaard and Østerdal 2009). *A continuous cost sharing rule on $\tilde{\mathcal{D}}$ satisfies Fixed Cost, Zero Cost, Additivity and Plateau Consistency if and only if it is the Decreasing Serial Cost Sharing Rule ϕ^{DS}.*

Before proving Theorem 2.10, we make a useful observation (omitting the straightforward proof). In case of plateau cost functions Δ^t, the decreasing serial rule has a particularly simple structure: Agents i, for which s_{n+1-i} (i.e., the total demand in case all agents j for which $j < i$ also demand q_i) exceeds the threshold t, all pay t/n, while agents with smaller demands pay their share as if there was a common average cost, plus an equal share of the residual cost. Formally:

Lemma 2.1. *Let $t > 0$, and let (N, Δ^t, q) be a cost sharing problem. If $s_1 < t$, then $\phi_j^{DS}(N, \Delta^t, q) = q_j$ for $j = 1, \ldots, n$. If $s_1 \geq t$, let i be the smallest positive integer for which $s_{n+1-i} \geq t$. Then*

$$\phi_j^{DS}(N, \Delta^t, q) = \frac{t}{n}, \quad j = i, \ldots, n,$$

and

$$\phi_j^{DS}(N, \Delta^t, q) = q_j + \frac{\sum_{k=i}^n q_k - (n+1-i)t/n}{i-1}, \quad j = 1, \ldots, i-1.$$

Proof of Theorem 2.10 (sketch). It is simple to demonstrate that ϕ^{DS} satisfies the properties in question. Hence, consider the converse claim.

Using the definitions $L(z) = z$, $\Delta^t(z) = \min\{z, t\}$ and $\Lambda^t(z) = \max\{0, z - t\}$ then, since Zero Cost together with Additivity and Plateau Consistency implies (a weak form of) Constant Returns,

$$\phi_i(N, \Delta^{nq_n}, q) = \phi_i(N, L, q) - \phi_i(N, \Lambda^{nq_n}, q) = q_i - 0 = q_i,$$

for all i.

Observe that $\Lambda^t = L - \Delta^t$ for all t. Let $t \geq nq_n$. By Zero Cost and Additivity,

$$\phi_i(N, \Delta^t, q) = \phi_i(N, \Delta^{nq_n}, q) + \phi_i(N, \Delta^t - \Delta^{nq_n}, q) = \phi_i(N, \Delta^{nq_n}, q),$$

since $\Delta^t - \Delta^{nq_n}$ is non-decreasing and has value 0 at nq_n. Thus, for $t \geq nq_n = s_1$ we have $\phi_i(N, \Delta^t, q) = q_i$, for all i, and consequently, $\phi(N, \Delta^t, q) = \phi^{DS}(N, \Delta^t, q)$ by Lemma 2.1. In the remainder of the proof we assume that $t < s_1$.

By Plateau Consistency we have $\phi_n(N, \Delta^t, q) = t/n$. Now, consider an arbitrary $i \neq n$, and suppose that $\phi_j(N, \Delta^t, q) = \phi_j^{DS}(N, \Delta^t, q)$ for all $j = i + 1, \ldots, n$. We will show that $\phi_i(N, \Delta^t, q) = \phi_i^{DS}(N, \Delta^t, q)$. For this, we consider two separate cases: (1) $t - \sum_{j=i+1}^n q_j \geq 0$, and (2) $t - \sum_{j=i+1}^n q_j < 0$.

Case (1). Repeated use of Fixed Cost, Additivity and Plateau Consistency gives

$$\phi_i(N, \Delta^t, q) = \phi_i\left(N \backslash \{i+1, ..., n\}, \Delta^{t - \sum_{j=i+1}^n q_j}, q^{N \backslash \{i+1,...,n\}}\right)$$

$$+ \frac{q_n - t/n}{n-1} + \frac{q_{n-1} - \frac{t - q_n}{n-1}}{n-2} + ... + \frac{q_{i+1} - \frac{t - \sum_{k=i+2}^n q_k}{i+1}}{i}$$

$$= \phi_i\left(N \backslash \{i+1, ..., n\}, \Delta^{t - \sum_{j=i+1}^n q_j}, q^{N \backslash \{i+1,...,n\}}\right)$$

$$+ \frac{\sum_{k=i+1}^n q_k - (n-i)t/n}{i}.$$

If $s_{n+1-i} \geq t$, then by Plateau Consistency we get

$$\phi_i(N \backslash \{i+1, ..., n\}, \Delta^{t - \sum_{j=i+1}^n q_j}, q^{N \backslash \{i+1,...,n\}}) = \frac{t - \sum_{k=i+1}^n q_k}{i},$$

hence

$$\phi_i(N, \Delta^t, q) = \frac{\sum_{k=i+1}^n q_k - (n-i)t/n}{i} + \frac{t - \sum_{k=i+1}^n q_k}{i}$$

$$= \frac{t}{n}.$$

If $s_{n+1-i} < t$ we have

$$\phi_i(N \backslash \{i+1, ..., n\}, \Delta^{t - \sum_{j=i+1}^n q_j}, q^{N \backslash \{i+1,...,n\}}) = q_i$$

and consequently

$$\phi_i(N, \Delta^t, q) = q_i + \frac{\sum_{k=i+1}^n q_k - (n-i)t/n}{i}.$$

By Lemma 2.1, we conclude that $\phi_i(N, \Delta^t, q) = \phi_i^{DS}(N, \Delta^t, q)$. $\square$

Case (2). By Lemma 2.1, we have $\phi_j^{DS}(N, \Delta^t, q) = \frac{t}{n}$ for $j = i+1, ..., n$. By Plateau Consistency, $\phi_i(N, \Delta^t, q) = t/n$. Now, using Plateau Consistency the residual cost function becomes fixed hence using Fixed Cost we get that $\phi_j(N, \Delta^t, q) = \frac{t}{n}$ for all $j < i$. Thus, $\phi_i(N, \Delta^t, q) = \phi_i^{DS}(N, \Delta^t, q)$.

We hence conclude that $\phi(N, \Delta^t, q) = \phi^{DS}(N, \Delta^t, q)$.

This may be now be generalized to the entire domain of non-decreasing cost functions as demonstrated in Hougaard and Østerdal (2009). $\square$

On the restricted domain of concave costs functions $\check{\mathcal{D}}$ it can be shown that ϕ^{DS} can be characterized by (continuity), Quasi-fixed Cost, Additivity, Plateau Consistency and Unanimity (Lower) Bound (stating that the cost share of any agent i cannot be smaller than the unanimity cost $C(nq_i)/n$).

Now, let $\nu_{\Gamma;\rho,\sigma}$ be a cost sharing rule on $\mathcal{D}^+$ using decomposition Γ and additive sub-rules ρ on $\hat{\mathcal{D}}$ and σ on $\check{\mathcal{D}}$. It turns out that mixed serial cost sharing can be characterized as the only rule that coincides with increasing and decreasing serial cost sharing on the respective domains $\hat{\mathcal{D}}$ and $\check{\mathcal{D}}$, is independent of cost levels below nq_1 and above nq_n, and additive with respect to fixed costs. Formally:

- *Extension:* The cost sharing rule $\nu_{\Gamma;\rho,\sigma}$ is identical to ϕ^{IS} on $\hat{\mathcal{D}}$ and ϕ^{DS} on $\check{\mathcal{D}}$.
- *Independence of irrelevant cost levels:* Let q be given. If two cost functions $C_1, C_2 \in \mathcal{D}^+$ coincide on the interval $[a, b]$ and $a \le nq_1 < nq_n \le b$, then $\nu_{\Gamma;\rho,\sigma}(q, C_1) = \nu_{\Gamma;\rho,\sigma}(q, C_2)$.
- *Fixed-cost additivity:* For any cost function $C \in \mathcal{D}^+$ and fixed-cost function $F \in \mathcal{D}^+$, $\nu_{\Gamma;\rho,\sigma}(q, C + F) = \nu_{\Gamma;\rho,\sigma}(q, C) + \nu_{\Gamma;\rho,\sigma}(q, F)$.

Theorem 2.11 (Hougaard and Thorlund-Petersen 2001). *A decomposition based cost sharing rule $\nu_{\Gamma;\rho,\sigma}$ (with additive sub-rules ρ and σ) on $\mathcal{D}^+$, satisfies Extension, Independence of irrelevant cost levels and Fixed-cost additivity if and only if it is the Mixed Serial Cost Sharing Rule φ^{MS}.*

Proof. It is easily verified that Mixed Serial Cost Sharing satisfies Extension, Independence of irrelevant cost levels and Fixed-cost additivity. To prove the converse: It suffices to consider a piecewise affine cost function C which is determined by some subdivision $0 < Q_1 < Q_2 \ldots$ of $[0, \infty)$. If C equals a convex angle function $C^{\alpha,\beta}(Q) = \max\{0, \alpha Q - \beta\}, \alpha, \beta > 0$, then C only has decomposition $C = C + 0$. Thus, by Extension $\nu_{\Gamma;\rho,\sigma}(q, C^{\alpha,\beta}) = \phi^{IS}(q, C^{\alpha,\beta})$. Since every piecewise affine convex cost function equals a finite sum of convex angle functions on any bounded interval and by assumption the sub-rule ρ is additive we get that $\rho = \phi^{IS}$. Similarly, considering concave angle functions we get $\sigma = \phi^{DS}$.

Now, consider a cost function C decomposed by Γ and demand q confined by the interval $[a, b]$ in the sense that $a \le nq_1 < nq_n \le b$. First, if C is convex on $[a, b]$ then there exists a convex function C^* and a fixed-cost function F^* such that $C^* + F^*$ coincides with C on $[a, b]$. Hence, by Extension and Fixed-cost additivity

$$\nu_{\Gamma;\phi^{IS},\phi^{DS}}(q, C^* + F^*) = \nu_{\Gamma;\phi^{IS},\phi^{DS}}(q, C^*) + \phi^{DS}(q, F^*),$$

and since $\nu_{\Gamma;\phi^{IS},\phi^{DS}}(q, C^*) = \phi^{IS}(q, R + S - F^*)$ we get that S must be affine on $[a, b]$. Likewise we can show that if C is concave on $[a, b]$ then R must be affine on this interval. Consequently, the piecewise affine function is decomposed according to the CS-decomposition. $\square$

Note, that even though ϕ^{IS} and ϕ^{DS} both are additive rules, mixed serial cost sharing does not satisfy Additivity but only Fixed-cost Additivity.

Now, among all cost sharing rules $\nu_{\Gamma;\phi^{IS},\phi^{DS}}$ on $\mathcal{D}^+$ using decomposition Γ and additive sub-rules ϕ^{IS} on $\hat{\mathcal{D}}$ and ϕ^{DS} on $\check{\mathcal{D}}$, mixed serial cost sharing can be characterized as resulting in the most unequal allocation of costs. A somewhat striking result since the CS-decomposition maximizes the concave component and thereby intuitively maximizes the role of ϕ^{DS} which might be expected to lead to more equally distributed cost shares. On the other hand, it follows from Proposition 2.4 that using increasing serial cost sharing on the entire domain of $\mathcal{D}^+$ results in more equal distributions than using mixed serial cost sharing.

Theorem 2.12 (Hougaard and Thorlund-Petersen 2001). *For any decomposition* Γ,

$$\nu_{\Gamma;\phi^{IS},\phi^{DS}} \succ_{LD} \phi^{MS}.$$

Proof. Let $\Gamma(C) = R^* + S^*$ and $\Gamma_{CS}(C) = R + S$ then it must be shown that for any $k = 1, \ldots, n$

$$\sum_{i=1}^{k}(\phi_i^{IS}(q,R) + \phi_i^{DS}(q,S)) \leq \sum_{i=1}^{k}(\phi_i^{IS}(q,R^*) + \phi_i^{DS}(q,S^*)).$$

Now, let $G = R^* - R = S - S^*$ then $\sum_{i=1}^{k}\phi_i^{DS}(q,G) \leq \sum_{i=1}^{k}\phi_i^{IS}(q,G)$ and since it can be shown that G is an increasing convex function (see, e.g., Thon and Thorlund-Petersen 1986) the theorem follows from $\phi^{IS} \succ_{LD} \phi^{DS}$ on $\hat{\mathcal{D}}$ cf. Proposition 2.4.   □

2.3.2.6 Manipulation

In case of homogeneous cost functions the only non-manipulable cost sharing rule is the average cost rule. Hence, all serial rules can be manipulated. In particular, it can be demonstrated that with *convex* cost functions, i.e., for problems in $\hat{\mathcal{D}}$, both increasing and decreasing serial cost sharing can be manipulated by coalitions *equalizing* their demand (for a fixed number of agents) and by agents *splitting* their demand (variable number of agents).

Example 2.8. Let $N = \{1, 2, 3\}$ and $q = (1, 2, 3)$. Then for the convex homogeneous cost function

$$C(Q) = \max\{0, Q - 4.5\},$$

we get the following cost shares using increasing serial cost sharing,

$$x^{IS} = (0, 0.25, 1.25).$$

Now, let agents 1 and 2 equalize their demand such that the new resulting demand vector becomes $\hat{q} = (1.5, 1.5, 3)$. In this case increasing serial cost sharing results in cost shares

$$\hat{x}^{IS} = (0, 0, 1.5),$$

making agents 1 and 2 better off as a group. Also, let agent 2 split his demand into two new demands such that the new demand vector becomes $\tilde{q} = (1, 1, 1, 3)$. In this case increasing serial cost sharing yield the following cost shares

$$\tilde{x}^{IS} = (0, 0, 0, 1.5),$$

making agent 2 better off. $\triangle$

Using a similar type of example it can be demonstrated that with *concave* cost functions, i.e., for problems in $\tilde{\mathcal{D}}$, both increasing and decreasing serial cost sharing can be manipulated by coalitions *spreading* their demand (for a fixed number of agents) and by agents *merging* their demand (variable number of agents).

2.3.3 Rules Based on the Incremental Principle

According to the serial principle above, demands are increasingly ordered and incremental costs (given that ordering) are shared *equally* between the relevant group of agents. Now, consider any ordering of demands: according to the idea of the *incremental principle* agent i *alone* must cover the incremental cost associated with satisfying i's demand given the demand of all agents prior to i in the ordering. In other words, agent i must pay the additional costs connected with a joint operation involving agents with demands prior to i's in the ordering.

Formally, let $\pi : \mathbf{R}^n_+ \to \mathbf{R}^n_+$ be an ordering of demands and let $S_{\pi,i} = \{j \in N | \pi(j) \leq i\}$ denote the set of indices of the first i demands given the ordering π. Now, for a *decomposable* cost function C the incremental principle results in cost shares,

$$x_i^\pi = C\left(\max_{j \in S_{\pi,i}} \{q_j\} \right) - C\left(\max_{j \in S_{\pi,i-1}} \{q_j\} \right). \tag{2.17}$$

Likewise, for a *homogeneous* cost function C the incremental principle results in cost shares,

$$x_i^\pi = C\left(\sum_{j \in S_{\pi,i}} q_j \right) - C\left(\sum_{j \in S_{\pi,i-1}} q_j \right). \tag{2.18}$$

To illustrate the principle, consider the simple case with three agents $N = \{1, 2, 3\}$ and increasingly ordered demands $q_1 \leq q_2 \leq q_3$. For a decomposable cost function the resulting cost shares according to the incremental principle become,

$$x_1 = C(q_1), \quad x_2 = C(q_2) - C(q_1), \quad x_3 = C(q_3) - C(q_2).$$

Likewise, the resulting cost shares for a homogeneous cost function become,

$$x_1 = C(q_1), \quad x_2 = C(q_2 + q_1) - C(q_1), \quad x_3 = C(q_3 + q_2 + q_1) - C(q_2 + q_1).$$

Clearly, the cost share of individual agents depends crucially on the ordering of demands and it is questionable whether such cost shares are fair to all agents for a given ordering (in particular in case of decomposable cost functions). In fact, note that there is a close connection between the incremental principle and the priority rules of the rationing model discriminating between agents.

However, since there are n agents there are $n!$ different orderings of demand vector q. Denote by $\Pi = \{\pi^j | j = 1, \ldots, n!\}$ the set of all such orderings. Consequently, there is a set of $n!$ possible cost shares for every agent, which are in accordance with the incremental principle. Just as the random priority rule of the rationing model was found by taking the average of awards over all the $n!$ possible priorities (see Sect. 2.2.5) we may, in the present model, define a cost sharing rule that takes the average of the incremental cost shares over the set of $n!$ different orderings of demand. Such a cost sharing rule will be called the Shapley rule due to its obvious relation to the Shapley value of a cooperative game, see, e.g., Shubik (1962).

- *The Shapley Cost Sharing Rule* ϕ^{Sh} is defined by cost shares,

$$x_i^{Sh} = \frac{1}{n!} \sum_{\pi \in \Pi} x_i^{\pi} \tag{2.19}$$

for all $i = 1, \ldots, n$.

Further analysis of incremental cost shares as well as the Shapley cost sharing rule is postponed to the next chapter where we consider cost allocation as cooperative games, that is, for the case where the cost function is defined for binary demands $C : \{0, 1\}^N \to \mathbf{R}_+$.

Remark 2.6. For decomposable cost functions $C(\mathcal{Q})$ it can be noted that the Shapley cost sharing rule as defined in (2.19) coincides with the serial rule as defined in (2.14).   △

Presently, an example will be used to compare the results of the different allocation rules of Sect. 2.3.

Example 2.9. Recall the situation of Example 2.6 where three agents ($n = 3$) with demands $q = (1, 3, 5)$ are operating under a homogeneous cost function $C(Q) = Q^2 + 64\sqrt{Q}$. Since the total cost is $C(9) = 273$, the equal split rule results in the cost shares $x^E = (91, 91, 91)$, but since agent 1's stand-alone cost of $C(1) = 65$ is smaller than x_1^E the restricted equal split rule results in the allocation $x^{RE} = (65, 104, 104)$. Now, cost shares using average cost sharing, increasing serial cost sharing and mixed serial cost sharing are respectively,

$x^{AC} = (30.33, 91, 151.67)$,
$x^{IS} = (39.95, 89.19, 143.86)$,
$x^{MS} = (40, 89.2, 143.8)$.

Clearly, the shares of mixed serial cost sharing are more equally distributed than the shares of increasing serial cost sharing (a general property according to Proposition 2.4) and in this case also more equally distributed than average cost sharing.

Finally, using the Shapley cost sharing rule, cost shares can be found by using the incremental principle with respect to all possible orderings of demand and take the average. Since we get that,

$x^{\pi^1} = (65, 79, 129)$,
$x^{\pi^2} = (65, 80.23, 127.76)$,
$x^{\pi^3} = (24.15, 119.85, 129)$,
$x^{\pi^4} = (27.98, 119.85, 125.15)$,
$x^{\pi^5} = (24.66, 80.23, 168.10)$,
$x^{\pi^6} = (27.98, 76.91, 168.10)$,

the resulting cost shares of the Shapley rule become,

$$x^{Sh} = (39.13, 92.68, 141.19).$$

$\triangle$

2.3.4 Comments

As mentioned in Moulin (2002) there is a clear formal relationship (a linear isomorphism) between order-preserving rationing rules and additive cost sharing rules. For example, the proportional rationing rule corresponds to the average cost rule, the random priority rule corresponds to the Shapley cost sharing rule, etc.

In terms of application, average cost sharing is very appealing in its simplicity and underlying notion of fairness (in proportion). Hence, it is often applied in practical cases along with its egalitarian counter part, the serial principle. For example, as mentioned in Sect. 1.3.2, Aadland and Kolpin (1998) record that both average cost sharing and the serial principle are used for sharing irrigation costs among farmers. Moreover, Herzog et al. (1997) demonstrate that the serial principle can be applied sharing multicast cost in computer networks according to the "Equal Link Split Downstream" method. Both papers provide an axiomatic analysis of the specific methods applied.

2.4 Summary

In this chapter we considered simple sharing problems where a group of agents, characterized by a one-dimensional individual factor such as a claim or a demand, should share a common cost (or value) which is either fixed or varies with the level of the characteristic.

In case of sharing a fixed cost (or value) rationing problems were considered. Basically, allocation rules are build around two principles of fairness; *proportionality* and *equality*. However, equality is not well-defined within the model since a rationing problem can be construed either as sharing what is left or as sharing what is lost. The Talmud allocation rule (building on the notion of equality) can be seen as an answer to this problem since this rule is constructed to be self-dual (like the proportional rule), i.e., independent of whether focus is on gains or losses.

It was shown that allocation rules based on both types of fairness satisfied fundamental principles like Equal Treatment of Equals and Consistency. However, only the proportional allocation rule were non-manipulable. Consequently, in cases where manipulation in the form of merging, splitting or reallocation of claims is a potential possibility, non-manipulability is a strong argument in favor of choosing the proportional allocation rule. Moreover, the proportional allocation also relates to the notion of equality although in a more indirect sense: the proportional rule were actually the only rule that preserved equality in the distribution of shares, that is, if characteristics (e.g., claims) become more equally distributed so does the allocated shares (and dually; losses).

In case of sharing a cost (or value) which varies with the level of characteristics, homogeneous (and decomposable) cost sharing problems were considered. Here, principles of proportionality and equality are still relevant but knowledge of the entire cost function introduces the possibility of constructing new allocation principles such as the *serial* and the *incremental* principle. In the present chapter we focussed on the serial principle while further analysis of the incremental principle is postponed to later chapters.

In both cases, however, the principles are based on a pre-specified ordering of agents characteristics (demand). Using the serial principle, the two natural orderings of increasing and decreasing demand defines two distinct allocation rules; increasing and decreasing serial cost sharing. As argued in the text the increasing serial rule seems most relevant on the domain of convex cost functions while the decreasing serial rules seems most relevant on the domain of concave cost functions. Generalizing this observation to the domain of all cost functions that can be decomposed into sums of convex and concave functions we analyzed a non-additive allocation rule called mixed serial cost sharing. On its relevant domain the cost shares resulting from mixed serial cost sharing were more equally distributed than those of both increasing and decreasing serial cost sharing.

Contrary to the proportional rule (average cost sharing), rules based on the serial principle may all be manipulated. Moreover, the proportional rule further satisfies a natural requirement of increasing cost shares for all agents when common costs are increasing – a property which is violated by the serial (and incremental) rules. The serial (and incremental) rules, however, all have the advantage that they are better in reflecting the underlying cost structure than average cost sharing where only information about the cost of total demand is utilized.

References

Aadland D, Kolpin V (1998) Shared irrigation costs: an empirical and axiomatic analysis, Math Soc Sci 35:203–218.

Aumann R, Maschler M (1985) Game theoretic analysis of a bankruptcy problem from the Talmud. J Econ Theory 36:195–213.

Banker R (1981) Equity considerations in traditional full-cost allocation practices: an axiomatic perspective. In: Moriarty S (ed) Joint Cost Allocation. University of Oklahoma, Norman.

Chun Y (1988) The proportional solution for rights problems. Math Soc Sci 15: 231–246.

Chun Y (1999) Equivalence of axioms for bankruptcy problems. Int J Game Theory 28:511–520.

De Frutos MA (1998) Decreasing serial cost sharing under economies of scale. J Econ Theory 79:245–275.

De Frutos MA (1999) Coalitional manipulations in a bankruptcy problem. Rev Econ Des 4:255–272.

Herzog I, Shenker S, Estrin D (1997) Sharing multicast costs. In: McKnight, Bailey (eds) Internet economics. MIT, Cambridge, MA.

Hougaard JL, Thorlund-Petersen L (2000) The stand-alone test and decreasing serial cost sharing. Econ Theory 16:355–362.

Hougaard JL, Thorlund-Petersen L (2001) Mixed serial cost sharing. Math Soc Sci 41:51–68.

Hougaard JL, Thorlund-Petersen L (2002) Bankruptcy rules, inequality and uncertainty, Working Paper 01-04. Department of Operations Management, Copenhagen Business School.

Hougaard JL, Østerdal LP (2005) Inequality preserving rationing. Econ Lett 87:355–360.

Hougaard JL, Østerdal LP (2009) Decreasing serial cost sharing: an axiomatic characterization, Int J Game Theory, (forthcoming).

Ju G-B (2003) Manipulation via merging and splitting in claims problems. Rev Econ Des 8:205–215.

Koster M (2009) Cost sharing. In: Meyers R (ed) Encyclopedia of complexity and systems science. Springer, Berlin.

Marshall A, Olkin I (1979) Inequalities: theory of majorization and its application. Academic, New York.

Moulin H (1987) Equal or proportional division of a surplus and other methods. Int J Game Theory 16:161–186.

Moulin H (1996) Cost sharing under increasing returns: a comparison of simple mechanisms. Games Econ Behav 13:225–251.

Moulin H (2000) Priority rules and other asymmetric rationing rules. Econometrica 68:643–684.

Moulin H (2002) Axiomatic cost and surplus sharing. In: Arrow, Sen, Suzumura (eds) Handbook of social choice and welfare, chap. 6. Elsevier, Amsterdam.

Moulin H, Shenker S (1992) Serial cost sharing. Econometrica 60:1009–1037.

Moulin H, Shenker S (1994) Average cost pricing versus serial cost sharing: an axiomatic comparison. J Econ Theory 64:178–201.

Moyes P (1989) Some classes of functions that preserve the inequality and welfare orderings of income distributions. J Econ Theory 49:347–359.

Moyes P (1994) Inequality reducing and inequality preserving transformations of incomes: symmetric and individualistic transformations. J Econ Theory 63: 271–298.

O'Neill B (1982) A problem of rights arbitration from the Talmud. Math Soc Sci 2:345–371.

Shenker S (1995) Making greed work in networks: a game theoretic analysis of gateway service disciplines. IEEE/ACM Trans Netw 3:819–831.

Shubik M (1962) Incentives, decentralized control, the assignment of joint costs and internal pricing, Manage Sci 8:325–343.

Thomson W (2003) Axiomatic and game-theoretic analysis of bankruptcy and taxation problems: a survey. Math Soc Sci 45:249–297.

Thomson W (2006) A Characterization of a family of rules for the adjudication of conflicting claims, Working Paper no. 530. Rochester Center for Economic Research.

Thon D, Thorlund-Petersen L (1986) Sums of increasing convex and increasing concave functions. Oper Res Lett 5:313–316.

Watts A (1996) On the uniqueness of equilibrium in Cournot oligopoly and other games. Games Econ Behav 13:269–285.

Young HP (1987) On dividing an amount according to individual claims or liabilities. Math Oper Res 12:398–414.

Young HP (1988) Distributive justice in taxation. J Econ Theory 44:312–335.

Chapter 3
Cost Allocation as Cooperative Games

3.1 Introduction

There is a wide range of situations where a group of agents (broadly interpreted as persons, departments, organizations or countries) benefit from cooperative actions, but is left with the problem of sharing the related costs. These situations range from everyday life problems such as people sharing a cab to international agreements like the Kyoto protocol where industrialized countries bargain over emission cuts. In everyday situations, like sharing a cab, there are rarely time to make use of sophisticated allocation rules even though the problem itself may be rather complex: typically the allocation becomes more or less random and people often tend to use rules of thumb. In situations like bargaining between countries over emission cuts, the final outcome will typically reflect the countries bargaining power rather than sophisticated considerations of fairness.

But even though there may be many obstacles to making fair allocations in practice, it is nevertheless worth pursuing the issue of fairness: Joint actions are often economically rational and when it is efficient to cooperate it becomes important to use cost sharing methods that encourage cooperative actions and sustain such cooperation in the long run. Therefore, the allocation of costs must be accepted by all participants by ensuring a certain level of fairness.

The following scenarios fit the framework:

1. "Agents" may, for example, refer to two municipalities that plan to build a joint facility. Building two separate facilities is more costly than the joint project so cooperation is economically efficient and should be encouraged. Therefore, it remains to find a reasonable and fair way to share the costs of the joint facility. Assuming that the municipalities are homogeneous except from their estimated costs (e.g., characterized by an equal number of citizens) it seems fair to require that no municipality shall pay more than the costs of building their own facility (the *stand-alone cost* of each municipality). Otherwise cooperation is not likely to take place (with resulting inefficiency). If the municipalities are not homogeneous, for example, if

they differ with respect to the number of citizens, and this ought to influence the allocation of costs, the problem can be reformulated in costs per capita.

2. "Agents" may also refer to units of the same type: Airport landing fees is a classical case in the cost sharing literature (see, e.g., Littlechild and Thompson 1977). Assume that the costs of building and maintaining runways shall be covered by airport landing fees. Typically, runways are used by many different types of planes where larger planes require longer runways. Obviously it is economically rational to build a runway that may serve all types of planes instead of separate runways for each type. But this raises the problem of sharing the costs between different types of aircrafts.

3. Finally, "agents" may refer to products or objectives as in the Tennessee Valley Authority case mentioned in Sect. 1.3.1. During the 1930s the US government launched a project building multi-purpose reservoirs to control flooding, provide electric power and improve navigational and recreational resources of the Tennessee River Basin. Once it is decided to undertake such a project and "optimal" target levels for each purpose are estimated it remains to share the total costs between the three main purposes. In Ransmeier (1942) it is explicitly stated that the cost share of any purpose, or combination of purposes, should not exceed the related stand-alone cost.

While it is rather clear that "agents", in the sense of persons or organizations, require a fair cost allocation in order to encourage and sustain cooperation in the long run it seems less obvious why fairness should play a crucial role in cases where "agents" are interpreted as products or objectives that cannot act strategically. But, it turns out that we may equivalently express the stand-alone cost conditions for products as conditions stating that no product (or group of products) must be subsidized by other products (or group of products), see Sect. 3.3 for further details. Thus, (indirectly) fairness in terms of the stand-alone cost conditions still play a crucial role in relation to firms business strategies, since a proper allocation of the costs of joint production (where no products are subsidized) prevents the management from misjudging the profitability of individual products.

Finally, note that compared to simple sharing problems (in Chap. 2) we may construe situations like (1)–(3) above as agents operating under a common cost function with binary demand $q_j \in \{0, 1\}$ for all j – that is, either agents get served at some preassigned level or not.

3.2 The Model

Let $N = \{1, \ldots, n\}$ be a group of n agents (interpreted as persons, organizations, branches or departments of a corporation, objectives, products, etc.) and let $\mathcal{P}(N)$ be the set of all coalitions (subsets) of N – there are $2^n - 1$ such coalitions disregarding the empty set $\emptyset$. Let $c : \mathcal{P}(N) \to \mathbf{R}$ be a discrete cost function where $c(S)$ represents the least costs of serving coalition $S \in \mathcal{P}(N)$ with $c(\emptyset) = 0$ by definition. Now, a pair (N, c) constitutes a *cost sharing problem*. Denote by Γ the set of all such cost sharing problems.

Given a cost allocation problem (N, c) we can associate a *cost savings problem* (N, v) where $v(S) = \sum_{i \in S} c(i) - c(S)$ for all $S \subset N$. Denote by $\hat{\Gamma}$ the set of all such cost savings problems (the cost savings problem is an ordinary coalitional game with transferable utility – a so-called TU-game, see, e.g., Peleg and Sudhölter 2003).

A cost sharing problem $(N, c) \in \Gamma$ is said to be *essential* if the cooperative solution is strictly preferred to the purely non-cooperative solution, i.e., if $c(N) < \sum_{i \in N} c(i)$. Likewise, a cost savings problem (N, v) is said to be *essential* if $v(N) > \sum_{i \in N} v(i)$.

Cost sharing (savings) problems are said to be *monotonic* if costs (savings) increase when the size of the coalition increases, i.e., if, for all $S' \subset S \subset N$ that $c(S') \leq c(S)$ (or $v(S') \leq v(S)$).

One way to state that cooperation is beneficial is to require that the costs connected with cooperation should always be smaller than adding up the costs of separate activities. In general, a cost sharing problem $(N, c) \in \Gamma$ is said to be *concave* if, for all $S, S' \subset N$ that

$$c(S \cup S') + c(S \cap S') \leq c(S) + c(S'). \tag{3.1}$$

In particular, if the condition holds for all S, S' where $S \cap S' = \emptyset$, (N, c) is said to be *subadditive*. Likewise, we could state that cooperation is beneficial by requiring that the cost savings connected with cooperation should always be larger than adding up the savings of separate activities. In general, a cost savings problem $(N, v) \in \hat{\Gamma}$ is said to be *convex* if, for all $S', S \subset N$ that

$$v(S \cup S') + v(S \cap S') \geq v(S) + v(S'). \tag{3.2}$$

In particular, if the condition holds for all S, S' where $S \cap S' = \emptyset$, (N, v) is said to be *superadditive*. Note, that if (N, c) is subadditive (concave) if and only if (N, v) is superadditive (convex).

A *cost allocation rule* is a function $\phi : \Gamma \to \mathbf{R}^n$ where

$$\phi_1(N, c) + \ldots + \phi_n(N, c) = c(N). \tag{3.3}$$

Likewise, a *savings allocation rule* is a function $\hat{\phi} : \hat{\Gamma} \to \mathbf{R}^n$ where

$$\hat{\phi}_1(N, v) + \ldots + \hat{\phi}_n(N, v) = v(N). \tag{3.4}$$

A *cost allocation* is a vector $x \in \mathbf{R}^n$ where $x_1 + \ldots + x_n = c(N)$. Likewise, a *savings allocation* is a vector $y \in \mathbf{R}^n$ where $y_1 + \ldots + y_n = v(N)$.

Finally, note that in practical applications of the model there may be difficulties involved in establishing the entire cost structure. In the worst case there will only be one realized cost, i.e., the total cost $c(N)$ of the common project (which has to be shared) and costs connected with all other coalitions $S \subset N$, are estimated on a hypothetical basis as some kind of expected costs in case S alone were to realize a common project. Since the number of coalitions may be very large even for a relatively small number of agents (e.g., 1,023 if $n = 10$) the task of estimating costs associated with all subsets may be very demanding (and often impossible) in practice. Consequently, there has been some doubt about the practical feasibility as well as relevance of the entire approach particularly in the accounting literature, see, e.g., Mirghani and Scapens (1995).

However, apart from issues of practical application the model plays an important role as an ideal approach to cost allocation in situations as specified above. Moreover, in practice, costs may turn out to be conveniently structured facilitating application of the model as demonstrated by the cases in Sect. 3.2.1.

3.2.1 Some Applications

Consider the following three applications of the model:

(1) Littlechild and Thompson (1977) model costs of aircraft movement (take-off's and landings) for a single airport (Birmingham) for a single time period (1968–1969). The costs of an airport movement area has a particularly simple structure since the costs of building a runway is determined by the largest aircraft for which it is designed and the costs of using the runway is proportional to the number of movements for each type of aircraft. Hence, let N be a set of movements by m aircraft types $j = 1, \ldots, m$ and assume that the costs of building a runway designed for aircrafts of type j is C_j where,

$$0 = C_0 < C_1 < \ldots < C_m,$$

since larger aircrafts (in terms of a higher index j) require longer, and thereby more expensive, runways.

Moreover, let N_j be the set of movements of aircrafts of type j, i.e.,

$$N = \bigcup_{j=1}^{m} N_j.$$

Further, for a given subset of movements $S \subseteq N$, let

$$j(S) = \max\{j | S \cap N_j \neq \emptyset\}$$

be the type of aircraft among the subset S with maximal runway building costs. Hence, the runway building costs of any subset of movements $S \subseteq N$ can be found as $\hat{c}(S) = C_{j(S)}$.

Now, let $n_j(S) = |S \cap N_j|$ be the number of type j movements among the set $S \subseteq N$ where the direct runway user costs of a movement of type j aircrafts is denoted z_j. Hence, allocating costs of building and operating a runway to specific movements (and thereby establish airport movement fees) can be modeled as a cost allocation problem (N, c) where

$$c(S) = \sum_{j \in S} z_j n_j(S) + C_{j(S)} \quad (c(\emptyset) = 0),$$

for all $S \subseteq N$. Hence, the entire cost structure is well established.

(2) Van den Nouweland et al. (1996) consider cost savings by rerouting international telephone calls. Instead of using direct circuits from the originating country to the destination country, costs may be saved by rerouting the calls via the international network. Due to time differences between Europe, America and Asia, circuits can be used more effectively if high traffic loads between some parts of the world can be rerouted via other parts of the world during their low traffic hours. Basically, this involves the cooperation of three international carriers; a carrier in the originating country, a transit carrier and a carrier in the destination country. This situation can be modeled as a cost saving problem (N, v) between a set N of international carriers with cost savings given by the function v. Since the cost savings are realized in 3-agent coalitions (that is between a carrier in the originating country, a transit carrier and a carrier in the destination country) the cost savings of an arbitrary coalition $S \subseteq N$ of carriers can be approximated as the sum of cost savings that can be obtained by any 3-agent subcoalition of S, i.e.,

$$v(S) = \sum_{T \subseteq S : |T| = 3} v(T),$$

for all $S \subseteq N$. Note that the cost savings of a given 3-carrier coalition $v(T)$ depends on the location of the carriers; costs are saved when the traffic from a carrier in one time zone to a carrier in another time is rerouted via a carrier in a third time zone while rerouting within the same time zone does not lead to any significant savings. This particular structure simplifies the subsequent savings allocation. Further considerations of network allocation problems can be found in Chap. 3.

(3) Bjørndal et al. (2004) consider networks of Automated Teller Machines (ATMs) where customers of one bank may use the ATMs of any other bank in the network to provide services such as cash withdrawals, etc. The related cost allocation problem is modeled in the following way: Let N denote the set of banks in the network and let L denote the set of possible locations (of the ATMs). Moreover, let n_i^l be the number of

transactions of bank $i \in N$ in location $l \in L$ and let $n^l(S) = \sum_{i \in S} n_i^l$ for $S \subset N$ be the total number of transactions in location l belonging to coalition S. Denote by A^l the set of banks that have ATMs at location l. Now, it is assumed that at any location l, customers of bank i will use the ATMs of bank i if these are available. Further it is assumed that transaction costs are the same for all banks: the transaction cost will be α if a customer uses an ATM of his own bank and β if he uses that of another bank where $\beta > \alpha$. The costs of a transaction which does not involve an ATM is assumed to be γ where $\gamma > \beta$ $(> \alpha)$.

If the banks $S \subset N$ form a network then for any location $l \in L$ their total amount of transaction costs is determined by

$$c^l(S) = \alpha n^l(S \cap A^l) + \beta n^l(S \setminus A^l)$$

if $S \cap A^l \neq \emptyset$ and $\gamma n^l(S)$ otherwise. Consequently, we may define a related cost savings problem (N, v) where, for each network (coalition) S, the saving is determined as total stand-alone cost minus network costs summed over all possible locations, i.e.,

$$v(S) = \sum_{l \in L} \left(\sum_{i \in S} c^l(i) - c^l(S) \right) = (\gamma - \beta) \sum_{l \in L: S \cap A^l \neq \emptyset} n^l(S \setminus A^l),$$

for all $S \subseteq N$. Thus, also in this case, there is a well established cost and saving structure.

3.3 The Stand-alone Cost Principle

Using the framework of Sect. 3.2 the stand-alone cost principle states that no coalition of agents S can be allocated total costs exceeding their stand-alone cost $c(S)$. Formally:

- *The stand-alone cost principle:* Let $x \in \mathbf{R}^n$ be a cost allocation related to the allocation problem (N, c), then for every coalition $S \subset N$,

$$\sum_{i \in S} x_i \leq c(S).$$

In other words, no coalition of agents has incentive to block cost allocations satisfying the stand-alone cost principle. Hence such allocations can be seen as sustaining cooperation among the agents in N.

Dually, we may consider the marginal cost principle stating that no coalition S must be subsidized by agents of the complement $N \setminus S$, i.e., no coalition can be allocated total costs lower than their marginal cost $c(N) - c(N \setminus S)$. Formally:

- *The marginal cost principle:* Let $x \in \mathbf{R}^n$ be a cost allocation related to allocation problem (N, c), then for every coalition $S \subset N$,

$$\sum_{i \in S} x_i \geq c(N) - c(N \setminus S).$$

Note that the marginal cost principle is equivalent to the stand-alone cost principle since,

$$\sum_{i \in S} x_i \geq c(N) - c(N \setminus S) = \sum_{i \in N} x_i - c(N \setminus S) \Leftrightarrow \sum_{i \in N \setminus S} x_i \leq c(N \setminus S).$$

For a given cost allocation problem (N, c), denote by core(N, c), the set of cost allocations satisfying the conditions of the stand-alone cost principle (or equivalently, those of the marginal cost principle), i.e.,

$$\text{core}(N, c) = \{x \in \mathbf{R}^n | \sum_{i \in N} x_i = c(N), \sum_{i \in S} x_i \leq c(S), \forall S \subset N\} =$$

$$\{x \in \mathbf{R}^n | \sum_{i \in N} x_i = c(N), \sum_{i \in S} x_i \geq c(N) - c(N \setminus S), \forall S \subset N\}.$$

Note that the core is a compact and convex subset of $\mathbf{R}^n$. Further, note that if, for example "agents" are interpreted as objectives or products then "agents" cannot choose strategically to block joint actions and are in some sense forced to cooperate. As such, the stand-alone cost principle seems to loose part of its relevance. However, due to the equivalence between the stand-alone cost and the marginal cost principle, one can still argue for the relevance of core allocations based on the no-subsidization argument behind the marginal cost principle as mentioned in Sect. 3.1.

Obviously, there may be situations where some coalitions violate the stand-alone cost principle, i.e., the core may be empty. If the core is empty, it means that there is no possibility of sharing the total cost, which sustain a joint action of all agents. For example, if there are no advantages from cooperation. However, even if the cost allocation problem is essential (i.e., $c(N) < \sum_{i \in N} c(i)$) we, generally, cannot guarantee that the core is non-empty as demonstrated by the following result.

Proposition 3.1. *Let (N, c) be an essential cost allocation problem where c has constant sum (i.e., $c(S) + c(N \setminus S) = c(N)$, $\forall S \subset N$), then core$(N, c) = \emptyset$.*

Proof. Let (N, c) be essential and have constant sum. Assume that $x \in$ core(N, c). Hence, for all $i \in N$ we have that

$$\sum_{j \in N \setminus i} x_j \leq c(N \setminus i).$$

Since c has constant sum $c(N \setminus i) = c(N) - c(i)$ and we get that

$$\sum_{j \in N \setminus i} x_j + c(i) \le c(N) = \sum_{j \in N} x_j \quad \Rightarrow \quad c(i) \le x_i.$$

Hence, $\sum_{i \in N} c(i) \le \sum_{i \in N} x_i = c(N)$ contradicting that the problem (N, c) is essential.   □

Looking for necessary and sufficient conditions for non-empty core we need some further definitions.

Given the set of agents N, a collection $\mathcal{B} = \{S_1, \ldots, S_m\}$ of non-empty subsets of N is called *balanced* if there exists positive numbers $\delta_1, \ldots, \delta_m$ such that

$$\sum_{j : i \in S_j} \delta_j = 1, \quad \text{for every } i \in N.$$

The collection δ is called a system of *balancing weights*.

Note that every partition of N is a balanced collection and, consequently, balanced collections can be viewed as generalized partitions. In case agents are interpreted as persons, we may think of balancing weights as indicating a percentage of the agents total time spend in given coalitions. The total costs of all such balanced arrangements can be shown to play a crucial role in relation to the existence of core elements.

Theorem 3.1 (Bondareva 1963; Shapley 1967). *There exists at least one cost allocation satisfying the stand-alone cost principle for cost allocation problem (N, c) (i.e., $\text{core}(N, c) \ne \emptyset$) if and only if, for all systems of balancing weights δ, that*

$$\sum_{S \subseteq \mathcal{B}} \delta_S c(S) \ge c(N).$$

Proof. Consider the following linear program

$\max z = \sum_{i \in N} x_i$
s.t. $\sum_{i \in S} x_i \le c(S) \ \forall S \subseteq N, \ S \ne \emptyset.$

Clearly, any solution x to this problem is in the core of (N, c) and conversely, if $x \in \text{core}(N, c)$ then $\sum_{i \in N} x_i = c(N)$. Thus, in optimum $z^* \ge c(N)$. By duality of linear programming the dual (linear) program is given by

$\min d = \sum_{S \subseteq N} \delta_S c(S)$
s.t. $\sum_{S : i \in S} \delta_S = 1, \ \forall i \in N, \ \delta_S \ge 0, \forall S \subseteq N, \ S \ne \emptyset.$

As both programs are feasible, it follows from the duality theorem (see, e.g., Taha 1989) that the optimal value is the same for both programs. Thus, (N, c) has non-empty core if and only if $\sum_{S \subseteq N} \delta_S c(S) = d^* = z^* \ge c(N)$. □

Consequently, if a cost sharing problem (N, c) has non-empty core, we say that (N, c) is balanced.

Example 3.1. In case of 3-agent problems $N = \{1, 2, 3\}$ all partitions of $\{1, 2, 3\}$ are balanced as well as the collection $(\{1, 2\}, \{1, 3\}, \{2, 3\})$. Balancing weights are given as solutions to the equations,

$$\delta_1 + \delta_{12} + \delta_{13} = 1,$$
$$\delta_2 + \delta_{12} + \delta_{23} = 1,$$
$$\delta_3 + \delta_{13} + \delta_{23} = 1.$$

Hence, according to Theorem 3.1, there exists allocations satisfying the stand-alone cost principle in case of 3-agent cost allocation problems if and only if,

$c(1) + c(2, 3) \geq c(1, 2, 3),$
$c(2) + c(1, 3) \geq c(1, 2, 3),$
$c(3) + c(1, 2) \geq c(1, 2, 3),$
$c(1) + c(2) + c(3) \geq c(1, 2, 3),$
$0.5(c(1, 2) + c(1, 3) + c(2, 3)) \geq c(1, 2, 3).$

It appears that subadditivity of (N, c) is a necessary condition for non-empty core since, in general, any partition of N is balanced. Moreover, note that the last condition is satisfied if (N, c) is concave. $\triangle$

Proposition 3.2 (Shapley 1971). *Let (N, c) be a concave cost allocation problem, then there exists at least one cost allocation satisfying the stand-alone cost principle (i.e., $\text{core}(N, c) \neq \emptyset$).*

Proof. Let π be a given ordering of the elements in N (since $N = \{1, \ldots, n\}$ there are $n!$ such orderings). Moreover, let $S_{\pi,k} = \{i \in N | \pi(i) \leq k\}$, $k = 0, \ldots, n$, be the k first elements of the ordering π. Thus, $S_{\pi,0} = \emptyset$ and $S_{\pi,n} = N$. Consider the incremental cost shares $x_i^\pi = c(S_{\pi,\pi(i)}) - c(S_{\pi,\pi(i)-1})$, $\forall i \in N$. We claim that $x^\pi \in \text{core}(N, c)$, when (N, c) is concave.

Indeed, let $T \subset N$, and j be the first element of $N \backslash T$ given π. All elements prior to j (given π) are consequently in T. Hence, $T \cup S_{\pi,\pi(j)} = T \cup j$, and $T \cap S_{\pi,\pi(j)} = S_{\pi,\pi(j)-1}$. By concavity of (N, c),

$$c(T) + c(S_{\pi,\pi(j)}) \geq c(T \cup S_{\pi,\pi(j)}) + c(T \cap S_{\pi,\pi(j)}) =$$

$$c(T \cup j) + c(S_{\pi,\pi(j)-1}).$$

Implying that,
$$x_j^\pi \geq c(T \cup j) - c(T).$$

Since
$$x_j^\pi = \sum_{h \in T \cup j} x_h^\pi - \sum_{h \in T} x_h^\pi,$$

we get that,
$$\sum_{h \in T} x_h^\pi - c(T) \leq \sum_{h \in T \cup j} x_h^\pi - c(T \cup j).$$

Repeating this argument $n - t - 1$ times (where $t = |T|$) we get,

$$\sum_{h \in T} x_h^\pi - c(T) \le \sum_{h \in N} x_h^\pi - c(N) = 0,$$

and since T was arbitrarily chosen, $x^\pi \in \text{core}(N, c)$. $\square$

In fact, as shown by Shapley (1971), when the problem (N, c) is concave the vertices of the core consist of the $n!$ incremental cost allocations x^π and conversely, (Ichiishi 1981) when all $n!$ incremental cost allocations x^π are contained in the core, then (N, c) is concave.

Remark 3.1. For interpretational reasons, it can be noted that concavity of (N, c) is equivalent to decreasing marginal contribution to coalitional costs for given agents i, i.e., $c(S \cup i) - c(S) \ge c(S' \cup i) - c(S')$ for all $i \in N$, all $S, S' \subset N \setminus \{i\}$ and $S \subset S'$. To see this, consider coalitions $S \cup i$ and S'. By concavity of (N, c), $c(S \cup i) + c(S') \ge c(S \cup i \cup S') + c(S \cup i \cap S') = c(S' \cup i) + c(S)$, since $S \subset S'$. Conversely, let $S \subset S'$, and let $T = N \setminus S'$ consist of agents $\{i_1, \dots, i_t\}$. Hence,

$$c(S \cup i_1) - c(S) \ge c(S' \cup i_1) - c(S')$$

$$c(S \cup \{i_1, i_2\}) - c(S \cup i_1) \ge c(S' \cup \{i_1, i_2\}) - c(S' \cup i_1)$$

$$\vdots$$

$$c(S \cup T) - c(S \cup T \setminus i_t) \ge c(S' \cup T) - c(S' \cup T \setminus i_t).$$

Adding these inequalities we have, for all $R \subset T$ that

$$c(S \cup R) - c(S) \ge c(S' \cup R) - c(S').$$

Consider arbitrary coalitions $\bar{S}$ and $\bar{S}'$, and let $S = \bar{S} \cap \bar{S}'$, $S' = \bar{S}'$ and $R = \bar{S} \setminus \bar{S}'$. Thus, $c(\bar{S} \cap \bar{S}' \cup \bar{S} \setminus \bar{S}') - c(\bar{S} \cap \bar{S}') \ge c(\bar{S}' \cup \bar{S} \setminus \bar{S}') - c(\bar{S}')$, yielding $c(\bar{S}) - c(\bar{S} \cap \bar{S}') \ge c(\bar{S} \cup \bar{S}') - c(\bar{S}')$, i.e., the conditions for concavity of (N, c). $\triangle$

Example 3.2. In the case of balanced cost allocation problems some core allocations may involve a transfer of money from some agents to others, i.e., core allocations may include negative cost shares even though $c(S) \ge 0$ for all $S \subseteq N$. For example, consider the following simple 2-agent problem (which is balanced): $c(1) = 8$, $c(2) = 2$ and $c(1, 2) = 1$. Clearly, in this case there are strong positive externalities from cooperation. The core consists of all allocations $\alpha(-1, 2) + (1 - \alpha)(8, -7), \alpha \in [0, 1]$. Thus, for example, the allocation $x = (-1, 2)$ satisfies the stand-alone cost principle but in this case agent 2 must cover all costs plus subsidize agent 1 with 1 unit in order to sustain cooperation.

In general, it is difficult to say whether such allocations are meaningful or not. On the one hand, it seems unreasonable that some agents should subsidize other agents in order to cooperate. Indeed, agent 2, of the above example, could simply cover all costs connected with the joint action himself and then let agent 1 free ride. Thus agent 1's threat to block the cooperation is an empty threat. In this sense it is difficult to argue that some agents should pay more than the total costs of the joint project. On the other hand, we cannot rule out the possibility of situations where some agents are willing to pay other agents to join the common project in order to obtain substantial savings. Therefore the relevance of core allocations with negative shares must depend of the specific situation. △

Since all $n!$ incremental cost shares $x_i^\pi = c(S_{\pi,\pi(i)}) - c(S_{\pi,\pi(i)-1})$ span the core when (N, c) is concave, we get that $\mathrm{core}(N, c) \subset \mathbf{R}_+^n$ if and only if c is monotonic. Unfortunately it is not as straightforward to find necessary and sufficient conditions for positive core elements in the general case of balanced problems.

Note, that for balanced cost savings problems (N, v) where $v(S) \geq 0$ for all $S \subseteq N$, the core will only contain non-negative allocations.

Example 3.3. For certain classes of allocation problems, the core plays a particular role from a purely operational point of view. For example, in the case of cost allocation in linear production: consider a production process where two inputs (a_1, a_2) are transformed into three outputs (b_1, b_2, b_3). The technology matrix is given by,

$$A = \begin{pmatrix} 0.25 & 0.10 \\ 8 & 5 \\ 4 & 6 \end{pmatrix}.$$

Input prices p are respectively \$200 and \$150 per unit.

Assume that three departments $\{1, 2, 3\}$ use this type of production process. Department $\{1\}$ must produce at least output vector $b(1) = (9, 260, 200)$. Department $\{2\}$ must produce at least output vector $b(2) = (5, 120, 200)$, and finally, department $\{3\}$ must produce at least output vector $b(3) = (14, 590, 400)$.

Hence, every department is faced with the problem of minimizing costs given input prices and the output requirement. For department $\{1\}$ this problem reads:

min $200a_1 + 150a_2$
s.t.
$0.25a_1 + 0.10a_2 \geq 9$
$8a_1 + 5a_2 \geq 260$
$4a_1 + 6a_2 \geq 200$.
$a_1, a_2 \geq 0$

Optimal solution is $(\hat{a}_1, \hat{a}_2) = (30.9, 12.7)$ yielding a total cost of $8,091.
For department $\{2\}$ the problem reads:

min $200a_1 + 150a_2$
s.t.
$0.25a_1 + 0.10a_2 \geq \quad 5$
$\quad 8a_1 + \quad 5a_2 \geq 120$
$\quad 4a_1 + \quad 6a_2 \geq 200$ '
$\qquad a_1, a_2 \geq \quad 0$

Optimal solution is $(\hat{a}_1, \hat{a}_2) = (9.1, 27.3)$ with total costs $5,909.
Finally, for department $\{3\}$ the problem reads:

min $200a_1 + 150a_2$
s.t.
$0.25a_1 + 0.10a_2 \geq \quad 14$
$\quad 8a_1 + \quad 5a_2 \geq 590$
$\quad 4a_1 + \quad 6a_2 \geq 400$ '
$\qquad a_1, a_2 \geq \quad 0$

Optimal solution is $(\hat{a}_1, \hat{a}_2) = (55, 30)$ with total costs $15,500.
The aggregate result of separate production is hence $b(1) + b(2) + b(3) =$
$(28, 970, 800)$ at a total cost of $

$$8091 + 5909 + 15500 = 29500.$$

Now, all three departments could agree to produce the aggregate output
requirement $(28, 970, 800)$ jointly, yielding the following joint problem:

min $200a_1 + 150a_2$
s.t.
$0.25a_1 + 0.10a_2 \geq \quad 28$
$\quad 8a_1 + \quad 5a_2 \geq 970$
$\quad 4a_1 + \quad 6a_2 \geq 800$ '
$\qquad a_1, a_2 \geq \quad 0$

Optimal solution is $(\hat{a}_1, \hat{a}_2) = (80, 80)$ with total costs $28,000, and conse-
quently the joint effort is less costly. In this way we can elicit a cost function
c and hence a cost allocation problem involving the three departments:

Department S	Cost $c(S)$
$\{1\}$	8,091
$\{2\}$	5,909
$\{3\}$	15,500
$\{1, 2\}$	14,000
$\{1, 3\}$	22,500
$\{2, 3\}$	19,909
$\{1, 2, 3\}$	28,000

It remains to allocate the total costs of joint production ($28,000) between the three departments. Now, it is easy to demonstrate that the above allocation problem is balanced. Thus, the core is non-empty. Core restrictions are given by $x_1 + x_2 + x_3 = 28000$ and,

$$x_1 = 8091,$$

$$5500 \leq x_2 \leq 5909,$$
$$14000 \leq x_3 \leq 15500.$$

A cost allocation satisfying the stand-alone cost principle can be found using the shadow prices resulting from the dual LP-problem:

max $28y_1 + 970y_2 + 800y_3$

s.t.
$$0.25y_1 + 8y_2 + 4y_3 \leq 200$$
$$0.10y_1 + 5y_2 + 6y_3 \leq 150,$$
$$y_1, y_2, y_3 \geq 0$$

with optimal solution $(\hat{y}_1, \hat{y}_2, \hat{y}_3) = (545.5, 0, 15.9)$.

Using these shadow prices we obtain the following cost allocation satisfying the stand-alone cost principle,

$$x_1 = 545.5 \cdot 9 \ + 0 \cdot 260 + 15.9 \cdot 200 = \ 8091,$$
$$x_2 = 545.5 \cdot 5 \ + 0 \cdot 120 + 15.9 \cdot 200 = \ 5909,$$
$$x_3 = 545.5 \cdot 14 + 0 \cdot 590 + 15.9 \cdot 400 = 14000.$$

This turns out to be a general result. Let N be the set of departments and let, for all coalitions $S \subseteq N$, the cost function be determined by

$$c(S) = \min\{p \cdot a \,|\, Aa \geq b(S) \text{ and } a \geq 0\},$$

where $b(S) = \sum_{i \in S} b(i)$. Let $\hat{y}$ be the optimal solution to the dual problem for coalition N, i.e., the solution to the problem

$$\max\{y \cdot b(N) \,|\, A^t y \leq p \text{ and } y \geq 0\}.$$

Then, we claim that the cost allocation $x_i = \hat{y} \cdot b(i)$, for all $i \in N$, is a core allocation of the problem (N, c). Indeed, by duality of linear programming

$$\hat{y} \cdot b(N) = c(N) = \sum_{i \in N} x_i.$$

Moreover, since for each $S \subset N$, that the solution y_S to the problem

$$\max\{y \cdot b(S) \,|\, A^t y \leq p \text{ and } y \geq 0\},$$

satisfies $c(S) = y_S \cdot b(S) \geq y \cdot b(S)$ for any y where $A^t y \leq p$, we have, in particular, that

$$\sum_{i \in S} x_i = \hat{y} \cdot b(S) \leq c(S), \; \forall S.$$

General results concerning LP-games and the core may, e.g., be found in Curiel (1997).   △

As demonstrated by the discussion and examples above the immediate impression is that we should focus on relevant cost allocations within the core (in case the core is non-empty). By the following example, however, we end this section showing that there may be arguments in favor of allocations which do *not* comply with the stand-alone cost principle.

Example 3.4. Consider the following cost allocation problem where $N = \{1, 2, 3\}$ and c is given by

$$c(\emptyset) = 0, \quad c(i) = 1, \quad i = 1, 2, 3,$$
$$c(1,2) = c(1,3) = 1, \quad c(2,3) = 2,$$
$$c(1,2,3) = 2.$$

Combined use of the stand-alone cost principle and the marginal cost principle results in the following restrictions on cost shares,

$$0 = c(1,2,3) - c(2,3) \leq x_1 \leq c(1) = 1,$$
$$1 = c(1,2,3) - c(1,3) \leq x_2 \leq c(2) = 1,$$
$$1 = c(1,2,3) - c(1,2) \leq x_3 \leq c(3) = 1.$$

Since $x_1 + x_2 + x_3 = c(1,2,3) = 2$ we get that $core(N, c) = (0, 1, 1)$. If cost allocations have to comply with the stand-alone cost principle, then the only possibility is the allocation $(0, 1, 1)$. But notice that it is costless for agent 2 and 3 to block cooperation with agent 1, while such an action would be very costly to agent 1. Hence, it could be argued that agent 1 has to pay a small share of the total cost in order to ensure that agent 2 and 3 will, in fact, cooperate. An allocation like $(\epsilon, 1 - \epsilon/2, 1 - \epsilon/2)$ would violate the stand-alone cost principle for coalitions $\{1, 2\}$ and $\{1, 3\}$ but there is no reason to expect that the extreme allocation $(0, 1)$ would be the result of "subproblems" $c(i) = c(j) = c(ij) = 1$, for $i = 1$ and $j = 2, 3$ – so maybe an allocation like $(\frac{1}{3}, \frac{5}{6}, \frac{5}{6})$ would be reasonable?   △

3.4 Four Allocation Rules

If the gains from cooperation are large enough there are many ways to share the common costs which satisfy the stand-alone cost principle and the challenge is rather to select one particular allocation. As examples of such selections from the core we introduce the nucleolus and the Lorenz allocation in Sects. 3.4.1 and 3.4.2. In general, however, there are also good arguments in favor of selections that potentially are in conflict with the stand-alone cost principle. As examples of such selections we introduce the Shapley value and τ-value in Sects. 3.4.3 and 3.4.4.

3.4.1 The Nucleolus

Consider a given allocation problem (N, c) and let x be a specific cost allocation (i.e., $x_1 + \ldots + x_n = c(N)$). Now, given (N, c) and x let, for all coalitions $S \subset N$,

$$e_S(x) = c(S) - \sum_{i \in S} x_i \qquad (3.5)$$

be the gains of coalition S from a cooperative action among the agents in N given the particular cost allocation x. Note that $e_S(x) \geq 0$, for all S, if and only if x satisfies the stand-alone cost principle. Hence, given the cost allocation x, coalition S is said to be better off than coalition T if S gains more than T from cooperation among N, i.e., if $e_S(x) > e_T(x)$.

One type of fairness requirement concerning a cost allocation x relates to favoring the worst off part, given the allocation x. As e indicates the gain from cooperation given x, we may require that the allocation x ought to maximize the value of e for the worst off coalition S. This is basically the idea behind the *nucleolus* introduced by Schmeidler (1969).

Formally, denote by $e(x) \in \mathbf{R}^{2^n - 2}$ the vector of gains given the allocation x and let $\theta : \mathbf{R}^{2^n - 2} \to \mathbf{R}^{2^n - 2}$ map vector elements in increasing order. Now, the nucleolus of cost allocation problem (N, c), denoted by x^{Nuc}, is defined as the allocation which lexicographically maximizes $\theta(e(x))$, i.e., the nucleolus is defined by the allocation rule,

$$\phi^{Nuc}(N, c) = \{x \in I(N, c) | \theta(e(x)) \succ_{lex} \theta(e(y)), \ \forall y \in I(N, c)\}, \qquad (3.6)$$

where $I(N, c) = \{x \in \mathbf{R}^n | \sum_{i \in N} x_i = c(N)\}$ and $\succ_{lex}$ is the lexicographic ordering: $x \succ_{lex} y$ if $x_1 > y_1$ or $x_1 = y_1$ and $x_2 > y_2$, etc.

For a given cost allocation problem (N, c), it can be shown that x^{Nuc} is unique and that $x^{Nuc} \in \text{core}(N, c)$ when (N, c) is balanced. Consequently $\phi^{Nuc}(N, c)$ is a core selection.

Remark 3.2. Computation of the Nucleolus can be done by solving a series of LP-problems (see, e.g., Owen 1995): First solve

$\max \epsilon$

s.t.

$\quad e_S(x) \geq \epsilon, S \subset N$
$\quad x \in I(N, c).$

Let ϵ_1 be the optimal solution and let A_1 be the set of coalitions S for which the coalitional gain is ϵ_1 for all optimal solutions (x, ϵ_1). If the optimal x is unique it is the nucleolus. If there are multiple optimal solutions x, then solve the following problem,

$$\max \epsilon$$
s.t.
$$e_S(x) \geq \epsilon, S \subset N$$
$$e_S(x) = \epsilon_1, \quad \forall S \in A_1$$
$$x \in I(N, c).$$

Let ϵ_2 be optimal solution and let A_2 be the set of coalitions S with coalitional gain ϵ_2 for all optimal solutions (x, ϵ_2). As long as there are multiple optimal solutions x, continue to solve the $(k+1)$'th LP-problem defined by adding to the k'th problem, the following restrictions,

$$e_S(x) = \epsilon_k \quad \forall S \in A_k,$$

where
$$A_k = \{S | e_S(x) = \epsilon_k \text{ for all optimal solutions } (x, \epsilon_k)\}.$$

A unique allocation, i.e., the nucleolus, is obtained after solving at most $n-1$ such LP-problems.   △

Example 3.5. Consider balanced 2-agent cost allocation problems. In this case the situation is particularly simple because

$$e(x) = (c(1) - x_1, c(2) - x_2) = (c(1) - x_1, c(2) - c(1,2) + x_1),$$

since $x_1 + x_2 = c(1,2)$. The nucleolus is hence determined by solving $c(1) - x_1 = c(2) - c(1,2) + x_1$, that is,

$$x_1^{Nuc} = \frac{c(1,2) - c(2) + c(1)}{2} = c(1) + \frac{c(1,2) - c(1) - c(2)}{2},$$

and similarly

$$x_2^{Nuc} = c(2) + \frac{c(1,2) - c(1) - c(2)}{2}.$$

Hence, in case of 2-agent problems, the nucleolus share the gain from cooperation equally between the two agents. Since the core is determined as all allocations $x(\alpha) = \alpha(c(1,2) - c(2), c(2)) + (1-\alpha)(c(1), c(1,2) - c(1))$, for $\alpha \in [0,1]$, the nucleolus corresponds to $x(0.5)$, i.e., the "mid-point" of the core when the problem is balanced.   △

The nucleolus may also be based on per capita gains

$$\hat{e}_S(x) = \frac{1}{|S|} e_S(x), \tag{3.7}$$

in which case it is denoted the *per capita nucleolus*. The per capita nucleolus is also a core selection for balanced cost allocation problems.

Remark 3.3. Consider the n-agent rationing model (q, E) of Chap. 2 and define, in the present setting, the related allocation problem $(N, v_{(q,E)})$ by

$$v_{(q,E)}(S) = \max\{E - \sum_{i \in N \setminus S} q_i, 0\}, \ \forall \ S \subset N.$$

That is, an allocation problem where the worth of each coalition of agents is determined as the non-negative amount left over when all other agents have satisfied their demands. Note that $v_{(q,E)}$ is a function expressing values which is convex and hence the core of $(N, v_{(q,E)})$ is non-empty. In Aumann and Maschler (1985) it is shown that the Talmud rule of the rationing model corresponds to the nucleolus of allocation problem $(N, v_{(q,E)})$. △

3.4.2 The Lorenz Allocation

Fairness can also be interpreted as distributional equality in the sense of Lorenz domination (see Sect. 2.2.2 in Chap. 2) and Lorenz maximization can consequently be a criterion for selection over the core. Unfortunately the set of Lorenz maxima, $L(N, c) = \{x \in \text{core}(N, c) | x \succ_{LD} y, \ \forall y \in \text{core}(N, c)\}$, over the core of a balanced cost allocation problem need not be unique. Uniqueness of $L(N, c)$ can only be guaranteed for concave cost allocation problems, see, e.g., Dutta and Ray (1989). As such, Lorenz maximization over the core will only lead to a selection if (N, c) is concave.

Thus, consider the class of *concave* cost allocation problems (N, c). Then the *Lorenz-allocation rule* ϕ^L is defined by cost shares $x^L = L(N, c)$.

Remark 3.4. Let (N, c) be a concave cost allocation problem. By Dutta and Ray (1989) the following algorithm determines x^L: Let $g(S, c) = c(S)/|S|$ be the average costs of coalition S:

(1) First, let $c_1 = c$. Define $S_1 \subset N$ as the largest coalition with the smallest average costs $g(S_1, c_1)$. Let $x_i^L = g(S_1, c_1)$, for all $i \in S_1$.
(k) Assume that $S_1, \ldots, S_{k-1}$ have been defined recursively where $S_1 \cup \ldots \cup S_{k-1} \neq N$. Define a new cost allocation problem where $c_k(S) = c_{k-1}(S_{k-1} \cup S) - c_{k-1}(S_{k-1})$ and let S_k be the largest coalition with the smallest average costs $g(S_k, c_k)$. Let $x_i^L = g(S_k, c_k)$, for all $i \in S_k$.

In $m \leq n$ such steps, $\{S_1, \ldots, S_m\}$ will be a partition of N, and x^L can be demonstrated to be the unique Lorenz maximal allocation in the core. △

Example 3.5 (continued). For the class of 2-agent balanced cost allocation problems, $L(N, c)$ is unique and hence a core selection. Compared to the nucleolus which is the "mid-point" of the core, the Lorenz allocation is either the equal split allocation (if this is in core) or that extreme point of the core which is "closest" to the equal split allocation. Formally, for 2-agent allocation problems,

$$x_i^L = \begin{cases} \min(c(i), \frac{c(ij)}{2}) & \text{if } c(j) \geq \frac{c(ij)}{2} \\ c(ij) - c(j) & \text{otherwise.} \end{cases}$$

△

Clearly, if the equal split allocation satisfies the stand-alone cost principle then this allocation is the Lorenz maximal core selection.

An important difference between the nucleolus and the Lorenz allocation relates to the property of "independence of irrelevant core alternatives" stating that if $x \in \text{core}(N, c)$ is selected for the allocation problem (N, c) then this allocation should also be selected for any cost allocation problem $(N, \hat{c})$ for which $x \in \text{core}(N, \hat{c}) \subseteq \text{core}(N, c)$. Since, by definition, the Lorenz allocation only depends on the core restrictions, ϕ^L satisfies independence of irrelevant core alternatives, whereas the nucleolus relates to the entire set of coalitional costs and thereby violates independence of irrelevant core alternatives as illustrated by the following example.

Example 3.6. Consider a 3-agent cost savings problem (N, v) defined by

$v(1) = v(2) = v(3) = 0,$
$v(1, 2) = v(1, 3) = 1, \quad v(2, 3) = 0,$
$v(1, 2, 3) = 2.$

Clearly, this problem is balanced and the equal split allocation is in the core. Therefore the Lorenz allocation is $x^L = (\frac{2}{3}, \frac{2}{3}, \frac{2}{3})$. The nucleolus is the allocation $x^{Nuc} = (1, \frac{1}{2}, \frac{1}{2})$. Now, there is a rather large family of cost allocation problems related to the cost savings problem above $(v(S) = \sum_{i \in S} c(\{i\}) - c(S))$. Take for example c and $\hat{c}$ defined as

$c(1) = c(2) = c(3) = 1,$
$c(1, 2) = c(1, 3) = 1, \quad c(2, 3) = 2,$
$c(1, 2, 3) = 1.$

and

$\hat{c}(1) = 1.5 \quad \hat{c}(2) = 1, \quad \hat{c}(3) = 0.5,$
$\hat{c}(1, 2) = \hat{c}(2, 3) = 1.5, \quad \hat{c}(1, 3) = 1,$
$\hat{c}(1, 2, 3) = 1.$

Note that in both cases the equal split allocation is in the core implying that the Lorenz allocation of both (N, c) and $(N, \hat{c})$ is $x^L = (\frac{1}{3}, \frac{1}{3}, \frac{1}{3})$.

Contrary to this we see that the nucleolus of (N, c) is $(0, \frac{1}{2}, \frac{1}{2})$ and of $(N, \hat{c})$ is $(\frac{1}{2}, \frac{1}{2}, 0)$. Since both c and $\hat{c}$ relate to the same savings problem it does not seem to agree with a principle of fairness that in the one case agent 1 is treated most favourable whereas in the other case agent 3 is treated most favourable. It could be argued that if, by a principle of fairness, the allocation $(0, \frac{1}{2}, \frac{1}{2})$ was selected for the problem (N, c) then this allocation should also be selected for the problem $(N, \hat{c})$ since it is still in the core and no coalition has an objection against it. But, clearly the nucleolus does not respect independence of irrelevant core alternatives. The Lorenz solution, on the other hand, does.

$\triangle$

In the general case of *balanced* cost allocation problems, results and characterizations concerning the set of Lorenz maxima over the core, $L(N, c)$, may be found in Hougaard et al. (2001).

Remark 3.3 (continued). Notice that if φ is an allocation rule with respect to the rationing model (q, E) (and hence satisfies $0 \leq x_i \leq q_i$ for all $i \in N$) then $\varphi \in \mathrm{core}(N, v_{(q,E)})$. Indeed, assume conversely that there exists a coalition S such that $\sum_{i \in S} x_i < v_{(q,E)}(S) = \max\{0, E - \sum_{i \in N \setminus S} q_i\}$. Since $x_i \geq 0$ for all $i \in N$ we must have that

$$\sum_{i \in S} x_i < E - \sum_{i \in N \setminus S} q_i \quad \Leftrightarrow \quad \sum_{i \in N \setminus S} q_i < \sum_{i \in N \setminus S} x_i,$$

contradicting that $q_i \geq x_i$ for all $i \in N$.

Since, by Theorem 2.1, the Constrained Equal Gains rule, φ^{CEG}, is the unique Lorenz maximizer among allocation rules of the rationing problem, it is equivalent to the Lorenz allocation of the problem $(N, v_{(q,E)})$. $\triangle$

3.4.3 The Shapley Value

The costs associated with any coalition of agents S are given by $c(S)$ and consequently it is possible to determine the marginal costs of letting agent i join an arbitrary coalition S, where $i \notin S$, i.e., $m_i(S) = c(S \cup i) - c(S)$. Clearly, the marginal costs may vary with coalition S. For example, by Remark 3.1 it is known that $m_i(S)$ is non-increasing in S when (N, c) is concave.

Now, one way of allocating the total costs $c(N)$ using these marginal costs $m_i(S)$ is, for example, by taking a weighted average of m_i over all coalitions $S \subseteq N \setminus i$. As such, define the *Shapley value* ϕ^{Sh} of a cost allocation problem (N, c) by the cost shares,

$$x_i^{Sh} = \sum_{S \subseteq N \setminus i} \frac{s!(n - s - 1)!}{n!} m_i(S), \quad \text{for all } i \in N, \tag{3.8}$$

(where $|S| = s$ and $0! = 1$). Note, that this is equivalent to taking the average of the incremental costs associated with agent i over all $n!$ possible orderings π of n agents (as done in case of simple sharing problems in Chap. 2, Sect. 2.3.3).

Example 3.5 (continued). Consider again the class of 2-agent cost allocation problems. Straightforward application of the definition yields, c

$$(x_1^{Sh}, x_2^{Sh}) = \left(\frac{c(1,2) - c(2) + c(1)}{2}, \frac{c(1,2) - c(1) + c(2)}{2} \right),$$

i.e., the gain from cooperation is shared equally between the two agents making the Shapley value coincide with the nucleolus on the class of 2-agent allocation problems.

Alternatively, there are $2! = 2$ possible orderings of two agents, i.e., $\pi^1 = 1, 2$ and $\pi^2 = 2, 1$. For agent 1, incremental cost shares are hence given by:

$$x_1^{\pi^1} = c(1) - c(\emptyset) = c(1)$$
$$x_1^{\pi^2} = c(1,2) - c(2).$$

Clearly, $x_1^{Sh} = 0.5 x_1^{\pi^1} + 0.5 x_1^{\pi^2} = 0.5(c(1,2) - c(2) + c(1))$. Likewise, $x_2^{Sh} = 0.5 x_2^{\pi^1} + 0.5 x_2^{\pi^2} = 0.5(c(1,2) - c(1) + c(2))$. △

Now, as it appears in Example 3.5, the Shapley value coincide with the nucleolus on the class of 2-agent allocation problems but this does not generalize to n-agent problems. In fact, the Shapley value need not even be a core selection for balanced problems, as demonstrated by the following simple example.

Example 3.7. Consider a 3-agent cost allocation problem given by

$$c(1) = 2, \quad c(2) = 1, \quad c(3) = 3,$$
$$c(1,2) = c(1,3) = c(2,3) = 3, \quad c(1,2,3) = 4.$$

The problem is balanced (and hence the core is non-empty) but *not* concave since, for instance, $c(1,2,3) + c(3) = 7 > c(1,3) + c(2,3) = 6$. The Shapley value is $x^{Sh} = (1.33, 0.83, 1.83)$, which violates the stand-alone cost principle for coalition $\{1,3\}$ since $x_1^{Sh} + x_3^{Sh} = 3.16 > c(1,3) = 3$. Note, however, that it is questionable whether coalition $\{1,3\}$ would actually block cooperation, since using the Shapley value to allocate costs in the projected problem involving only agent 1 and 3 ($c(1) = 2, c(3) = 3$ and $c(1,3) = 3$) results in the cost allocation $x_{c|\{1,3\}}^{Sh} = (1,2)$. Thus, agent 3 is actually worse off by "standing-alone" with agent 1 (paying 2) than in the fully cooperative case (paying 1.83). Hence, the threat by agent 1 and 3 to block cooperation does not seem credible as agent 3 will be worse off. △

In general, when (N,c) is concave, the vertices of the core consist of the $n!$ incremental cost allocations x^π, and since the Shapley value is the average of the incremental cost allocations, concavity of (N,c) consequently ensures that the Shapley value satisfies the stand-alone cost principle and becomes a core selection.

Remark 3.5. Hart and Mas-Colell (1989) provide an alternative interpretation of the Shapley value. For every allocation problem (N, c) let $P(N, c)$ be the single valued so-called *potential* of the problem where $P(\emptyset, c) = 0$ and let $M_i^P(N, c) = P(N, c) - P(N \setminus i, c)$ be the marginal contribution of agent i in terms of potential. Now, requiring that $\sum_{i \in N} M_i^P(N, c) = c(N)$ uniquely determines the potential of (N, c) as

$$P(N, c) = \sum_{S \subseteq N} \frac{(s-1)!(n-s)!}{n!} c(S).$$

Indeed, since $P(\emptyset, c) = 0$ we get that $P(i, c) = c(i)$ and consequently that

$$P(ij, c) = \frac{c(ij) + P(i, c) + P(j, c)}{2} = \frac{c(ij) + c(i) + c(j)}{2}$$

and further

$$P(ijk, c) = \frac{c(ijk)}{3} + \frac{c(ij) + c(ik) + c(jk)}{6} + \frac{c(i) + c(j) + c(k)}{3},$$

etc. It is easily seen that the Shapley value is the marginal contribution in terms of potential, i.e., $\phi_i^{Sh}(N, c) = P(N, c) - P(N \setminus i, c) = M_i^P(N, c)$. $\triangle$

Remark 3.3 (continued). As already indicated the Shapley value of allocation problem $(N, v_{(q,E)})$ is equivalent to the so-called the random priority rule of the rationing model (q, E), see Chap. 2, Sect. 2.2.5. $\triangle$

Remark 3.6. Note that for *concave* cost allocation problems, the Lorenz allocation rule, ϕ^L, Lorenz-dominates the both the nucleolus and the Shapley value while these latter rules cannot be ranked using the partial Lorenz ordering, i.e.

$$\phi^L \succeq_{LD} \{\phi^{Nuc}, \phi^{Sh}\}.$$

In other words, for some concave allocation problems the cost shares of the nucleolus are more equally distributed than those of the Shapley value while for others the cost shares of the Shapley value are more equally distributed than those of the nucleolus. The Lorenz-allocation, on the other hand, is always Lorenz-dominating all other allocations in the core. $\triangle$

3.4.4 The τ-Value

For a given cost allocation problem, let $M_i = c(N) - c(N \setminus i)$ denote the marginal cost of agent i joining the complement $N \setminus i$ and let $M = (M_1, \ldots, M_n)$ be the vector of such marginal costs for all n agents.

Following the argument of the marginal cost principle (see Sect. 3.3), M_i can be interpreted as a lower bound for agent i's cost share.

For any coalition $S \subseteq N$, let $g(S) = c(S) - \sum_{i \in S} M_i$ denote the cost gap related to S, i.e., the difference between the stand-alone cost of S and the total lower bound of cost shares. It can be argued that, if $i \in S$, then agent i should never pay more than $M_i + g(S)$ and, consequently, an upper bound for i's cost share can be found as $M_i + w_i$ where $w_i = \min_{S:i \in S} g(S)$.

Consider the class of cost allocation problems for which $g(S) \geq 0$ for all $S \subseteq N$ and $\sum_{i \in N} w_i \geq g(N)$. In particular, these conditions are satisfied for balanced cost allocation problems. Now, following Tijs (1981), define the τ-value of cost allocation problem (N, c) by the cost shares

$$x_i^\tau = M_i + \frac{w_i}{\sum_{i \in N} w_i} g(N), \quad \text{for all } i \in N. \tag{3.9}$$

That is, the τ-value of agent i is determined by agent i's marginal cost plus a share of the total cost gap $g(N)$ which is proportional to the minimal cost gap related to coalitions containing i.

Example 3.5 (continued). Consider 2-agent cost allocation problems. Following the definitions above we get that

$M_1 = c(1,2) - c(2),$
$M_2 = c(1,2) - c(1),$
$g(\{1\}) = c(1) - c(1,2) + c(2),$
$g(\{2\}) = c(2) - c(1,2) + c(1),$
$g(\{1,2\}) = c(2) + c(1) - c(1,2),$

implying that $w_1 = w_2 = c(1) + c(2) - c(1,2)$. Note, that if c is essential then $g(S) \geq 0$ for $S \subseteq \{1,2\}$ and $\sum_{i \in N} w_i \geq g(N)$. Consequently, the τ-value, ϕ^τ, is determined by cost shares

$$x_1^\tau = c(1,2) - c(2) + \frac{c(1) + c(2) - c(1,2)}{2} = \frac{1}{2} \left(c(1) - c(2) + c(1,2) \right),$$

$$x_2^\tau = c(1,2) - c(1) + \frac{c(1) + c(2) - c(1,2)}{2} = \frac{1}{2} \left(c(2) - c(1) + c(1,2) \right).$$

Thus, on the class of 2-agent cost allocation problems the τ-value coincides with the Shapley value and the nucleolus. Moreover, it can be shown that the τ-value is a core selection for all balanced 3-agent cost allocation problems. △

In the particular case of concave cost allocation problems, where (according to Remark 3.1)

$$c(S \cup i) - c(S) \geq c(S' \cup i) - c(S') \quad \text{for } S \subset S' \subset N \setminus i,$$

we have that

$$c(S \cup i) - c(S) \geq M_i \quad \Leftrightarrow \quad g(S \cup i) \geq g(S)$$

and consequently $w_i = g(i)$ for all $i \in N$. Therefore

$$x_i^\tau = M_i + \frac{g(i)}{\sum_{i=1}^n g(i)} g(N), \tag{3.10}$$

which is also known as the *Alternate-Cost-Avoided method* used in the Tennessee Valley project mentioned in Sects. 1.3.1 and 3.1 (3). See, e.g., Tijs and Driessen (1986) for further details.

On the class of balanced cost allocation problems the τ-value need not satisfy the stand-alone cost principle as demonstrated by the following example.

Example 3.8. Consider the following 5-agent cost allocation problem where,

$c(i) = 10$ for $i \in \{1, 2, 3, 4, 5\}$,
$c(1, 3) = c(1, 4) = c(1, 5) = c(2, 3) = c(2, 4) = c(2, 5) = 19$,
$c(3, 4) = c(3, 5) = c(4, 5) = 18$,
$c(1, 2) = 15$,
$c(3, 4, 5) = 20$,
$c(S) = c(S \cap \{1, 2\}) + c(S \cap \{3, 4, 5\})$ for all $S \subseteq N = \{1, 2, 3, 4, 5\}$ where $|S| \geq 3$.

(in particular; $c(N) = 35$). Note that $w_i = g(i)$ for all $i \in N$ but the problem is *not* concave since, for instance, $c(2, 3) + c(3, 4, 5) < c(2, 3, 4, 5) + c(3)$. The problem, however, is balanced and the core is hence non-empty. Determining the τ-value of cost allocation problem (N, c) we note that $M = (5, 5, 2, 2, 2)$ and

$$w = (g(1), g(2), g(3), g(4), g(5)) = (5, 5, 8, 8, 8).$$

Hence, $\sum_{i=1}^5 w_i = 34$, and $g(N) = 35 - 16 = 19$ yielding

$$x^\tau = (7.794, 7.794, 6.470, 6.470, 6.470).$$

But x^τ violates the stand-alone cost principle, e.g., for coalition $\{1, 2\}$ since $x_1^\tau + x_2^\tau = 15.588 > 15 = c(1, 2)$. For comparison the Shapley value is given by

$$x^{Sh} = (7.45, 7.45, 6.70, 6.70, 6.70)$$

which also violates the stand-alone cost principle, e.g., for coalition $\{3, 4, 5\}$ since $x_3^{Sh} + x_4^{Sh} + x_5^{Sh} = 20.1 > 20 = c(3, 4, 5)$. Due to the particular structure of c, there is a unique Lorenz maximizing allocation in the core given by

$$x^L = (7.5, 7.5, 6.667, 6.667, 6.667).$$

$\triangle$

Even on the class of concave problems the τ-value may violate the stand-alone cost principle as hinted by the fact that the τ-value coincides with the Alternate-Cost-Avoided method on this class.

Remark 3.3 (continued). The τ-value of the cost allocation problem $(N, v_{(q,E)})$ is equivalent to the so-called *adjusted proportional rule* of the rationing model (q, E), defined in Curiel et al. (1987). $\triangle$

3.5 Monotonicity Vs. the Stand-alone Cost Principle

Typically, cooperative actions require repeated use of a given allocation rule based on periodical reassessments of the costs involved. Qualitative evaluation of particular cost allocation rules therefore also includes an analysis of how such rules respond to changes in the costs. Loosely speaking, it seems that if the costs change in a certain way the resulting cost allocation should change in a parallel fashion. For example, assume that the corporate center of some company searches for a cost allocation rule to share the joint costs related to n branches. An important criterion for the selection of such a rule is that it induces the right incentives among the branches once the rule is implemented. Since the corporate center will be interested in cost reductions it is important that the allocation rule ensures that no branch will have incentive to block a cost reduction because its resulting cost share will increase as a consequence of reducing costs. This can be expressed in two equivalent fashions: first, assume that the costs of all coalitions containing branch i has been reduced while the costs of all other coalitions remain fixed, then i cannot receive a larger cost share. Formally:

- A cost allocation rule ϕ is *coalitionally monotonic* if, for all $i \in N$ that,

$$[c(S) \geq \hat{c}(S) \text{ for all } S \supseteq i \text{ and } c(T) = \hat{c}(T) \text{ otherwise}]$$
$$\Rightarrow \; \phi_i(N, c) \geq \phi_i(N, \hat{c}).$$

Alternatively, if the costs are reduced for a given coalition (the costs of all other coalitions kept fixed) then the resulting cost share of any member of that coalition cannot increase. Formally, for a particular coalition $S \subset N$:

- A cost allocation rule ϕ is *S-monotonic* if, for all $i \in S$,

$$[c(S) \geq \hat{c}(S) \text{ and } c(T) = \hat{c}(T) \text{ for all } T \neq S] \; \Rightarrow \; \phi_i(N, c) \geq \phi_i(N, \hat{c}).$$

We say that an allocation rule ϕ is *coalitionally monotonic* if ϕ is S-monotonic for all coalitions $S \subseteq N$.

Broadly speaking, we may view the stand-alone cost principle as ensuring that cooperation is not blocked by conflicting interests, as *given* by the participation constraints of all coalitions, while the property of coalitional monotonicity relates to conflicting interests among members of a coalition when the participation constraints *vary*. As it turns out, there is a trade-off between these conditions, in the sense that, no allocation rule can satisfy both the stand-alone cost principle and coalitional monotonicity on the class of balanced cost allocation problems.

Theorem 3.2 (Young 1985). *For $n \geq 4$ no core allocation rule satisfies coalitional monotonicity (i.e., S-monotonicity for all $S \subseteq N$).*

Proof. Young proved the theorem for $n \geq 5$ but this result is extended in Housman and Clark (1998) to $n \geq 4$ using the following proof for $n = 4$: By contradiction, let ϕ be a core allocation rule which is coalitionally monotonic on 4-agent problems. Consider the cost allocation problem $c(1) = c(2) = c(3) = c(4) = 10$, $c(1,2) = c(3,4) = 20$, $c(1,3) = c(1,4) = c(2,3) = c(2,4) = 19$, $c(1,2,3) = c(1,2,4) = c(1,3,4) = c(2,3,4) = 29$ and $c(1,2,3,4) = 38$. In addition, define c^1, c^2, c^3 and c^4 by c except for $c^1(1,3,4) = c^2(2,3,4) = c^3(1,2,3) = c^4(1,2,4) = 28$. Now, $\text{core}(N, c^1) = \text{core}(N, c^2) = \{(10, 10, 9, 9)\}$ and $\text{core}(N, c^3) = \text{core}(N, c^4) = \{(9, 9, 10, 10)\}$, and consequently, $\phi(N, c^1) = \phi(N, c^2) = (10, 10, 9, 9)$ and $\phi(N, c^3) = \phi(N, c^4) = (9, 9, 10, 10)$.

Since $c(1,3,4) = 29 > 28 = c^1(1,3,4)$ and $c(S) = c^1(S)$ for $S \neq \{1,3,4\}$ we have, by coalitional monotonicity, that $\phi_1(N, c) \geq \phi_1(N, c^1) = 10$. Likewise, we get $\phi_i(N, c) \geq \phi_i(N, c^i) = 10$ for $i = 2, 3, 4$, contradicting that $\sum_{i=1}^{4} \phi_i(N, c) = c(N) = 38$.   □

Remark 3.7. As demonstrated in Housman and Clark (1998) there is an infinite class of core allocation rules that are coalitionally monotonic on the class of 3-agent allocation problems. Moreover, note that N-monotonicity – that is,

$$[c(N) \geq \hat{c}(N) \text{ and } c(T) = \hat{c}(T) \text{ for all } T \neq N] \Rightarrow \phi_i(N, c) \geq \phi_i(N, \hat{c}),$$

for all $i \in N$ – is inherently different from S-monotonicity with respect to any proper subcoalition. By increasing the costs related to coalition N a new set of feasible cost allocations emerge whereas increasing the costs related to any proper subcoalition reduces the set of core allocations.   △

As a direct consequence of Theorem 3.2, we see that neither the nucleolus nor the per capita nucleolus (which are core selections) can be coalitionally monotonic on the class of balanced cost allocation problems. In fact, the nucleolus is not even N-monotonic (but the per capita nucleolus is). The Shapley value, on the other hand, is clearly coalitionally monotonic by the way it is defined, but it is not a core selection on the class of balanced problems. The τ-value is neither coalitionally nor N-monotonic.

Since coalitional monotonicity is a desirable property based on consideration of fairness, as well as incentives, it once more indicates that there are good arguments in favor of allocations, which do not necessarily comply with the stand-alone cost principle (as the Shapley value $(\frac{1}{3}, \frac{5}{6}, \frac{5}{6})$ in Example 3.4). To find such compliance we need to restrict attention to subclasses of allocation problems.

On the subclass of concave cost allocation problems the Lorenz allocation is a well defined core selection, which is coalitionally monotonic, see, e.g., Hougaard et al. (2005) for a more general result. Note also, that on this class the Shapley value is another example of a core selection which is coalitionally monotonic. Again, the nucleolus fails to satisfy N-monotonicity (Hokari 2000).

Remark 3.8. In Hougaard and Østerdal (2006) the nature of S-monotonicity is further examined for the particular case where some central planner (HQ) is imagined to select a core allocation by maximizing a (strictly concave and differentiable) objective function over the set of allocations satisfying the stand-alone cost principle. In this case it is demonstrated that for suitably large problems ($|N| \geq 4$ and $|S| \geq 3$) S-monotonicity is tantamount to a favoring of coalition S in the sense that the selected cost allocation must minimize the aggregate costs of coalition S, given the core constraints. It therefore follows that coalitional monotonicity is impossible, since the central planner cannot favor all coalitions simultaneously. It is furthermore shown that no choice of objective function can ensure N-monotonicity, i.e., we cannot exclude situations where some agents have the incentive to block cost reductions related to the entire group of agents. Since there are many N-monotonic allocation methods and N-monotonicity is a desirable property, it highlights the "costs" of insisting on maximizing a (strictly concave and differentiable) objective function over the set of allocations satisfying the stand-alone cost principle. $\triangle$

Another relevant monotonicity property of cost allocation rules concerns variation in the population. For instance, imagine a situation where joint costs are shared among a group of agents facing positive network externalities. In this case, it is natural to require that the selected allocation rule should support the inclusion of new members into the network, for example, by requiring that no coalition of the original members should be worse off by an enlargement and hence have an incentive to block it. Formally, consider N as any non-empty finite subset of the set of natural numbers $\mathbf{N}$ and let $c_{|S}$ be the restriction of c to $S \subset N$. Now:

- A cost allocation rule ϕ is *population-monotonic* if, for all S, N with $S \subset N$ that

$$\phi_i(S, c_{|S}) \geq \phi_i(N, c),$$

for all $i \in S$.

For the particular case of concave cost allocation problems it can be shown that both the Shapley value and the Lorenz-allocation (as well as generalizations hereof) are population monotonic, see, e.g., Sprumont (1990) and Hougaard et al. (2005) respectively, while the nucleolus is not, see, e.g., Hokari (2000). The τ-value also fails population monotonicity.

3.6 Axiomatic Characterizations

There is a large literature characterizing the four allocation rules above by various sets of axioms. In order to make these characterizations as comparable as possible, we shall focus on distributional characteristics for 2-agent problems and the property of consistency (see also Sect. 2.2.3 for the consistency property related to rationing models).

3.6.1 Consistency and Reduced Problems

Loosely speaking, consistency requires that reallocation of costs among a subcoalition of agents should result in cost shares identical to those resulting from the original allocation problem. In other words, for members of any coalition $T \subset N$, cost shares should be the same regardless of whether we apply some allocation rule ϕ on the original problem (N, c) or on a reduced problem (T, c_T^ϕ) where members in the complement of T have been "bought off". Formally, consistency is defined as follows:

- *Consistency*: Let (T, c_T^ϕ) be a reduced problem and let ϕ be a cost allocation rule. Then,

$$\phi_i(T, c_T^\phi) = \phi_i(N, c),$$

for every problem (N, c), every coalition $T \subset N$, and all $i \in T$.

Clearly, we have to be more precise in defining the exact form of the reduced problem since members in $N \backslash T$ may be "bought off" in several different ways. In particular, we shall focus on two standard forms, i.e., the Davis–Maschler and the Hart–Mas-Colell reduced problems.

Consider a given cost allocation problem (N, c) and a specific cost allocation $\phi(N, c) = x$. For any coalition $T \subset N$ define the *Davis–Maschler Reduced Problem* (T, c_T^ϕ) by

$$c_T^\phi(S) = \min_{S' \subseteq N \backslash T} \{ c(S \cup S') - \sum_{i \in S'} \phi_i(N, c) \}, \tag{3.11}$$

for all $S \subset T$, and $c_T^\phi(T) = c(N) - \sum_{i \in N \backslash T} \phi_i(N, c)$.

The Davis–Maschler reduced problem (T, c_T^ϕ) may be interpreted as follows: the members of coalition T are going to share their related aggregate costs $\sum_{i \in T} x_i$, given allocation x, on the basis of an underlying cost structure which is determined by all subcoalitions S of T being free to "buy out" members of the complement of T (including the empty set) in the way which minimize their own costs. For example if $N = \{1, 2, 3, 4, 5\}$ and $T = \{1, 2, 3\}$, then agent 1 is free to minimize $\{c(1), c(1, 4) - x_4, c(1, 5) - x_5, c(1, 4, 5) - x_4 - x_5\}$.

Alternatively, consider a given cost allocation problem (N,c) and some cost allocation rule ϕ. For any coalition $T \subset N$ define the *Hart–Mas-Colell Reduced Problem* (T, c_T^ϕ) by

$$c_T^\phi(S) = c(S \cup S') - \sum_{i \in S'} \phi_i(S \cup S', c_{|S \cup S'}), \qquad (3.12)$$

for all $S \subseteq T$, where $S' = N \backslash T$ and $c_{|S \cup S'}$ is the restriction of c to $S \cup S' \subseteq N$.

The Hart–Mas-Colell reduced problem (T, c_T^ϕ) may be interpreted as follows: the members of subcoalitions S of T must "buy out" all members of the complement of T according to their aggregate cost share in the appropriate restricted problem $(S \cup (N \backslash T), c_{|S \cup (N \backslash T)})$. For example if $N = \{1,2,3,4,5\}$ and $T = \{1,2,3\}$, then $c(1) = c(1,4,5) - \phi_4(\{1,4,5\}, c_{|\{1,4,5\}}) - \phi_5(\{1,4,5\}, c_{|\{1,4,5\}})$.

Hence, the Hart–Mas-Colell and the Davis–Maschler reduced problems differ in two main aspects. First, the Hart–Mas-Collel form relates to a general cost allocation rule ϕ used on restricted problems and not a specific cost allocation $\phi(N,c) = x$. Second, the members of S are not free to "buy out" members of the complement of T such as to minimize their costs.

Which of the two reduced forms is most relevant depends on the particular context being modeled. For instance, Hart and Mas-Colell (1989) mention that their reduced form seems reasonable in cases where a company has branches in several countries (or states) and wants to perform country specific cost studies knowing that the branches of the other countries are "active". Here, consistency requires that cost allocation among the branches of the specific country should remain the same whether the accountants of the corporate center consider the reduced allocation problem of the country itself or the allocation problem related to the company's global (or nation wide) activities. Contrary to this consider the Davis–Maschler reduced form: imagine a situation where a subgroup of agents wants to reallocate the result of a given allocation between themselves. Here, consistency requires that the allocation should remain the same although all coalitions of the subgroup are free to buy out members of the complement as they prefer (i.e., by minimizing their costs). As such, the difference can be seen as relating to a difference in planning level where the Hart–Mas-Colell form fits a neutral third party evaluator while the Davis–Maschler form is more suitable for reallocation among the involved agents themselves.

Remark 3.9. Note, that there are two additional reduced forms: The Moulin reduced problem, where $c_T^\phi(S) = c(S \cup S') - \sum_{i \in S'} \phi_i(N,c)$ with $S' = N \setminus T$, and the reduced problem, where $c_T^\phi(S) = \min_{S' \subseteq N \backslash T} \{c(S \cup S') - \sum_{i \in S'} \phi_i(S \cup S', c_{|S \cup S'})\}$, for all $S \subset T$, and $c_T^\phi(T) = c(N) - \sum_{i \in N \backslash T} \phi_i(N,c)$. None of the four allocation rules of Sect. 3.4 satisfies consistency with respect to the Moulin reduced problem. Moreover, in Hart and Mas-Colell (1989) it is shown that no allocation rule, which shares the gain from cooperation equally for all 2-agent allocation problems can be consistent with respect to the last type of reduced game. $\triangle$

3.6.2 Characterizing the Nucleolus

In case of 2-agent problems the nucleolus and the Shapley value coincide and become the allocation that shares the gains from cooperation equally among the two agents (see Example 3.5). We denote this the 2-agent standard allocation:

- 2-agent standard allocation: Consider 2-agent cost allocation problems $(\{i, j\}, c)$. Then

$$\phi_i(\{i, j\}, c) = c(i) + \frac{1}{2}(c(i, j) - c(i) - c(j))$$

for $i \neq j$.

Together with consistency with respect to the Davis–Maschler reduced form this property can be shown to characterize the nucleolus.

Theorem 3.3 (Sobolev 1975). *A cost allocation rule ϕ satisfies the 2-agent standard allocation and consistency with respect to the Davis–Maschler reduced problem if and only if ϕ is the nucleolus.*

Variations of the theorem, as well as related proofs, may be found in Peleg and Sudhölter (2003).

Example 3.7 (continued). Recall the cost allocation problem in Example 3.7 where

$$c(1) = 2, \quad c(2) = 1, \quad c(3) = 3,$$
$$c(1, 2) = c(1, 3) = c(2, 3) = 3, \quad c(1, 2, 3) = 4.$$

In this case, the nucleolus is found to be $x^{Nuc} = (1.5, 1, 1.5)$, which coincides with the Lorenz maximal allocation in the core. It is simple to confirm that this allocation is consistent with respect to the Davis–Maschler reduced problems. Consider for instance the reduced problem $(\{1, 2\}, c^x_{\{1,2\}})$ where $c^x_{\{1,2\}}(1, 2) = 2.5$ and

$$c^x_{\{1,2\}}(1) = \min\{c(1) = 2, c(1, 3) - x_3^{Nuc} = 1.5\} = 1.5$$
$$c^x_{\{1,2\}}(2) = \min\{c(2) = 1, c(2, 3) - x_3^{Nuc} = 1.5\} = 1.$$

Thus, $\phi^{Nuc}(\{1, 2\}, c^x_{\{1,2\}}) = (1.5, 1) = (x_1^{Nuc}, x_2^{Nuc})$. On the other hand, consider the Hart–Mas-Colell reduced problem $(\{1, 3\}, c^{Nuc}_{\{1,3\}})$ where $c^{Nuc}_{\{1,3\}}(1, 3) = 3$ and

$$c_{\{1,3\}}^{Nuc}(1) = c(1,2) - \phi_2^{Nuc}(\{1,2\}, c_{|1,2}) = 3 - 1 = 2$$
$$c_{\{1,3\}}^{Nuc}(3) = c(2,3) - \phi_2^{Nuc}(\{2,3\}, c_{|2,3}) = 3 - 0.5 = 2.5.$$

Thus, $\phi^{Nuc}(\{1,3\}, c_{\{1,3\}}^{Nuc}) = (1.25, 1.75) \neq (x_1^{Nuc}, x_3^{Nuc})$. Consequently the nucleolus is *not* consistent with respect to the Hart–Mas-Colell reduced problem.

Finally, note that if we consider the related cost savings problem $v(S) = \sum_{i \in S} c(i) - c(S)$ we get

$$\phi^{Nuc}(N, v) = (0.5, 0, 1.5),$$

which differs from the Lorenz maximal allocation in the core $x^L = (1, 0, 1)$. In general, $\phi_i^{Nuc}(N, c) = c(i) - \phi_i^{Nuc}(N, v)$ for all i. $\triangle$

3.6.3 Characterizing the Shapley Value

Since the Shapley value coincides with the nucleolus on 2-agent allocation problems it cannot be consistent with respect to the Davis–Maschler reduced problem (by Theorem 3.3). However, it is in fact consistent with respect to the Hart–Mas-Colell reduced problem which turns out to be a characterizing property.

Theorem 3.4 (Hart and Mas-Colell 1989). *A cost allocation rule ϕ satisfies the 2-agent standard allocation and consistency with respect to the Hart–Mas-Colell reduced problem if and only if ϕ is the Shapley value.*

Sketch of Proof. We show only that an allocation rule ϕ satisfying 2-agent standard allocation and consistency with respect to the Hart–Mas-Colell reduced problem must be the Shapley value, following the argument in Hart and Mas-Colell (1989).

We claim that there exists a potential P where $P(\emptyset, c) = 0$ such that $\phi_i = P(N, c) - P(N \setminus i, c)$ hence proving that ϕ is the Shapley value (see Remark 3.5 in Sect. 3.4.3). The claim follows easily by 2-agent standard allocation for $n \le 2$ where $P(i, c) = c(i)$ and $P(ij, c) = 0.5(c(ij) + c(i) + c(j))$. Hence consider generalization to $n \ge 3$ by induction: Assume that P is defined for problems up to dimension $n - 1$ and consider a problem (N, c) with $|N| = n$. By consistency $\phi_i(N, c) - \phi_j(N, c) = \phi_i(N \setminus k, c_{|N \setminus k}) - \phi_j(N \setminus k, c_{|N \setminus k})$. Since $\phi_i = P(N, c) - P(N \setminus i, c)$ for all coalitions of size $n - 1$ we get that

$$\phi_i(N \setminus k, c_{|N \setminus k}) - \phi_j(N \setminus k, c_{|N \setminus k}) =$$
$$P(N \setminus \{k, j\}, c_{|N \setminus k}) - P(N \setminus \{k, i\} c_{|N \setminus k}) =$$
$$\phi_i(N \setminus \{k, j\}, c_{|N \setminus k}) - \phi_j(N \setminus \{k, i\}, c_{|N \setminus k}).$$

Now, by consistency

$$\phi_i(N \setminus \{k, j\}, c_{|N \setminus k}) - \phi_j(N \setminus \{k, i\}, c_{|N \setminus k}) = \phi_i(N \setminus j, c) - \phi_j(N \setminus i, c).$$

Hence,

$$\phi_i(N,c) - \phi_j(N,c) = \phi_i(N \setminus j, c) - \phi_j(N \setminus i, c) =$$
$$P(N \setminus j, c) - P(N \setminus \{i,j\}, c) - [P(N \setminus i, c) - P(N \setminus \{i,j\}, c)] =$$
$$P(N \setminus j, c) - P(N \setminus i, c),$$

proving the case for $n \geq 3$.   □

Remark 3.10. There are several other characterizations of the Shapley value, for example, in Shapley (1953) relating to the additivity property stating that an allocation rule is additive if $\phi(N, c_1 + c_2) = \phi(N, c_1) + \phi(N, c_2)$ (which is *not* satisfied by the nucleolus) and in Young (1985) relating to a strong monotonicity property stating that if $c(S) - c(S \setminus i) \geq \hat{c}(S) - \hat{c}(S \setminus i)$ for all $S \supseteq i$ then $\phi_i(N, c) \geq \phi_i(N, \hat{c})$ (which is *not* satisfied by the nucleolus).   △

Example 3.7 (continued). Recall that the Shapley value of the cost allocation problem (N, c) where

$$c(1) = 2, \quad c(2) = 1, \quad c(3) = 3,$$
$$c(1,2) = c(1,3) = c(2,3) = 3, \quad c(1,2,3) = 4,$$

is given by $x^{Sh} = (1.33, 0.83, 1.83)$, which violates the stand-alone cost principle for coalition $\{1,3\}$. Now, it is simple to confirm that this allocation is consistent with respect to the Hart–Mas-Colell reduced problems. Consider for instance the reduced problem $(\{1,2\}, c^{Sh}_{\{1,2\}})$ where $c^{Sh}_{\{1,2\}}(1,2) = 2.17$ and

$$c^{Sh}_{\{1,2\}}(1) = c(1,3) - \phi^{Sh}_3(\{1,3\}, c_{|1,3}) = 3 - 2 = 1$$
$$c^{Sh}_{\{1,2\}}(2) = c(2,3) - \phi^{Sh}_3(\{2,3\}, c_{|2,3}) = 3 - 2.5 = 0.5.$$

Clearly, $\phi^{Sh}(\{1,2\}, c^{Sh}_{\{1,2\}}) = (1.33, 0.83) = (x^{Sh}_1, x^{Sh}_2)$. On the other hand, consider the Davis–Maschler reduced problem $(\{2,3\}, c^x_{\{2,3\}})$ where $c^x_{\{2,3\}}(2,3) = 2.66$ and

$$c^x_{\{2,3\}}(2) = \min\{c(2) = 1, c(1,2) - x^{Sh}_1 = 1.66\} = 1,$$
$$c^x_{\{2,3\}}(3) = \min\{c(3) = 3, c(1,3) - x^{Sh}_1 = 1.66\} = 1.66.$$

Thus, $\phi^{Sh}(\{2,3\}, c^x_{\{2,3\}}) = (1, 1.66) \neq (x^{Sh}_2, x^{Sh}_3)$. Hence, the Shapley value is *not* consistent with respect to Davis–Maschler reduced problems.

△

3.6.4 Characterizing the Lorenz Allocation

As demonstrated by Example 3.7 neither the nucleolus nor the Shapley value were consistent with respect to both the Davis–Maschler and the Hart–Mas-Colell reduced problems. However, it turns out that on the subclass of *concave* allocation problems the Lorenz allocation is in fact consistent with respect to both types of reduced problems. But according to Example 3.5 the

Lorenz allocation does not satisfy the 2-agent standard allocation. Rather it satisfies the following type of 2-agent allocation called *2-agent constrained egalitarianism*:

- *2-agent constrained egalitarianism:* Consider 2-agent cost allocation problems $(\{i, j\}, c)$. Then

$$\phi_i(\{i, j\}, c) = \begin{cases} \min(c(i), \frac{c(ij)}{2}) \text{ if } c(j) \geq \frac{c(ij)}{2} \\ c(ij) - c(j) \qquad \text{otherwise.} \end{cases}$$

As mentioned in Example 3.5 an allocation satisfying 2-agent constrained egalitarianism is identical to the equal split if this allocation is in the core. Otherwise it is the core allocation which is "closest" to the equal split, i.e., the Lorenz maximizing allocation in the core.

Theorem 3.5 (Dutta 1990). *A cost allocation rule ϕ satisfies 2-agent constraint egalitarianism and consistency with respect to the Davis–Maschler reduced problem (as well as the Hart–Mas-Colell reduced problem) if and only if ϕ is the Lorenz-allocation.*

Remark 3.11. In Arin et al. (2003) it is shown that the Lorenz allocation is the only continuous and anonymous allocation rule which satisfies independence of irrelevant core alternatives (see Sect. 3.4.2). In Hougaard et al. (2001) the Lorenz set $L(N, c)$ is characterized on the general domain of balanced problems using consistency.

3.6.5 Characterizing the τ-Value

In terms of characterizing properties the τ-value is not directly comparable with the other allocation rules. By Example 3.5 in Sect. 3.4.4 the τ-value satisfies 2-agent standard allocation but is not consistent with respect to neither the Davis–Maschler nor the Hart–Mas-Colell reduced problems. Tijs (1987) provides a characterization based on properties, which are somewhat closely related to the τ-value itself.

3.7 Comments

Closing this chapter we shall briefly mention a couple of deviations from the standard model above. First, the model above is static of nature. Dynamic aspects, as for example when imposing various monotonicity properties, are really just considered in terms of a repetition of the static framework. However, there may be (dynamic) allocation problems where prior allocations become relevant and the applied allocation rule hence becomes a function of the history of allocations as well as of the present cost or value structure. For example, fair allocation of scarce health care resources according to needs among a group of persons or institutions may be influenced by the size of prior allocations. Lehrer (2002), as the exception in the literature, considers such a dynamic framework.

Second, uncertainty often characterize real-life situations that involve allocation problems while the above model is deterministic. To the extent that allocation can await the realization of actual costs this does not pose a problem. On the other hand, if costs are random variables C with probability distribution functions $F_{C(S)}(t) = Prob\{C(S) \leq t\}$ then a cooperative decision problem (under risk) is introduced since the stand-alone cost principle is no longer straightforwardly defined. However, as focus is somehow moved away from the issue of allocation in as far as it influences the decision of the involved coalitions, we shall not go into further details but refer to the existing literature, which roughly speaking consists of two separate tracks: the "chance constrained games" by Charnes and Granot (1973) involving prior allocations and second step reallocation after realization of costs and the "stochastic cooperative games" incorporating agents risk attitudes as, e.g., in Suijs (2000) and Timmer et al. (2003).

Finally, situations may occur where the allocation problem is restricted in coalition structure either since the costs (or worth) of some coalitions are unavailable or because the existence of some coalitions are excluded due to geographical, social or other types of restrictions. There is a large literature concerning such problems (games) with given coalition structures and related allocation rules. Since some types of restricted coalition structures may conveniently be represented by networks we shall return to this issue in Chap. 3.

3.8 Summary

Since cooperative actions are often economically rational, rules for sharing costs and benefits associated with these actions must encourage and sustain the cooperation. In this context, the stand-alone cost principle is quite fundamental since it states that no agent, or group of agents, can be forced to pay more than their stand-alone cost when the total cost of the cooperative scheme is shared, and consequently has no incentive to block the cooperative effort. Necessary and sufficient conditions for the existence of allocations that satisfy the stand-alone cost principle were provided by the Bondareva–Shapley theorem (Theorem 3.1).

When the gains from cooperation are large enough, many allocation rules will satisfy the stand-alone cost principle. The nucleolus and the Lorenz allocation (only defined on concave problems) are examples of such rules. However, there are also (otherwise) desirable rules, such as the Shapley- and the τ-value, which may violate the stand-alone cost principle (unless there are gains from cooperation related to all underlying coalition structures, i.e., the problem is concave).

Moreover, when changes are made in the cost structure, cost shares ought to change in a similar way. For example, if costs are reduced for a given group of agents, the cost share of every agent in the group ought to be non-increasing. Otherwise some agents will have incentives to block a potential cost reduction. There are allocation rules that satisfy such monotonicity requirements (e.g., the Shapley value), but unfortunately they are, in general, incompatible with the stand-alone cost principle (unless the problem is concave).

The potential conflict between monotonicity requirements and stand-alone cost requirements can also be illustrated by the four allocation rules that were singled out for further analysis: The nucleolus generally satisfies the stand-alone cost requirements but violates the monotonicity requirements while the opposite is true for the Shapley value. The τ-value generally satisfies neither the monotonicity requirements nor the stand-alone cost requirements while the Lorenz allocation satisfies both but only on the restricted domain of concave problems (as do the Shapley value).

However, it can be argued that monotonicity in cost shares for all coalitions is are rather strong requirement. Likewise, it seems questionable whether the stand-alone requirements are reasonable in all situations. Thus, the apparent conflict between the stand-alone cost principle and the monotonicity requirements seems less serious than what appears at first sight. Moreover, as mentioned, the stand-alone cost principle and the monotonicity requirements can be reconciled for concave problems (e.g., using the Shapley value or the Lorenz allocation).

The four rules mentioned above all relate to different aspects of fairness: The nucleolus favors the worst off coalition, the Lorenz allocation is egalitarian subject to the stand-alone cost requirements, the Shapley value considers the average of all incremental costs associated with each agent and the τ-value relates to both the marginal cost of each agent and the total cost gap. Furthermore, it turns out that the nucleolus, the Lorenz allocation and the Shapley value differ in the way they are consistent (relating to different types of reduced problems) and treat 2-agent problems.

References

Arin J, Kuipers J, Vermeulen D (2003) Some characterizations of egalitarian solutions on classes of TU-games. Math Soc Sci 46:327–345.

Aumann R, Maschler M (1985) Game theoretic analysis of a bankruptcy problem from the Talmud. J Econ Theory 36:195–213.

Bjondal E, Hamers H, Koster M (2004) Cost allocation in a bank ATM network. Math Methods Oper Res 59:405–418.

Bondareva ON (1963) Certain applications of the method of linear programming to the theory of cooperative games. Problemy Kibernitiki 10:119–139.

Charnes A, Granot D (1973) Prior solutions: extensions of convex nucleolus solutions to chance-constrained games. In: Proceedings of the Computer Science and Statistics Seventh Symposium at Iowa State University, 323–332.

Curiel I (1997) Cooperative game theory and applications. Kluwer, Dordrecht.

Curiel I, Maschler M, Tijs SH (1987) Bankruptcy games. Z Oper Res 31:A143–A159.

Dutta B (1990) The egalitarian solution and reduced game properties in convex games. Int J Game Theory 19:153–169.

Dutta B, Ray D (1989) A concept of egalitarianism under participation constraints. Econometrica 57:615–635.

Hart S, Mas-Colell A (1989) Potential, value, and consistency. Econometrica 57:589–614.

Hokari T (2000) The nucleolus is not aggregate monotonic on the class of convex games. Int J Game Theory 29:133–137.

Hougaard JL, Østerdal LP (2006) Monotonicity of social welfare optima. Games Econ Behav (to appear).

Hougaard JL, Peleg B, Thorlund-Petersen L (2001) On the set of Lorenz-maximal imputations in the core of a balanced game. Int J Game Theory 30:147–165.

Hougaard JL, Peleg B, Østerdal LP (2005) The Dutta–Ray solution on the class of convex games: a generalization and monotonicity properties. Int Game Theory Review 7:1–12.

Housman D, Clark L (1998) Core and monotonic allocation methods. Int J Game Theory 27:611–616.

Ichiishi T (1981) Super modularity: applications to convex games and the greedy algorithm. J Econ Theory 25:283–286.

Lehrer E (2002) Allocation processes in cooperative games. Int J Game Theory 31:341–351.

Littlechild SC, Thompson GF (1977) Aircraft landing fees: a game theory approach. Bell J Econ 8:186–204.

Mirghani AN, Scapens RW (1995) Cost allocation theory and practice: the continuing debate. In: Ashton, Hopper, Scapens (eds) Issues in management accounting, chap. 3. Prentice-Hall, London, pp. 39–60.

Owen G (1995) Game theory, 3rd edn. Academic, New York.

Peleg B, Sudhölter P (2003) Introduction to the theory of cooperative games. Kluwer, Dordrecht.

Ransmeier JS (1942) The Tennessee Valley Authority: a case study in the economics of multiple purpose stream planning. Vanderbilt University Press, Nashville, TN.

Schmeidler D (1969) The Nucleolus of a characteristic function game. SIAM J Appl Math 17:1163–1170.

Shapley L (1953) A value for n-person games. Ann Math Stud 28:307–318.

Shapley L (1967) On balanced sets and cores. Naval Res Logist Q 14:453–460.

Shapley L (1971) Cores of convex games. Int J Game Theory 1:11–26.

Sobolev AI (1975) The characterization of optimality principles in cooperative games by functional equations. In: Vorobiev NN (ed) Mathematical methods in social sciences, vol 6. Academy of Sciences of the Lithunian SSR, Vilnius, pp. 95–151 (in Russian).

Sprumont Y (1990) Population monotonic allocation schemes for cooperative games with transferable utility. Games Econ Behav 2:378–394.

Suijs J (2000) Cooperative decision-making under risk. Kluwer, New York.

Taha HA (1989) Operations research, 2nd edn. Maxwell Macmillan, New York.

Tijs SH (1981) Bounds for the core and the τ-value. In: Moeschlin O, Pallaschke D (eds) Game theory and mathematical economics. North-Holland, Amsterdam, pp. 123–132.

Tijs SH (1987) An axiomatization of the τ-value. Math Soc Sci 13:177–181.

Tijs SH, Driessen TSH (1986) Game theory and cost allocation problems. Manage Sci 32:1015–1024.

Timmer J, Borm P, Tijs S (2003) On three Shapley-like solutions for cooperative games with random payoffs. Int J Game Theory 32:595–613.

van den Nouweland A, Borm P, van den Golstein Brouwers W, Groot Bruinderink R, Tijs S (1996) A game theoretic approach to problems in telecommunication. Manage Sci 42:294–303.

Young P (1985) Monotonic solutions of cooperative games. Int J Game Theory 14: 65–72.

Chapter 4
General Sharing Problems

4.1 Introduction

Generalizing the cost sharing scenario to cover a multiple goods situation, the complexity of the cost allocation model increases significantly compared to the one-good (or homogeneous) case treated in Chap. 2.

The first problem arises because there are at least two ways to construe the situation that we intend to model:

- We may consider the scenario as one where n agents $i = 1, \ldots, n$ each demand a basket of m different types of goods. That is, each agent i is characterized by a demand vector $q^i = (q_1^i, \ldots, q_m^i)$. Total cost is determined by a cost function over the aggregate demand of all the agents for each good, i.e., as $C\left(\sum_{i=1}^n q_1^i, \ldots, \sum_{i=1}^n q_m^i\right)$. Typically, we shall think of the m goods as being measured in different units, but it may also be interpreted as demand for the same (homogeneous) good, e.g., delivered at m different locations or points in time.
- We may also choose to consider the situation as one where n agents each demand a different (or "personal") type of good such that the total demand is a profile written as $q = (q_1, \ldots, q_n)$. Total cost is determined by a cost function over the demand profile, i.e., as $C(q_1, \ldots, q_n)$. The immediate interpretation of a "personal" good is that of a good which is different from the other personal goods and hence makes interpersonal comparisons of demand meaningless. But, as above, we could also interpret the situation as involving demand for the same good, i.e., as the homogeneous case but with an asymmetric cost function where the agents are held responsible for these asymmetries.

Clearly, these are two distinct scenarios, which in principle require two different models. However, notice that if a cost sharing rule relates to a fixed unit price for each particular good then the choice of modeling framework becomes indifferent. Indeed, let $n = m$, let j be the index of agents and let i be the index of goods. Assume that the scenario of personalized goods is chosen and that cost sharing rules are defined with respect to this model.

For a given demand profile $(q_1, \ldots, q_n)$ and a given cost function $C(q)$ we obtain the cost allocation $(x_1, \ldots, x_n)$ where x_i is the cost share associated with good i. Now, referring to the scenario of baskets of goods, the demand for each personal good q_i can be seen as the aggregate demand of all the agents for good i, i.e., as $q_i = \sum_{j=1}^{n} q_i^j$. Assuming that all agents pay the same unit price for a given good independent of their size of demand we may determine such unit prices for each good as $p_i = x_i/q_i$ based on the cost allocation $(x_1, \ldots, x_n)$. These unit prices can then be used to assess the cost share of agent j, x^j, related to any basket of goods since $x^j = \sum_{i=1}^{n}(x_i/q_i)q_i^j$. But, as we shall see in the following, many cost sharing rules do not relate to fixed unit prices. Moreover, when discussing desirable properties of allocation rules the normative appeal of such properties may be totally different in the different scenarios as considered in Sect. 4.4.

The second problem arises because none of the cost sharing rules analysed for simple sharing problems (Chap. 2) can be directly applied in the generalized scenarios: the proportional rule requires that the demand of each agent can be compared to the total demand of the group, and while this works fine when all agents demand the same type of good the ratios are not defined for demands of multiple goods. Moreover, rules based on the incremental and serial principles typically require that demands can be ordered according to the size of demand and/or interpersonally compared. Again, this works fine when all agents demand the same type of good, but is no longer well defined for demands of multiple goods. The challenge is therefore to extend the rules of Chap. 2 to the case of multiple goods and (unfortunately) there is no unique way of doing this as it will become clear in the following.

As an alternative approach to extending the allocation rules from simple sharing problems, we may transform the problem into one of binary demands as in Chap. 3, simply by defining the cost allocation problem (N, c) by $N = \{1, \ldots, n\}$ and

$$c(S) = C\left(\sum_{i \in S} q_1^i, \ldots, \sum_{i \in S} q_m^i\right),$$

for all $S \subseteq N$, in the case where agents demand baskets of goods, or as

$$c(S) = C(\{q_i\}_{i \in S}, 0, \ldots, 0),$$

for all $S \subseteq N$, in the case of personalized goods. Now, the rules analysed in Chap. 3 can be applied and the cost share x_j related to each agent $j = 1, \ldots, n$ determined, for example using the Shapley value, here called the Shapley–Shubik cost sharing rule (Sect. 4.3.2).

In order to emphasize the connection with the framework of Chap. 2, we shall model the general sharing problem as the situation where n agents each demand a different (or "personal") good and costs are given by a (heterogeneous) cost function $C : \mathbf{R}_+^n \to \mathbf{R}_+$.

The following scenarios may be imagined:

1. In a given company the department of administrative services offer in-service training programs to n other departments of the company. Each department i demands a specific type of program in the quantity q_i and the total cost $C(q_1, \ldots, q_n)$ of running the training programs must be allocated between the n departments. Note that cost allocation would be simple if the cost function is additive (i.e., $C(q_1, \ldots, q_n) = c_1(q_1) + \ldots + c_n(q_n)$). However, it is easy to imagine that the same teachers are used in different courses and parts of a given training program may be common for two or more departments, etc. – all aspects that creates joint costs.

2. One of the departments of the company is a production department where n different types of products are being produced in different quantities q_i under joint production. The total costs of production is given by the cost function $C(q_1, \ldots, q_n)$. In order to analyse the company's strategic position on the market the management need unit production costs p_i of all products and these can be found by taking the cost share related to product i, x_i, and adjust for differences in quantity, i.e., $p_i = x_i/q_i$. Apart from the literature on managerial economics and accounting, internal pricing of products has been a major topic in the literature on optimal pricing and regulation of multi-product natural monopolies such as electricity production and telecommunication.

3. Although we stick to the context of cost allocation, the model has an equally natural interpretation within output (or surplus) sharing problems: Imagine, for example, n agents each delivering working effort q_i in a joint project where the output is modeled by a production function $P : \mathbf{R}_+^n \to \mathbf{R}_+$ and total output has to be shared according to effort. Since efforts do not enter homogeneously in the production process we cannot use the rules of Chap. 2 directly.

4.2 The Model

Let $N = \{1, \ldots, n\}$ be the set of agents as well as "personal" (heterogeneous) goods. A demand profile (related to N) is a vector $q \in \mathbf{R}_+^n$ where q_i specifies the demand of agent i for good i. For $S \subset N$, let q^S be the projection of q on $\mathbf{R}^S$.

For fixed N, costs (related to demand profiles) are modeled by a non-decreasing[1] cost function $C : \mathbf{R}_+^n \to \mathbf{R}$ that satisfies $C(0, \ldots, 0) = 0$. Let $\mathcal{C}_0$ denote the set of such functions. In particular, let $\partial_i C(q)$ be the first order derivative of $C \in \mathcal{C}_0$ at q with respect to the ith argument if it exists. Let $\mathcal{C}_1$ be the set of continuously differentiable functions in $\mathcal{C}_0$. Moreover, let $\mathcal{C}_2$ be

---

[1] That is, $q \geq^* q'$ implies that $C(q) \geq C(q')$ where $q \geq^* q' \Leftrightarrow q_i \geq q_i' \ \forall i = 1, \ldots, n$.

the set of all twice continuously differentiable functions in $\mathcal{C}_0$ with bounded derivatives (i.e., there exists numbers $a(C)$ and $b(C)$ such that $0 < a(C) \leq \partial_i C \leq b(C)$ for all $i \in N$). In practice C may be estimated as shown in Sect. 4.5.

Further, we say that the cost function $C \subset \mathcal{C}_0$ is *submodular* (*supermodular*) if $C(q) + C(q') \geq (\leq) C(q \wedge q') + C(q \vee q')$, where $(q \wedge q')_i = \min\{q_i, q'_i\}$ and $(q \vee q')_i = \max\{q_i, q'_i\}$. For $C \in \mathcal{C}_2$ submodularity (supermodularity) is tantamount to $\frac{\partial^2 C}{\partial q_i \partial q_j} \leq (\geq) 0$ for all $i \neq j$.

For fixed N, let (q, C) be a (heterogeneous) cost sharing problem and let ϕ be a cost sharing rule which specifies a unique vector of cost shares $x = (x_1, \ldots, x_n) = \phi(q, C)$ where the cost shares x_i add up to the total cost $C(q)$.

For fixed N and some domain of cost functions, say $\mathcal{Z} \subset \mathcal{C}_0$, let f be a separable bijection from $\mathbf{R}_+^n$ onto itself, i.e., a list $(f_1, \ldots, f_n)$ of n bijections from $\mathbf{R}_+$ onto itself. For each cost function $C \in \mathcal{Z}$, define $C^f(t) = C(f(t))$ for all $t \in \mathbf{R}_+^n$. Now, f is an *ordinal transformation* if $C^f \in \mathcal{Z}$. Moreover, two problems (q, C) and (q', C') are said to be *ordinally equivalent* if there exists an ordinal transformation f such that $C' = C^f$ and $q = f(q')$.

In particular, if $f_i^\lambda = \lambda_i q_i$ for all $i \in N$ and $\lambda_i \in \mathbf{R}_+$, two problems (q, C) and (q', C') are said to be *scale equivalent* if there exists a transformation f^λ such that $C' = C^{f^\lambda}$ and $q = f^\lambda(q')$.

4.3 Three Allocation Rules

As mentioned in the Introduction there are no obvious ways to extend average cost sharing and cost sharing rules based on the incremental and serial principles to the case of multiple goods. Therefore the literature has primarily focused on extensions satisfying certain desirable properties (as we shall see in Sect. 4.4) and three such extensions are the Aumann–Shapley rule being an extension of average cost sharing (the proportional rule), the Shapley–Shubik rule being an extension of the Shapley-value (or random priority rule) and the Friedman–Moulin rule being an extension of serial cost sharing.

4.3.1 The Aumann–Shapley Rule

The Aumann–Shapley rule (Aumann and Shapley 1974) was for long the unanimous recommendation in the cost sharing literature and has been the subject of numerous papers focussing on both theoretical and applied aspects. While it can be seen as an extension of average cost sharing it is also closely related to the notion of the Shapley value being its continuous ("non-atomic") generalization.

Consider cost functions $C \in \mathcal{C}_1$. Fixing N and q, the idea is to replace the average cost in the homogeneous case (which is not well defined in the multiple goods case since total demand is not an economically meaningful term) with the average of i's marginal costs on a path joining 0 and q by raising coordinates in proportion to q. To be more precise:

- The *Aumann–Shapley Rule* ϕ^{AS} is defined by the cost shares,

$$x_i^{AS}(q,C) = \int_0^{q_i} \partial_i C\left(\frac{t}{q_i}q\right) dt = q_i \int_0^1 \partial_i C(tq) dt \quad \text{for all } i \in N. \quad (4.1)$$

Note that $\sum_{i=1}^n x_i^{AS}(q,C) = C(q)$. In particular, $p_i^{AS} = \int_0^1 \partial_i C(tq) dt$ can be seen as the unit cost of good i – also known as the Aumann–Shapley price. Since "agent" i pays the same price for all units demanded, use of the Aumann–Shapley rule makes the choice between the scenario of demand for personal goods (as in the present model) and the scenario of demand for a basket of goods, indifferent: the demand for good i (q_i) in the present model can simply be interpreted as the aggregate demand for good i among m individual agents demanding baskets of n different goods and using the Aumann–Shapley prices the cost share related to any basket of goods can be determined.

Moreover, note that when all agents except for agent i demand zero, agent i will cover all costs and consequently the Aumann–Shapley price coincides with the average cost $C(q_i, 0, \ldots, 0)/q_i$ in the homogeneous case.

In order to emphasize that the Aumann–Shapley rule is closely related to the Shapley value, we shall also define a discrete version of the Aumann–Shapley rule: Let each agent i demand an *integer* quantity q_i. For a given set agents $N = \{1, \ldots, n\}$ and (integer) demand vector q, let $N_1, \ldots, N_n$ be pairwise disjoint sets such that $|N_i| = q_i$ for each $i \in N$, and let $N_q = \cup_{i \in N} N_i$. Hence, we have constructed a new set of pseudo-agents – one for each good demanded. Now, for each subset of pseudo-agents $S \subseteq N_q$, define the discrete cost function $\Gamma_q(S) = C(|S \cap N_1|, \ldots, |S \cap N_n|)$. The (discrete version of the) Aumann–Shapley rule is then defined as

$$\phi_i^{AS}(q,C) = \sum_{j \in N_i} \phi_j^{Sh}(N_q, \Gamma_q) \quad \text{for all } i \in N, \quad (4.2)$$

where $\phi^{Sh}(\cdot, \cdot)$ is the Shapley value of the related cost sharing problem as defined in (3.8) in Chap. 3. That is, the Aumann–Shapley cost share of each agent $i \in N$ can be found by adding up the Shapley values (with respect to Γ_q) of all pseudo-agents derived from the demand of agent i.

Example 4.1. Consider the 2-agent case $|N| = 2$ and let costs be determined by the (concave) cost function

$$C(q) = q_2 + (q_1 + q_2)^{0.5}.$$

If, for instance, demand is given by $q = (q_1, q_2) = (1, 2)$ the total cost is $C(1, 2) = 2 + 3^{0.5} = 3.73$. Using the Aumann–Shapley rule to allocate total costs we observe that,

$$\partial_1 C(q) = 0.5(q_1 + q_2)^{-0.5} \quad \text{and} \quad \partial_2 C(q) = 1 + 0.5(q_1 + q_2)^{-0.5}.$$

Hence,

$$x_1^{AS}((1, 2), C) = \int_0^1 0.5(3t)^{-0.5} dt = [3^{-0.5} t^{0.5}]_0^1 = 3^{-0.5} = 0.58$$

and

$$x_2^{AS}((1, 2), C) = 2 \int_0^1 (1 + 0.5(3t)^{-0.5}) dt = 2[t + 3^{-0.5} t^{0.5}]_0^1 = 2(1 + 3^{-0.5}) = 3.15,$$

with corresponding unit costs (Aumann–Shapley prices) of 0.58 and 1.58 respectively.

Now, consider instead the cost function $\hat{C}(q) = q_1^2 + (q_1 + q_2)^{0.5}$ (which is neither concave nor convex). For $q = (1, 2)$ we get $x_1^{AS}((1, 2), \hat{C}) = 1.58$ and $x_2^{AS}((1, 2), \hat{C}) = 1.15$. Thus, contrary to average cost sharing in the homogeneous case, the Aumann–Shapley rule is *not* order-preserving.

Finally, consider the discrete version of the Aumann–Shapley rule: Given $N = \{1, 2\}$, $C(q) = q_2 + (q_1 + q_2)^{0.5}$ and $q = (1, 2)$ we get two sets $N_1 = \{i_1\}$ and $N_2 = \{i_2, i_3\}$ such that $N_q = \{i_1, i_2, i_3\}$. Hence, the sharing problem (N_q, Γ_q) is given by

$\Gamma_q(i_1) = C(1, 0) = 1,$
$\Gamma_q(i_2) = \Gamma_q(i_3) = C(0, 1) = 2,$
$\Gamma_q(i_1, i_2) = \Gamma_q(i_1, i_3) = C(1, 1) = 1 + 2^{0.5},$
$\Gamma_q(i_2, i_3) = C(0, 2) = 2 + 2^{0.5}$
$\Gamma_q(i_1, i_2, i_3) = C(1, 2) = 2 + 3^{0.5}.$

Now, the Shapley value of (N_q, Γ_q) is given by $(x_{i_1}^{Sh}, x_{i_2}^{Sh}, x_{i_3}^{Sh}) = (3^{-0.5}, 1 + 3^{-0.5}, 1 + 3^{-0.5})$ and consequently we get the resulting Aumann–Shapley cost shares $x_1^{AS} = x_{i_1}^{Sh} = 0.58$ and $x_2^{AS} = x_{i_2}^{Sh} + x_{i_3}^{Sh} = 3.15$. Note that we could have labeled the demands differently but anonymity of Shapley value (see, e.g., Peleg and Sudhölter 2003) guarantees that all possible choices are equivalent. △

Example 4.2. The case of internal telephone billing rates at Cornell University by Billera et al. (1978) is a early example of an application of Aumann–Shapley pricing. Loosely speaking, Cornell buy telephone services in bulks at reduced prices and need to allocate those costs among the users.

Now, telephone calls are not homogeneous: prices depend on the time of day (most expensive at peak hours), the destination and whether it is a weekend or workday call: that is, there are $n = 24 \times k \times 2 = 48k$ different types of calls when there are k different destinations. Given any (monthly) demand $q = (q_1, \ldots, q_n)$ for the n different call types, the lowest costs connected with q can be determined, $C(q)$, as well as the associated Aumann–Shapley prices for all call types. $\triangle$

Remark 4.1. As mentioned in the Introduction the cost allocation problem can equivalently be construed as a problem of internal pricing (for example in natural monopolies). Hence, it is natural to compare the Aumann–Shapley prices with prices that are consistent with economic efficiency, i.e., the marginal cost prices, $p_i^{MC} = \partial_i C(q)$ for all i.

If the cost function is homogeneous of degree k (i.e., $C(tq) = t^k C(q)$, $t \in [0,1]$) the connection between Aumann–Shapley pricing and marginal cost pricing is clear. In particular,

$$\partial_i C(tq) = \frac{C(tq + t\Delta q_i) - C(tq)}{t\Delta q_i} = \frac{t^k C(q + \Delta q_i) - t^k C(q)}{t\Delta q_i} =$$

$$t^{k-1} \frac{C(q + \Delta q_i) - C(q)}{\Delta q_i} = t^{k-1} \partial_i C(q),$$

and consequently

$$p_i^{AS} = \partial_i C(q) \int_0^1 t^{k-1} dt = p_i^{MC} \frac{1}{k}.$$

Hence, if $k < 1$ – in the one-dimensional case corresponding to C being concave – then $p_i^{MC} < p_i^{AS}$ for all i and the use of marginal cost pricing will result in a budget deficit (since use of the Aumann–Shapley prices results in budget balance). If $k = 1$ – in the one-dimensional case corresponding to C being linear – then marginal cost pricing coincides with Aumann–Shapley pricing. Finally, if $k > 1$ – in the one-dimensional case corresponding to C being convex – then $p_i^{MC} > p_i^{AS}$ for all i resulting in a budget surplus if marginal cost prices are used. $\triangle$

As demonstrated by the example above, marginal cost prices cannot be used directly to allocate costs since they do not necessarily result in budget balance. However, budget balance can be ensured using various *adjusted versions* of marginal cost pricing, as for example

$$x_i^{PMC} = \frac{q_i p_i^{MC}}{\sum_{j=1}^n q_j p_j^{MC}} C(q), \quad \text{for all } i \in N, \tag{4.3}$$

where the residual is shared in proportion to marginal cost or

$$x_i^{EMC} = q_i p_i^{MC} + \frac{1}{n} \left(C(q) - \sum_{j=1}^n q_j p_j^{MC} \right), \quad \text{for all } i \in N, \tag{4.4}$$

where the residual is shared equally. Both these rules are extensions of average cost sharing and thereby alternatives to the Aumann–Shapley rule.

4.3.2 The Shapley–Shubik Rule

To extend the Shapley value (of Chap. 3 and/or the Shapley cost sharing rule of Chap. 2) to the model with demand for "personal" goods is straightforward (Shubik 1962). The same formulas as in (3.8), in Chap. 3, can be used replacing $c(S)$ with $C(\{q_i\}_{i \in S}, 0, \ldots, 0)$ for all $S \subseteq N$. Let $m_i(S) = C(\{q_j\}_{j \in S \cup i}, 0, \ldots, 0) - C(\{q_j\}_{j \in S}, 0, \ldots, 0)$ and define:

- *The Shapley–Shubik Rule ϕ^{SS}* by the cost shares,

$$x_i^{SS} = \sum_{S \subseteq N \setminus i} \frac{s!(n-s-1)!}{n!} m_i(S), \qquad (4.5)$$

for all $i \in N$ (where $|S| = s$ and $0! = 1$).

Note that $\sum_{i=1}^{n} x_i^{SS}(q, C) = C(q)$. Moreover, considering a given ordering π of demands, cost sharing according to the incremental principle can be obtained as,

$$x_i^{\pi} = C(q_{\pi_1}, \ldots, q_{\pi_i}, 0, \ldots, 0) - C(q_{\pi_1}, \ldots, q_{\pi_{i-1}}, 0, \ldots, 0)$$

for all $i \in N$. The Shapley–Shubik rule may also be defined as the average of x^{π} over all $n!$ orderings (as in 2.19 in Chap. 2).

Example 4.1 (continued). Recall the cost function $C(q) = q_2 + (q_1 + q_2)^{0.5}$ of Example 4.1. With total demand $q = (1, 2)$ we get the allocation problem (N, c) where $N = \{1, 2\}$ and $c(1) = 1$, $c(2) = 3.42$ and $c(1, 2) = 3.73$. Using the Shapley–Shubik rule therefore results in cost shares $x_1^{SS} = 0.66$ and $x_2^{SS} = 3.07$ – that is, cost shares are more equally distributed than using the Aumann–Shapley rule in this case (where $x_1^{AS} = 0.58$ and $x_2^{AS} = 3.15$).

Now, consider instead the cost function $\hat{C}(q) = q_1^2 + (q_1 + q_2)^{0.5}$. For $q = (1, 2)$ we get $x_1^{SS}((1, 2), \hat{C}) = 1.66$ and $x_2^{SS}((1, 2), \hat{C}) = 1.07$. Thus, contrary to the Shapley value in the homogeneous case, the Shapley–Shubik rule is *not* order-preserving. Moreover, note that in this case the cost shares are more spread than using the Aumann–Shapley rule (where $x_1^{AS} = 1.58$ and $x_2^{AS} = 1.15$).   △

Remark 4.2. As mentioned in the Introduction any of the allocation rules examined in Chap. 3 can be applied replacing $c(S)$ with $C(\{q_i\}_{i \in S}, 0, \ldots, 0)$ for all $S \subseteq N$, as above.   △

4.3.3 The Friedman–Moulin Rule

Consider cost functions $C \in \mathcal{C}_1$. Fix N and q and label the agents in increasing order according to the size of their demands, i.e., such that $q_1 \leq \ldots \leq q_n$. Note, that even though this ordering is mathematically meaningful the economic interpretation is obscure in case the goods are measured in different units of measurement.

Like the Aumann–Shapley rule, the Friedman–Moulin rule ϕ^{FM} (Friedman and Moulin 1999) can be seen as generated by a production path from 0 to q: The cost share of each agent i, x_i^{FM}, is the integral of the marginal cost $\partial_i C$ along a path joining 0 and q by raising all coordinates at the same speed and freezing a coordinate once it reaches q_j, $j \leq i$. That is, in general cost shares are found by integration of marginal costs along the general path:
$$0 \to (q_1, \ldots, q_1) \to (q_1, q_2, \ldots, q_2) \to (q_1, q_2, q_3, \ldots, q_3) \to \ldots \to (q_1, \ldots, q_n).$$
To be more precise:

- *The Friedman–Moulin Rule* is defined by cost shares,

$$x_i^{FM}(q, C) = \int_0^{q_i} \partial_i C((te) \wedge q) dt, \quad \text{for all } i \in N, \qquad (4.6)$$

  where $e = (1, \ldots, 1)$ and $(a \wedge b) = (\min\{a_i, b_i\})_{i \in N}$.

  Note, that

$$\sum_{i=1}^{n} x_i^{FM}(q, C) = C(q).$$

Further, since the cost share of agent i only depends on the marginal costs along the path

$$0 \to (q_1, \ldots, q_1) \to (q_1, q_2, \ldots, q_2) \to \ldots \to (q_1, q_2, \ldots, q_{i-1}, q_i, \ldots, q_i),$$

it is independent of the demand from agents with a higher demand than i, in line with the serial principle mentioned in Sect. 2.3.2 of Chap. 2.

For example, in the 2-agent case ($N = \{1, 2\}$) we get,

$$x_1^{FM} = \int_0^{q_1} \partial_1 C(t, t) dt$$

and

$$x_2^{FM} = \int_0^{q_1} \partial_2 C(t, t) dt + \int_{q_1}^{q_2} \partial_2 C(q_1, t) dt =$$

$$\int_0^{q_1} \partial_2 C(t, t) dt + C(q_1, q_2) - C(q_1, q_1) = C(q_1, q_2) - x_1^{FM}.$$

When all agents demand the same good and the cost function C is *homogeneous* (i.e., is a function of the total demand), then the definition in (4.6) is equivalent to the definition of increasing serial cost sharing x^{IS} (defined in (2.14) in Chap. 2): The cost share of agent 1 is determined as q_1 times the average of the marginal costs from 0 to nq_1 – that is,

$$x_1^{FM} = q_1 \frac{C(nq_1) - C(0)}{nq_1} = \frac{C(nq_1)}{n} = x_1^{IS}.$$

The cost share of agent 2 is determined as x_1^{FM} plus the incremental demand $q_2 - q_1$ times the average of the marginal cost from nq_1 to $q_1 + (n-1)q_2$, i.e.,

$$x_2^{FM} = x_1^{FM} + (q_2 - q_1) \frac{C(q_1 + (n-1)q_2) - C(nq_1)}{(n-1)(q_2 - q_1)}$$

$$= x_1^{IS} + \frac{C(q_1 + (n-1)q_2) - C(nq_1)}{n-1} = x_2^{IS},$$

and so forth. Hence, in general for a homogeneous cost function we get

$$x_i^{FM} = \int_0^{q_i} \partial_i C((te) \wedge q) dt$$

$$= \sum_{k \le i} \int_{q_{k-1}}^{q_k} \partial_i C((te) \wedge q) dt$$

$$= \sum_{k \le i} \int_{q_{k-1}}^{q_k} C' \left(\sum_{i \in N} \min\{t, q_i\} \right) dt$$

$$= \sum_{k \le i} \int_{q_{k-1}}^{q_k} C' \left((n+1-k)t + \sum_{l=1}^{k-1} q_l \right) dt$$

$$= \sum_{k \le i} \frac{C((n+1-k)q_k + \sum_{l=1}^{k-1} q_l) - C\left((n-k)q_{k-1} + \sum_{l=1}^{k-2} q_l \right)}{n+1-k}$$

$$= x_i^{IS}.$$

In this sense, ϕ^{FM} extends ϕ^{IS} to the case of heterogeneous demands.

Thus, it also clear that the agents do not pay a constant unit price for all units demanded (as in Aumann–Shapley pricing) and, consequently, using the Friedman–Moulin rule does not make the choice between the scenarios of demand for personal goods and for baskets of goods, indifferent. Of course, for a given demand vector and cost function we could determine unit prices for good i as $p_i = x_i^{FM}/q_i$, but such unit prices cannot be used in connection with a disaggregation of q_i into m individual demands for good i without violating the spirit of the Friedman–Moulin rule (and the serial principle).

Example 4.1 (continued). Recall the case in Example 4.1 where $|N| = 2$ and costs are determined by the function

$$C(q) = q_2 + (q_1 + q_2)^{0.5}$$

with partial derivatives

$$\partial_1 C(q) = 0.5(q_1 + q_2)^{-0.5} \quad \text{and} \quad \partial_2 C(q) = 1 + 0.5(q_1 + q_2)^{-0.5}.$$

Let $q = (q_1, q_2) = (1, 2)$ yielding total cost $C(1, 2) = 2 + 3^{0.5} = 3.73$. Applying the Friedman–Moulin rule results in the following cost shares:

$$x_1^{FM}((1, 2), C) = \int_0^1 \partial_1 C(t, t)dt = \int_0^1 0.5(2t)^{-0.5}dt$$
$$= [2^{-0.5}t^{0.5}]_0^1 = 0.71,$$

and

$$x_2^{FM}((1, 2), C) = \int_0^1 \partial_2 C(t, t)dt + \int_1^2 \partial_2 C(1, t)dt$$
$$= \int_0^1 (1 + 0.5(2t)^{-0.5})dt + \int_1^2 (1 + 0.5(1 + t)^{-0.5})dt$$
$$= [t + 2^{-0.5}t^{0.5}]_0^1 + [t + (1 + t)^{0.5}]_1^2 = 3.02.$$

Compared to the result of the Aumann–Shapley and Shapley–Shubik rule, the resulting allocation $x^{FM}((1, 2), C)$ is more equally distributed than $x^{SS}((1, 2), C)$, which again is more equally distributed than $x^{AS}((1, 2), C)$. This Lorenz-dominance relationship, however, does not hold generally for concave cost functions.

Now, consider instead the cost function $\hat{C}(q) = q_1^2 + (q_1 + q_2)^{0.5}$. For $q = (1, 2)$ we get $x_1^{FM}((1, 2), \hat{C}) = 1.707$ and $x_2^{FM}((1, 2), \hat{C}) = 1.025$. Thus, contrary to increasing serial cost sharing in the homogeneous case, the Friedman–Moulin rule is *not* order-preserving. Moreover, compared to the result of the Aumann–Shapley and Shapley–Shubik rule, the resulting allocation $x^{FM}((1, 2), \hat{C})$ is more spread than $x^{SS}((1, 2), \hat{C})$, which again is more spread than $x^{AS}((1, 2), \hat{C})$. Since both C and $\hat{C}$ are submodular, this Lorenz-relation does not hold generally for submodular cost functions.

Finally, let $\bar{q} = (2, 1)$ and consider the permuted vector with increasing demands $\bar{q}_{(\cdot)} = (\bar{q}_{(1)}, \bar{q}_{(2)}) = (1, 2)$. Total cost is $C(\bar{q}) = 2.73$, which is shared as,

$$x_{(1)}^{FM}(\bar{q}_{(\cdot)}, C) = \int_0^{\bar{q}_{(1)}} \partial_{(1)} C(t, t)dt = \int_0^1 (1 + 0.5(2t)^{-0.5})dt = 1.71,$$

and

$$x_{(2)}^{FM}(\bar{q}(\cdot), C) = \int_0^{\bar{q}(1)} \partial_{(2)} C(t, t) dt + \int_{\bar{q}(1)}^{\bar{q}(2)} \partial_{(2)} C(1, t) dt$$

$$= \int_0^1 0.5(2t)^{-0.5} dt + \int_1^2 0.5(1+t)^{-0.5} dt = 1.02.$$

Hence agent 1 pays 1.02, while agent 2 pays 1.71.   △

Remark 4.3. Since the Friedman–Moulin rule is based on an *increasing* ordering of demands there is a natural counterpart based on a *decreasing* ordering of demands (as in the case of decreasing serial cost sharing (2.15) in Chap. 2).

Let the Decreasing Friedman–Moulin rule ϕ^{DFM} be defined by cost shares:

$$x_n^{DFM}(q, C) = \int_0^{q_n} \partial_n C(t, \dots, t) dt,$$

$$x_{n-1}^{DFM}(q, C) = \int_0^{q_n} \partial_{n-1} C(t, \dots, t) dt - \int_{q_{n-1}}^{q_n} \partial_{n-1} C(t, \dots, t, q_n) dt,$$

and

$$x_i^{DFM}(q, C) = \int_0^{q_n} \partial_i C(t, \dots, t) dt -$$

$$\int_{q_{n-1}}^{q_n} \partial_i C(t, \dots, t, q_n) dt - \dots - \int_{q_i}^{q_{i+1}} \partial_i C(t, \dots, t, q_{i+1}, \dots, q_n) dt,$$

for $i = 1, \dots, n-2$. Note that $\sum_{i=1}^n x_i^{DFM}(q, C) = C(q)$. Moreover, note that the increasing and decreasing versions of the Friedman–Moulin rule coincide when the cost function is additive, i.e., when $C(q) = \sum_{j=1}^n c_j(q_j)$, and that the cost shares of the decreasing version may be negative contrary to the cost shares of the (increasing) Friedman–Moulin rule.   △

Example 4.3. In order to compare the increasing and decreasing version of the Friedman–Moulin rule, consider the case with $N = \{1, 2\}$ and a Cobb-Douglas cost function $C(q) = q_1^{\alpha_1} q_2^{\alpha_2}$, for positive numbers α_1 and α_2. Using the (increasing) Friedman–Moulin rule in this case, we get that the agent with the smallest demand pays a fixed proportion of the total cost in case both agents had demanded q_1, i.e.,

$$x_1^{FM} = \frac{\alpha_1}{\alpha_1 + \alpha_2} q_1^{\alpha_1 + \alpha_2},$$

(and consequently agent 2 pays the residual). Using the decreasing rule we get the natural mirror image being that the agent with the largest demand pays a fixed proportion of the total cost in case both agents had demanded q_2, i.e.,

$$x_2^{DFM} = \frac{\alpha_2}{\alpha_1 + \alpha_2} q_2^{\alpha_1 + \alpha_2}$$

(and consequently agent 1 pays the residual). Note that unlike the decreasing serial cost sharing rule of the homogeneous case, concavity of C is not enough to guarantee non-negative cost shares of the decreasing version of the Moulin–Friedman rule. In the present example, concavity is tantamount to $\alpha_1 + \alpha_2 \leq 1$ which does not guarantee that the cost share of agent 1 is positive, i.e., that

$$x_1^{DFM} = q_1^{\alpha_1} q_2^{\alpha_2} - \frac{\alpha_2}{\alpha_1 + \alpha_2} q_2^{\alpha_1 + \alpha_2} \geq 0.$$

For example, if $q = (1, 5)$ and $\alpha = (0.5, 0.5)$ then $x_1^{DFM} = -0.26$. It is conjectured, however, that submodularity of C is a sufficient condition for non-negative cost shares of the decreasing version of the Friedman–Moulin rule (e.g., notice that the Cobb-Douglas cost function is supermodular and that the cost shares x^{DFM} related to the submodular cost functions C and $\hat{C}$ of Example 4.1 are all positive). △

Remark 4.4. Koster et al. (1998) and Tejedo and Truchon (2002) represent two attempts to extend increasing serial cost sharing to the scenario where agents demand baskets of goods. In case agents demand baskets of goods there is simply no obvious way to rank these baskets and consequently no obvious way to redefine the serial principle. Thus, there is potentially an infinite number of possible serial extensions. For example, demands may be ordered according to their stand-alone costs $C(q^i)$ and the intermediate production levels determined as $r_0 = 0$ and $r_k = \sum_{z=1}^{k} q^z + \sum_{z=k+1}^{n} \rho^R(C, q^k, q^z)$ for $k = 1, \ldots, n$, where $\rho^R(C, q^k, q^z) = \frac{C(q^k)}{C(q^z)} q^z$. Now, using the formula for Increasing Serial Cost sharing (defined in (2.14) of Chap. 2) with respect to these intermediate production levels defines a rule, which is called the Radial Serial Rule in Koster et al. (1998). A generalization of this type of rule is further analysed in Tejedo and Truchon (2002). △

4.4 Axiomatic Characterization

The Aumann–Shapley, Shapley–Shubik and Friedman–Moulin cost sharing rules have many appealing properties in common. For example, Friedman (2003) (see also Haimanko 2000) demonstrates that these three rules are distinguished members of a rich class of cost sharing rules satisfying Additivity (defined as usual with respect to cost functions) and

- *Dummy:* Agent i's costs share $\phi_i(q, C) = 0$ whenever $\partial_i C(z) = 0$ for all z.

Loosely speaking, this class consists of convex combinations of "path generated" rules (like the Aumann–Shapley and Friedman–Moulin rule – the

Shapley–Shubik rule is a convex combination of path generated incremental rules). In this connection it is worth to note that under Additivity, the property of Dummy is equivalent to the normatively compelling property of

- *Separability:* If $C(z) = \sum_{j=1}^{n} c_j(z_j)$ where c_j is non-decreasing and $c_j(0) = 0$ for all j, then $\phi_i(q, C) = c_i(q_i)$ for all $i \in N$.

In Chaps. 2 and 3, concerning the cases of homogeneous and binary demands, the axiomatic characterizations of cost sharing rules were centered around various versions of the *consistency* property. Basically, consistency requires that removing an agent, and adjusting the cost function properly for that agents' cost share, does not alter the cost shares of the remaining agents. There are many ways to adjust the cost function, but as argued in Friedman (2003) it seems natural to suggest a straightforward extension of consistency as defined for the model with homogeneous demand (in Moulin and Shenker 1994– and for binary demands by Hart and Mas-Colell 1989). Therefore, let consistency be defined as follows:

- *Consistency:* For cost sharing problems (q, C) where $C \in \mathcal{C}_2$,

$$\phi_j(q, C) = \phi_j(q^{N \setminus i}, C^{N \setminus i})$$

for $j \neq i$, where $C^{N \setminus i} = C(q^{N \setminus i}, q_i) - \phi_i((q^{N \setminus i}, q_i), C)$.

Given that the cost sharing rule satisfies Additivity and Dummy we get that $C^{N \setminus i}(0) = 0$ and that $C^{N \setminus i}$ can be made non-decreasing by adding terms of the form $F = \sum_{j \in N} f(x_j)$ which are then rendered irrelevant by Additivity and Dummy. Friedman (2003) shows that Consistency is satisfied by all three rules of Sect. 4.3.

However, there are also important properties, which separates the Aumann–Shapley, the Shapley–Shubik and the Friedman–Moulin rule.

As mentioned in Sect. 2.2.3 (Chap. 2), scale invariance seems to be a rather fundamental property since it states that cost shares are independent of the units of measurement. In the rationing model this was a quite obvious requirement but it seems reasonable also in the present set-up since the way to share costs still ought to be independent of units of measurement even though demand now concerns different goods. Formally:

- *Scale Invariance:* Let (q, C) and (q', C') be two scale equivalent cost sharing problems. Then $\phi_i(q, C) = \phi_i(q', C')$ for all $i \in N$.

Scale invariance is satisfied by both the Aumann–Shapley and the Shapley–Shubik rule. In fact, as shown in Sprumont (1998) the Shapley–Shubik rule satisfies the stronger property of ordinal invariance (i.e., invariance for ordinally equivalent problems) and is the only additive such rule.

However, considering the model where agents demand baskets of goods, Kolpin (1996) demonstrates that we cannot find a scale invariant and additive extension of serial cost sharing. With respect to the present model it can also be shown that the Friedman–Moulin rule does *not* satisfy scale invariance as done in the example below.

Example 4.1 (continued). Consider a simple rescaling where $(q_1', q_2') = (q_1, 0.5q_2)$ and $C'(q') = 2q_2' + (q_1' + 2q_2')^{0.5}$. Let $q = (1, 2)$ and consequently $q' = (1, 1)$. Using the Friedman–Moulin rule with respect to the problem (q', C') we get,

$$
\begin{aligned}
x_1^{FM}((1,1), C') &= \int_0^1 \partial_1 C'(t, t)dt = \int_0^1 0.5(3t)^{-0.5}dt \\
&= [3^{-0.5}t^{0.5}]_0^1 = 0.58 \neq x_1^{FM}((1,2), C) = 0.71,
\end{aligned}
$$

and

$$
\begin{aligned}
x_2^{FM}((1,1), C') &= \int_0^1 \partial_2 C'(t, t)dt = \int_0^1 (2 + (3t)^{-0.5})dt \\
&= [2t + 3^{-0.5}2t^{0.5}]_0^1 = 3.15 \neq x_2^{FM}((1,2), C) = 3.02.
\end{aligned}
$$

However, note that $x_i^{FM}((1,1), C') = x_i^{AS}((1,1), C') = x_i^{AS}((1,2), C)$ for $i \in \{1, 2\}$.   △

Demand monotonicity is another relevant property stating that if the demand of a given agent increases (ceteris paribus) then this agent cannot end up paying less than before. As such, the property is clearly linked to incentive issues: in case Demand Monotonicity is violated, and goods are freely disposable, some agents may have incentive to misrepresent their demand and thereby waste resources for the group as a whole. Moreover, it can be argued that by requiring Demand Monotonicity the agents are made at least weakly responsible for their own demand. Formally we have:

- *Demand Monotonicity:* Let (q, C) and (q', C) be two cost sharing problems and let $i \in N$. If $q_i \leq q_i'$ and $q_j = q_j'$ for all $j \in N \setminus i$ then $\phi_i(q, C) \leq \phi_i(q', C)$.

Demand monotonicity is satisfied by the Shapley–Shubik and the Friedman–Moulin rule but *not* by the Aumann–Shapley rule as demonstrated in Friedman and Moulin (1999) using the following example.

Example 4.4. Let $N = \{1, 2\}$ and let $\hat{C} = (q_1 q_2)/(q_1 + q_2)$. For agent 1 the Aumann–Shapley cost share is determined by

$$
x_1^{AS}(q, \hat{C}) = q_1 \int_0^1 \partial_1 C(tq_1, tq_2)dt = \frac{q_1 q_2^2}{(q_1 + q_2)^2},
$$

which is not monotonic in q_1 (increases for $q_1 \in [0, q_2]$ and then decreases for $q_1 > q_2$).   △

Note, however, that the Aumann–Shapley rule satisfies Demand Monotonicity on the particular class of Cobb-Douglas cost functions, i.e., functions $\bar{C}(q) = q_1^{\alpha_1} q_2^{\alpha_2} \ldots q_n^{\alpha_n}$ for positive numbers α_j. In this case $x_i^{AS}(q, \bar{C}) = \alpha_i C(q) / \sum_{j=1}^{n} \alpha_j$ for all $i \in N$, so all agents pay a fixed fraction of total costs. Hence, it is very likely that agents will demand too much compared to what is optimal from the point of view of the group as whole, highlighting that Demand Monotonicity is a rather weak requirement for making agents responsible for their own demand.

Moreover, recall that the Aumann–Shapley rule relates to a fixed unit price and consequently makes the choice between modeling agent specific demands, and demands for baskets of goods, indifferent. It is an open question whether Demand Monotonicity is a relevant property if we construe demands q_i as aggregates of individual demands, i.e., as in the case where agents demand baskets of goods. Imagine for example, that one agent starts demanding some good (demand used to be zero), then why should all other agents with unchanged demands for this (and all other) good(s) suddenly risk paying a larger unit price for this particular good? As such the relevance of Demand Monotonicity is less obvious for rules that relate to a fixed unit price as, e.g., the Aumann–Shapley rule.

In the cost sharing literature, there exists a number of characterizations of the individual cost sharing rules. Theorem 4.1, presents a selection of those related to the properties discussed above.

Theorem 4.1 (Billera and Heath 1982; Mirman and Tauman 1982; Sprumont 1998; Friedman and Moulin 1999). *Fix N. For cost sharing problems where $q \in \mathbf{R}_+^n$ and $C \in \mathcal{C}_1$, then among cost sharing rules satisfying the Additivity and the Dummy axiom:*

1. *The Aumann–Shapley rule ϕ^{AS} is the unique rule that satisfies Scale Invariance and extends the average cost rule ϕ^{AC}.*
2. *The Shapley–Shubik rule ϕ^{SS} is the unique rule that satisfies Ordinal Invariance and Equal Treatment[2] (alternatively, Ordinal Invariance may be replaced by Scale Invariance and Demand Monotonicity).*
3. *The Friedman–Moulin rule ϕ^{FM} is the unique rule that satisfies Demand Monotonicity and extends the increasing serial cost sharing rule ϕ^{IS}.*

The first part of the theorem (1) is proved in Billera and Heath (1982) and Mirman and Tauman (1982). The second part (2) is proved in Sprumont (1998) while the alternative statement is proved in Friedman and Moulin (1999). Finally the third part (3) is proved Friedman and Moulin (1999).

Besides the property of Demand Monotonicity, other monotonicity properties of cost sharing rules may be relevant in order to create the right incentives when applied in decentralized organizations. Indeed it could be argued, as in

---

[2] In the sense that, if C is symmetrical in the demands of i and j and $q_i = q_j$ then $\phi_i(q, C) = \phi_j(q, C)$.

Young (1985), that a more efficient technique of production (one with lower marginal costs) should never lead to higher imputed costs. Formally, this could be interpreted as if, for any two problems (q, C) and (q, G) where $C, G \in C_1$, and any $i \in N$, that $\partial_i C(z) \geq \partial_i G(z)$ for $0 \leq z \leq q$ (that is, G is more efficient producing good i than C, given the level of demand) then we should require that $\phi_i(q, C) \geq \phi_i(q, G)$. It can be shown that all three rules of Sect. 4.3 satisfies this requirement, see, e.g., Friedman (2004). However, if the same logic is used to allow for a comparison between *unit prices* of different products in different cost functions, a unique rule is singled out. Formally, we define the property of cross monotonicity in unit prices as follows:

- *Cross Monotonicity in Unit Prices:* If, for any two problems (q, C) and (q, G) where $C, G \in C_1$ and for any $i, j \in N$ that $\partial_i C(z) \geq \partial_j G(z)$ for $0 \leq z \leq q$ then $p_i = \phi_i(q, C)/q_i \geq \phi_j(q, G)/q_j = p_j$.

Monotonicity in this form is a rather strong requirement stating that, given actual demand q, if it is more efficient to produce good j on machine G, than good i on machine C, then the unit price associated with good j should be smaller than the unit price associated with good i.

Theorem 4.2 (Young 1985). *The Aumann–Shapley rule ϕ^{AS} is the unique cost sharing rule that satisfies Cross Monotonicity in Unit Prices.*

A proof can be found in Young (1985).

Yet another kind of monotonicity condition, which concerns agents incentives to misrepresent their true demand is the following: If agent i increases his demand then any coalition of agents that includes agent i should experience increasing total costs (that is, the sum total of the cost shares of agents in the coalition should increase). Otherwise the coalition has incentives to let agent i increase his demand. For example, if a cost sharing rule is used that satisfies Demand Monotonicity, then the other agents are simply able to compensate agent i for his increasing costs and still benefit from the action.

In a discrete model (that is, a model with integer demands) it is demonstrated in Moulin and Sprumont (2005) that (for $n \geq 3$) no cost sharing rule satisfies Additivity, Dummy and monotonicity in the above sense and consequently non of the three rules of Sect. 4.3 (in discrete versions) satisfy this kind of monotonicity condition. It is tempting to conjecture that this result holds true in the present model. Consider Example 4.4., which demonstrates that the Friedman–Moulin rule (that satisfies Additivity and Dummy) violates the above notion of monotonicity.

Example 4.5. Let $N = \{1, 2, 3\}$ and let $q = (q_1, 2, 3)$ where $q_1 \in [0, 2]$. Consider the following (non-decreasing) cost function: Let $f(x) = (1 + 10e^{-10x})^{-1}$ and

$$C(q) = q_1 + (0.1 + 2f(q_1 - 0.8))q_2 + (1 - f(q_1 - 0.8)f(10q_2 - 5q_3))q_3.$$

Letting the parameter q_1 start to increase from 0, the Friedman–Moulin cost share of agent 1 increases (ϕ^{FM} satisfies Demand Monotonicity). However, the sum of Friedman–Moulin cost shares of agent 1 and 3 ($x_1^{FM} + x_3^{FM}$) decreases for $q_1 \in [0.8, 1.2]$.   △

4.4.1 Non-additive Extensions

In Friedman and Moulin (1999) it is demonstrated that Additivity is the cause of many incompatibilities when extending the average and serial cost sharing rules. For example, an additive extension of average cost sharing cannot satisfy Demand Monotonicity and an additive extension of serial cost sharing cannot satisfy Scale Invariance. Thus, Additivity must be abandoned if such properties are to be compatible.

Consider first non-additive extensions of average cost sharing: Clearly, not all non-additive extensions of average cost sharing satisfies both Demand Monotonicity and Scale Invariance. For instance, proportionally adjusted marginal cost pricing, x^{PMC}, as defined in (4.3), is a non-additive extension of average cost sharing that satisfies Scale Invariance but *not* Demand Monotonicity.

It is therefore striking that Sprumont (1998) presents a non-additive extension of average cost sharing that satisfies both Demand Monotonicity and Ordinal Invariance (an thereby Scale Invariance) defined as follows.

Restrict attention to 2-agent problems (q, C) where $q \in \mathbf{R}_+^2$ and $C \in \mathcal{C}_2$. A cost sharing problem (q, C) is said to be *proportionally normalized* if $\partial_i C(rq) = 1$ for $i = 1, 2$ and all $r \geq 0$. Sprumont proves that to each problem (q, C) there is a unique proportionally normalized problem which is ordinally equivalent to (q, C) – let this problem be denoted (q^*, C^*).

Now, the *ordinally proportional rule* ϕ^{OP} is defined using the average cost sharing rule ϕ^{AC} with respect to the proportionally normalized (and ordinally equivalent) problem, i.e., given by cost shares

$$x_i^{OP}(q, C) = \frac{q_i^*}{q_1^* + q_2^*} C(q) \tag{4.7}$$

for $i = 1, 2$.

In the homogeneous case where $C(q) = c(q_1 + q_2)$ it can be shown that $q_i^* = q_i / c^{-1}(1)$ and hence

$$x_i^{OP}(q, C) = \frac{q_i^*}{q_1^* + q_2^*} C(q) = \frac{q_i / c^{-1}(1)}{(q_1^* + q_2^*)/c^{-1}(1)} C(q) = \frac{q_i}{q_1 + q_2} C(q),$$

i.e., ϕ^{OP} is indeed an extension of average cost sharing ϕ^{AC}.

It is tempting to generalize this approach to n-agent cost sharing problems but with more than two agents we are no longer guaranteed that a unique proportionally normalized (and ordinally equivalent) problem exists for each cost sharing problem. Sufficient conditions for this are provided in Wang and Zhu (2002).

For specific cost sharing problems it may be very hard to determine the problem (q^*, C^*) so unfortunately practical use of the rule seems rather limited.

Next, consider non-additive extensions of serial cost sharing. Sprumont (1998) argues that a natural extension of the serial principle relates to a ranking of cost shares rather than a ranking of demands as in homogeneous case. As mentioned earlier it is economically meaningless to compare the size of demands for different goods while it makes sense to compare monetary values. The serial principle could therefore be reinterpreted as requiring that an agent's cost share should be independent of changes in the demands of agents who *pay* (and not demand) more than him.

While this seems a natural extension of the serial principle it clearly excludes the straightforward candidate for an extension of the increasing serial rule, i.e., the Friedman–Moulin rule, since ϕ^{FM} is not order-preserving (cf. Example 4.1). However, as shown in Sprumont (1998) there is a related version, called the Moulin–Shenker rule, which satisfies this (new) version of the serial principle as well as Ordinal Invariance and (as do any rule that satisfies the (new) serial principle) Demand Monotonicity.

Formally, fix N and consider a cost sharing problem (q, C) where $C \in \mathcal{C}_2$. Instead of raising all "active" coordinates at the same speed as done using the path $P(t) = (te) \wedge q$ related to the Friedman–Moulin rule, we now use a path $\tilde{P}(t)$ determined by the unique solution to the following system of differential equations for each agent i,

$$\tilde{P}'_i(t) = \begin{cases} \frac{1}{\partial_i C(\tilde{P}(t))} & \tilde{P}_i(t) < q_i \\ 0 & \text{otherwise} \end{cases}$$

for which $\tilde{P}(0) = 0$. In this way, "active" coordinates are raised at a speed, which equals the marginal cost among all agents with "active" coordinates.

The Moulin–Shenker rule ϕ^{MS} is now defined by the cost shares,

$$x_i^{MS}(q, C) = \int_0^\infty \partial_i C(\tilde{P}(t)) \tilde{P}'_i(t) dt, \tag{4.8}$$

for $i = 1, \ldots, n$.

Sprumont (1998) offers a characterization based directly on the serial principle. An alternative characterization based on a version of consistency is found in Koster (2007).

Also in this case it may be very hard to determine the cost shares for specific problems limiting the practical relevance of the rule.

4.5 Practical Application by Convex Envelopment of Cost Data

Following Hougaard and Tind (2009), the present section will demonstrate that practical application of the cost sharing rules of Sect. 4.3 is simple using a non-parametric approach to estimate the cost function based on registered cost data.

Let $\{(q_j, C_j)\}_{j=1,\ldots,h}$ be a set of h observations of (output) vectors $q_j \in \mathbf{R}_+^n$ and their associated production cost $C_j \in \mathbf{R}_+$. These observations can be construed as originating either from the same firm over h time periods or from h different firms at a given point in time.

We may consider costs C as the result of producing output vector q. Hence, a "cost" possibility z is a data point $(q, C) \in \mathbf{R}_+^n \times \mathbf{R}_+$ where C is the possible cost associated with producing q. Denote by $\mathcal{C} \subset \mathbf{R}^{n+1}$ the cost possibility set and assume:

Convexity: If $z, z' \in \mathcal{C}$ then $\lambda z + (1 - \lambda)z' \in \mathcal{C}$ for $\lambda \in [0, 1]$.
Decreasing returns: If $z \in \mathcal{C}$ then $\lambda z \in \mathcal{C}$ for $\lambda \in [0, 1]$.
Free disposability: Let $z = (q, C) \in \mathcal{C}$ and let $q' \leq q$ and $C' \geq C$ then $z' = (q', C') \in \mathcal{C}$.

For a given data set $\{(q_j, C_j)\}_{j=1,\ldots,h} \in \{\mathbf{R}^{n+1}\}^h$ we obtain an empirical estimate $\mathcal{C}^*$ of the cost possibility set $\mathcal{C}$ as the intersection of sets satisfying the three conditions above, which contains all the data points, i.e., as,

$$\mathcal{C}^* = \{(\hat{q}, \hat{C}) \in \mathbf{R}_+^{n+1} | \sum_{j=1}^h \lambda_j q_j \geq \hat{q}, \sum_{j=1}^h \lambda_j C_j \leq \hat{C}, \sum_{j=1}^h \lambda_j \leq 1, \ \lambda_j \geq 0, \forall j\}.$$

Let $\mathcal{Q}^* = \{q | \exists \bar{C} : (q, \bar{C}) \in \mathcal{C}^*\}$ be the set of possible productions q given the observed data set.

Alternatively we may replace the assumption of decreasing returns (in production) with the assumption:

Constant returns: If $z \in \mathcal{C}$ then $\lambda z \in \mathcal{C}$ for $\lambda \geq 0$.

In this case we get

$$\mathcal{C}^* = \{(\hat{q}, \hat{C}) \in \mathbf{R}_+^{n+1} | \sum_{j=1}^h \lambda_j q_j \geq \hat{q}, \sum_{j=1}^h \lambda_j C_j \leq \hat{C}, \lambda_j \geq 0, \forall j\}.$$

Now, the (efficient) boundary of $\mathcal{C}^*$ is a non-parametric estimate of the cost function $C(q)$. Note that due to convexity of $\mathcal{C}^*$ the estimated cost function $C^*(q)$ will be convex and piecewise linear. The convexity assumption may be relaxed (see, e.g., Bogetoft 1996, Bogetoft et al. 2000) but, for the present purpose we continue with the convex version above.

Note that even though the estimate C^* is not differentiable in general, it is continuously differentiable along a line segment $[0, z]$, except perhaps for finitely many points. Thus, both the Aumann–Shapley and the Friedman–Moulin rule are well defined with respect to the estimate C^*.

4.5.1 Cost Allocation Using Data Envelopment

First consider calculation of the Aumann–Shapley cost shares with respect to the estimate C^*. In connection with transportation problems, Samet et al. (1984) suggested to use parametric programming (see, e.g., Taha 1989) to determine the Aumann–Shapley cost shares. Here the same technique is used to determine the Aumann–Shapley prices, which are easily found as a finite sum of gradients of the linear pieces of C^* along the line segment $[0, q]$ weighted with the normalized length of the subintervals where C^* has constant gradient.

Select a given demand vector $\hat{q} \in \mathcal{Q}^*$. In our case, we first consider parameter values $t \in [0, 1]$ and solve

$$\min \ \sum_{j=1}^{h} \lambda_j C_j \tag{4.9}$$

$$\text{s.t.} \ \sum_{j=1}^{h} \lambda_j q_j \geq t\hat{q} \tag{4.10}$$

$$\sum_{j=1}^{h} \lambda_j \leq 1 \tag{4.11}$$

$$\lambda_j \geq 0, \forall j. \tag{4.12}$$

As a result we get the relevant subintervals of $[0, \hat{q}]$ for which the gradients are constant, i.e., a series of values t_m for which the gradient is constant on the interval $[t_{m-1}, t_m]$. The values of the gradients are equal to the values of the optimal dual variables corresponding to the constraints (4.10). The optimal dual variable corresponding to the convexity constraint (4.11) is usually nonzero. In technical terms, we may consider the Aumann–Shapley allocation procedure as a way to transfer and allocate the value of this dual variable to the dual variables corresponding to (4.10) as illustrated in Example 4.5.

If the convexity constraint (4.11) is removed, we get a constant returns to scale version of the problem, i.e.

$$\min \sum_{j=1}^{h} \lambda_j C_j$$

$$\text{s.t.} \sum_{j=1}^{h} \lambda_j q_j \geq t\hat{q}$$

$$\lambda_j \geq 0, \forall j.$$

In this model the gradients are the same all over the interval $[0, \hat{q}]$ with values determined by the optimal dual variables, and by linear programming duality they can be applied directly in the cost sharing problem as Aumann–Shapley prices.

Example 4.6. Consider the following cost data from four observations:

Obs.	q_1	q_2	C
1	2	3	6
2	3	1	5
3	4	5	15
4	5	2	10

Consider demand vector $\hat{q} = (4, 3)$ and define $\bar{q} = (\bar{q}_1(t), \bar{q}_2(t)) = (\hat{q}_1 t, \hat{q}_2 t) = (4t, 3t)$. Hence, we solve the following problem:

$$\min 6\lambda_1 + 5\lambda_2 + 15\lambda_3 + 10\lambda_4$$
$$2\lambda_1 + 3\lambda_2 + 4\lambda_3 + 5\lambda_4 \geq 4t$$
$$3\lambda_1 + 1\lambda_2 + 5\lambda_3 + 2\lambda_4 \geq 3t$$
$$\lambda_1 + \lambda_2 + \lambda_3 + \lambda_4 \leq 1$$
$$\lambda_i \geq 0 \text{ for } i = 1, \dots, 4.$$

By parametric linear programming we get, omitting the t argument in the $\bar{q}$ variables:

t	Objective function
$0 \leq t \leq \frac{7}{11} = 0.64$	$\frac{9}{7}\bar{q}_1 + \frac{8}{7}\bar{q}_2$
$\frac{7}{11} \leq t \leq \frac{11}{13} = 0.85$	$\frac{9}{5}\bar{q}_1 + \frac{7}{5}\bar{q}_2 - \frac{9}{5}$
$\frac{11}{13} \leq t \leq 1$	$\frac{17}{8}\bar{q}_1 + \frac{19}{8}\bar{q}_2 - \frac{43}{8}$

From the above table we get Aumann–Shapley cost shares

$$x_1^{AS} = 4 \times \{\frac{9}{7} \times \frac{7}{11} + \frac{9}{5} \times (\frac{11}{13} - \frac{7}{11}) + \frac{17}{8} \times (1 - \frac{11}{13})\} = 6.09$$

and

$$x_2^{AS} = 3 \times \{\frac{8}{7} \times \frac{7}{11} + \frac{7}{5} \times (\frac{11}{13} - \frac{7}{11}) + \frac{19}{8} \times (1 - \frac{11}{13})\} = 4.16.$$

Observe that total cost is $x_1^{AS} + x_2^{AS} = 10.25$ which is equal to the objective function value of the above program when $t = 1$, as it should be.

The third convexity constraint is binding and receives in this case a non-zero dual variable value which is equal to the element $-\frac{43}{8}$ in the last row of the table. Again from the last row we see that the optimal dual variable corresponding to the first element in the demand vector is equal to $\frac{17}{8} = 2.125$. Multiplication of this price by the demand $\hat{q}_1 = 4$ gives the value of 8.50. The difference between x_1^{AS} and this value is -2.41. The similar difference corresponding the second element of the demand vector is -2.96. The two differences add to $-5.37 = -\frac{43}{8}$ which is equal to the value of the optimal dual variable corresponding to the convexity constraint, as it should be. In this way the dual variable for the convexity constraint is distributed on to the values of the demand vector.

The corresponding constant returns to scale model, obtained by removal of the convexity constraint, is

$$
\begin{aligned}
\min\; & 6\lambda_1 + 5\lambda_2 + 15\lambda_3 + 10\lambda_4 \\
& 2\lambda_1 + 3\lambda_2 + 4\lambda_3 + 5\lambda_4 \geq 4t \\
& 3\lambda_1 + 1\lambda_2 + 5\lambda_3 + 2\lambda_4 \geq 3t \\
& \lambda_i \geq 0 \text{ for } i = 1, \ldots, 4.
\end{aligned}
\tag{4.13}
$$

In this case we get the same objective function for all t as shown by the table:

t	Objective function
$0 \leq t \leq 1$	$\frac{9}{7}\bar{q}_1 + \frac{8}{7}\bar{q}_2$

The optimal dual variables for the two constraints of the program (4.13) are $\left(\frac{9}{7}, \frac{8}{7}\right)$ and they are equal to the coefficients of the objective function in the above table, as they should be. This confirms that the cost allocation by the Aumann–Shapley method in the case of constant return to scale is equivalent to a cost allocation based on the optimal dual variables of the model. In this case it is not necessary to allocate dual variables arising from an additional (convexity) constraint. $\triangle$

The same type of technique can be used to determine the cost shares of the Friedman–Moulin rule. Consider a demand vector $\hat{q} \in \mathcal{Q}^*$ and let $\hat{q}_{(\cdot)} = (\hat{q}_{(1)}, \ldots, \hat{q}_{(n)})$ be the vector $\hat{q}$ where the indices have been permuted such that they are in increasing order, i.e., $\hat{q}_{(1)} \leq \ldots \leq \hat{q}_{(n)}$. Moreover, define vectors $v_0 = (0, \ldots, 0)$, $v_1 = (\hat{q}_{(1)}, \ldots, \hat{q}_{(1)})$, $v_2 = (\hat{q}_{(1)}, \hat{q}_{(2)}, \ldots, \hat{q}_{(2)}), \ldots$, $v_i = (\hat{q}_{(1)}, \ldots, \hat{q}_{(i-1)}, \hat{q}_{(i)}, \ldots, \hat{q}_{(i)}), \ldots, v_n = \hat{q}_{(\cdot)}$.

We now have to solve n problems for $s = 0, \ldots, n-1$, and parameter values $t \in [0, 1]$,

$$
\min \sum_{j=1}^{h} \lambda_j C_j
$$

$$
\text{s.t.} \sum_{j=1}^{h} \lambda_j q_j \geq v_s + t(v_{s+1} - v_s)
\tag{4.14}
$$

$$\sum_{j=1}^{h} \lambda_j \le 1$$

$$\lambda_j \ge 0, \forall j.$$

Again we obtain the relevant subintervals of the path

$$[v_0, v_1], [v_1, v_2], \ldots, [v_{n-1}, v_n]$$

for which the gradients are constant, i.e., a series of values t_m for which the gradient is constant on the interval $[t_{m-1}, t_m]$. We may then determine the gradients on all such subintervals and determine the Friedman–Moulin cost shares as illustrated by the following example.

Example 4.6 (continued). Continuing the previous example we get that $(\hat{q}_{(2)}, \hat{q}_{(1)}) = (\hat{q}_1, \hat{q}_2) = (4, 3)$, $v_1 = (3, 3)$ and $v_2 = (3, 4)$. Hence for $s = 0$ we shall solve

$$
\begin{aligned}
\min\ & 6\lambda_1 + 5\lambda_2 + 15\lambda_3 + 10\lambda_4 \\
& 2\lambda_1 + 3\lambda_2 + 4\lambda_3 + 5\lambda_4 \ge 3t \\
& 3\lambda_1 + 1\lambda_2 + 5\lambda_3 + 2\lambda_4 \ge 3t \\
& \lambda_1 + \lambda_2 + \lambda_3 + \lambda_4 \le 1 \\
& \lambda_i \ge 0 \text{ for } i = 1, \ldots, 4.
\end{aligned}
$$

This results in the table:

t	Objective function
$0 \le t \le \frac{7}{9} = 0.78$	$\frac{9}{7}\bar{q}_1 + \frac{8}{7}\bar{q}_2$
$\frac{7}{9} \le t \le \frac{11}{12} = 0.92$	$\frac{9}{5}\bar{q}_1 + \frac{7}{5}\bar{q}_2 - \frac{9}{5}$
$\frac{11}{12} \le t \le 1$	$\frac{17}{8}\bar{q}_1 + \frac{19}{8}\bar{q}_2 - \frac{43}{8}$

The contribution to x_1^{FM} from this table is

$$3 \times \left\{ \frac{9}{7} \times \frac{7}{9} + \frac{9}{5} \times \left(\frac{11}{12} - \frac{7}{9}\right) + \frac{17}{8} \times \left(1 - \frac{11}{12}\right) \right\} = 4.281$$

and to x_2^{FM}

$$3 \times \left\{ \frac{8}{7} \times \frac{7}{9} + \frac{7}{5} \times \left(\frac{11}{12} - \frac{7}{9}\right) + \frac{19}{8} \times \left(1 - \frac{11}{12}\right) \right\} = 3.843.$$

Next for $s = 1$ we shall solve

$$
\begin{aligned}
\min\ & 6\lambda_1 + 5\lambda_2 + 15\lambda_3 + 10\lambda_4 \\
& 2\lambda_1 + 3\lambda_2 + 4\lambda_3 + 5\lambda_4 \ge 3 + t \\
& 3\lambda_1 + 1\lambda_2 + 5\lambda_3 + 2\lambda_4 \ge 3 \\
& \lambda_1 + \lambda_2 + \lambda_3 + \lambda_4 \le 1 \\
& \lambda_i \ge 0 \text{ for } i = 1, \ldots, 4.
\end{aligned}
$$

implying the table:

t	Objective function
$0 \le t \le 1$	$\frac{17}{8}\bar{q}_1 + \frac{19}{8}\bar{q}_2 - \frac{43}{8}$

The contribution to x_1^{FM} is

$$1 \times \frac{17}{8} \times 1 = 2.125$$

and to x_2^{FM}

$$0 \times \frac{19}{8} \times 1 = 0.$$

Hence, in total, the Friedman–Moulin cost shares are given by

$$x_1^{FM} = 4.281 + 2.125 = 6.41$$

and

$$x_2^{FM} = 3.843 + 0 = 3.84.$$

Again total cost is $x_1^{FM} + x_2^{FM} = 10.25$ as it should be. So the Friedman–Moulin case puts a larger cost share on q_1 in comparison to the Aumann–Shapley case. Again we see that the value of the dual variable of the convexity constraint $-\frac{43}{8} = -5.37$ is allocated to the values of the demand vector, but this time with the shares -2.09 and -3.28 respectively for output 1 and output 2. $\triangle$

4.6 Comments

Contrary to the (homogeneous) one-good model in Chap. 2, manipulability in the form of reshuffling, merging or splitting of demands does not make sense in the present "personalized" goods framework. Merging (and reshuffling) of demands would imply that goods measured in different units should be added, which is meaningless and splitting would require the definition of a "new" cost function over $\mathbf{R}_+^{n+1}$ instead of $\mathbf{R}_+^n$. Allocations can therefore only be manipulated by the agents' strategic choice of demand q_i. To some extent this problem has been highlighted by the monotonicity conditions in Sect. 4.4, but further analysis of such situations requires the knowledge of agents preferences, which is not available in the present model. Notice, however, that if we consider the model where agents demand baskets of goods and we use, for instance, the Radial Serial rule (defined in Remark 4.4.) agents may manipulate through merging and splitting of demands.

Contrary to the (binary demands) model in Chap. 3, it is debatable whether the stand-alone cost requirements are relevant in the present model since typically it will not be possible for agents to "stand-alone" and the relevance of the no-subsidy argument may be questionable. Translated to the present framework the stand-alone cost principle states that

$$\sum_{i \in S} x_i \leq C(\{q_i\}_{i \in S}, 0, \dots, 0) \quad \text{for all} \quad S \subseteq N.$$

As mentioned in Moulin (2002) there is a conflict between additive rules and the stand-alone cost principle. However, additivity and the stand-alone cost principle may be reconciled when the cost function C is submodular.

Finally, we have ignored the scenario where a fixed amount F must be allocated among a group of agents $i = 1, \dots, n$ with multiple characteristics q_{ij}, $j = 1, \dots, m$. For example, in the case where a set of branches, characterized by similar (multiple) production activities, must share the costs of a common marketing campaign. Clearly, there is no straightforward solution to this problem and consequently there has been many *ad hoc* suggestions. However, Beasley (2003) presents an interesting approach: Imagine that there existed a set of common characteristic weights α_j. Then, for instance, costs could be allocated in proportion to weighted characteristics. Now, as these weights typically do not exist we may elicit such weights under the assumption that the weighted characteristics per unit of cost is identical for all agents. To be more specific, for each agent i we may determine cost shares x_i and weights α_j such that the cost share of i is minimized (maximized) subject to constraints stating that $\sum_{j=1}^{m} \alpha_j q_{ij}/x_i = 1$ for all i and $\sum_{h=1}^{n} x_h = F$ (with $x_h \geq 0$ and $\alpha_j > 0$). In this way we obtain, for each agent, a lower and an upper bound on the cost share which is compatible with the assumption that weighted characteristics per unit of cost is identical for all agents. A specific allocation can now be chosen according to various additional criteria as discussed in Beasley (2003). Note that the approach is operational in the sense that all computations only involve linear programming.

4.7 Summary

Generalizing the one-good cost sharing model of Chap. 2 to a multiple goods framework, as in the present chapter, considerably increases the complexity of the model. It is no longer obvious how to interpret the allocation problem and there are no straightforward and uniquely determined way to extend the cost sharing rules known from the one-good model. Basically the allocation problem can be interpreted either as that of a group of agents each demanding baskets of goods and sharing the common cost of the aggregate demand or as that of a group of agents each demanding a specific type of good ("personalized" good) and sharing the common cost of the groups demand profile. The present chapter focuses on the latter scenario while the former scenario is relatively unexplored in the literature.

Once it is decided which type of allocation problem that is most relevant it is simple to transform the problem into one of binary demands as in Chap. 3 and then use the allocation rules associated with this model (for instance the Shapley value – to be called the Shapley–Shubik rule in the present framework). Loosely speaking, it can be shown that if additivity and ordinal invariance are important properties of the allocation rule then the Shapley–Shubik rule is the one to apply. There are also *non*-additive and ordinally invariant rules, but they are quite complex and difficult to apply in practice. In any case, ordinal invariance is a very convenient and desirable (though very strong) property in a type of modeling framework where we basically try to compare demand for apples with demand for oranges.

Now, in the economics literature the Aumann–Shapley rule has been the dominating recommendation in a multiple goods framework. This rule extends the average cost sharing rule of the one-good model and hence has the advantage of having a clear cut economic interpretation as well as being easy to use in practice (as demonstrated in Sect. 4.5). It is not ordinally invariant (which is a rather strong requirement) but satisfies scale invariance which seems to be a quite fundamental property with respect to any version of the model. Moreover, since the Aumann–Shapley rule implies that all agents pay a fixed price per unit of demand, the model where agents demand baskets of goods becomes equivalent to the model where agents demand "personalized" goods.

Lately, however, the Aumann–Shapley rule has been criticized on the basis of the fact that it does not satisfy a weak form of demand monotonicity (i.e., if demand increases so does the cost share). Loosely speaking, this can be seen as the "price" for having a rule that assigns cost shares according to fixed unit prices and while demand monotonicity seems relevant in the scenario where agents demand personalized goods its relevance is questionable in the scenario where agents demand baskets of goods. Demand monotonicity is satisfied by the Shapley–Shubik rule as well as the Friedman–Moulin rule (being an extension of the increasing serial cost sharing rule of the one-good model). But the latter rule does not satisfy scale invariance and the fact that this rule requires that demands are increasingly ordered makes the economic interpretation somewhat obscure in the framework of personalized goods.

References

Aumann R, Shapley L (1974) Values of non-atomic games. Princeton University Press, Princeton.

Beasley JE (2003) Allocating fixed costs and resources via data envelopment analysis. Eur J Oper Res 147:198–216.

Billera LJ, Heath C (1982) Allocation of shared costs: a set of axioms yielding a unique procedure. Math Oper Res 7:32–39.

Billera LJ, Heath DC, Raanan J (1978) Internal telephone billing rates – a novel application of non-atomic game theory. Oper Res 26:958–965.

Bogetoft P (1996) DEA on relaxed convexity assumptions. Manage Sci 42:457–465.

Bogetoft P, Tama JM, Tind J (2000) Convex input and output projections of non-convex production possibility sets. Manage Sci 46:858–869.

Friedman EJ (2003) Paths and consistency in additive cost sharing. Int J Game Theory 32:501–518.

Friedman EJ (2004) Strong monotonicity in surplus sharing. Econ Theory 23:643–658.

Friedman EJ, Moulin H (1999) Three methods to share joint costs or surplus. J Econ Theory 87:275–312.

Haimanko O (2000) Partially symmetric values. Math Oper Res 25:573–590.

Hart S, Mas-Colell A (1989) Potential, value, and consistency. Econometrica 57:589–614.

Hougaard JL, Tind J (2009) Cost allocation and convex data envelopment. Eur J Oper Res 194:939–947.

Kolpin V (1996) Multi-product serial cost sharing: an incomparability with the additivity axiom. J Econ Theory 69:227–233.

Koster M (2007) The Moulin–Shenker rule. Soc Choice Welf 29:271–293.

Koster M, Tijs S, Borm P (1998) Serial cost sharing methods for multi-commodity situations. Math Soc Sci 36:229–242.

Mirman L, Tauman Y (1982) Demand compatible equitable cost sharing prices. Math Oper Res 7:40–56.

Moulin H, Shenker S (1994) Average cost pricing versus serial cost sharing: an axiomatic comparison. J Econ Theory 64:178–201.

Moulin H (2002) Axiomatic cost and surplus sharing. In: Arrow, Sen, Suzumura (eds) Handbook of social choice and welfare, chap. 6. Elsevier, Amsterdam.

Moulin H, Sprumont Y (2005) On demand responsiveness in additive cost sharing. J Econ Theory 125:1–35.

Peleg B, Sudhölter (2003) Introduction to the theory of cooperative games. Kluwer, Dordrecht.

Samet D, Tauman Y, Zang I (1984) An application of the Aumann–Shapley prices for cost allocation in transportation problems. Math Oper Res 9:25–42.

Shubik M (1962) Incentives, decentralized control, the assignment of joint costs and internal pricing. Manage Sci 8:325–343.

Sprumont Y (1998) Ordinal cost sharing. J Econ Theory 81:126–162.

Taha HA (1989) Operations research, 4th edn. Maxwell MacMillan, New York.

Tejedo C, Truchon M (2002) Serial cost sharing in multidimensional context. Math Soc Sci 44:277–299.

Young HP (1985) Producer incentives in cost allocation. Econometrica 53:757–764.

Wang Y-T, Zhu D (2002) Ordinal proportional cost sharing. J Math Econ 37:215–230.

Chapter 5
Sharing in Networks

5.1 Introduction

Various forms of networks have always played important roles in the economy, and in view of the recent growth of telecommunication and economic activities related to the Internet, an understanding of network formation and allocation problems within networks seems particularly challenging.

Networks have been studied intensively in Physics (in order to understand and predict behaviour in such systems, see, e.g., Newman 2003 for a survey) and in Operations Research (where focus is on algorithm design and computational complexity, see, e.g., Magnanti and Wolsey 1995 for a survey). Both streams of literature typically use graphs as a convenient representation of networks. Economic issues such as allocation, efficiency and network formation, on the other hand, have primarily been addressed by economists and game theorists.

In the present chapter we shall focus on the latter approach and consider three main scenarios: The first concerns the minimum cost spanning tree model where a group of agents shall be connected to a common source (sometimes considered as the supplier) in the least costly way. It is assumed that there are no externalities in the network so the problem can be represented solely by the costs of connecting all pairs of agents (including the source) represented by a link cost matrix. Allocating the total cost associated with the least costly way to connect all agents to the source can then be done using an allocation rule ϕ defined over the set of possible link cost matrices, given the set of agents.

The second scenario concerns a model of demand-based cost allocation. The network is characterized by network externalities and a proxy for these are given by a "communication" matrix stating the amount of communication between every pair of agents in the network. Each agent is further characterized by an individual connection cost, i.e., the cost of being connected to the entire network. In this sense the cost structure is much simpler than in the first scenario. The total cost of the network (i.e., the sum of individual connection costs) is then allocated among the agents using an allocation rule ϕ, which takes the profile of individual connection costs and/or the "communication" matrix into account.

J.L. Hougaard, *An Introduction to Allocation Rules*,
DOI 10.1007/978-3-642-01828-2_5, © Springer-Verlag Berlin Heidelberg 2009

Finally, the third scenario concerns the quite general case where any network related to a given group of agents has a value modeled by a value function (positive or negative). In other words, the particular way that the agents are connected is important for the value of their network relation. This is, for example, quite obviously the case for various types of social networks. An allocation rule then allocates the value of the network among the agents involved.

Consider the following examples related to the scenarios above:

1. Recall the case of airport landing fees mentioned in Chap. 3 where the cost structure related to the building of runways was simplified by the fact that larger aircrafts require longer runways. Therefore the least costly way to build a runway can be modeled by a simple network where a number of nodes (here being types of aircrafts) are connected as a chain. The "source" of the network represents the beginning of the runway, the first node represents the length required by the smallest type of aircraft, etc. With every link between two nodes in the network there is an associated cost of building that particular incremental part of the runway. Clearly, there are no network externalities. The "runway" network is a *minimal cost spanning tree* in the sense that it minimizes the costs of connecting every node to the source (where nodes may be connected indirectly, that is, connected to the source via other nodes that are connected to the source). Clearly, a star-shaped network representing the case where all types of aircrafts have their own runway is the opposite and most costly alternative to the chain.

2. Consider a telecommunication network where the traffic between agents is given by a traffic matrix measuring, for instance, hours of communication between any pair of agents per month. This information will typically be available from the network operator. Moreover, each agent is characterized by a connection cost, which is the cost in terms of local wires, switching cards, etc. Assume that there are no other costs connected with the network. Because of the externalities as indicated by the traffic matrix, agents may have an incentive to share the connection cost of other agents.

3. Consider any kind of business (or social) relationship where the particular network structure determines the value for those involved. For example a relationship, which forms a network with the shape of a star, i.e., one agent is the center and the other, say n, agents are connected to the center by their own link. Assume that each of the n agents i obtain the utility u from a direct link to the center and δu from an indirect link to another agent j via the center where $\delta \in [0, 1]$. Let the value of the network be the sum of utilities of all agents involved. Hence, the increase in network value from adding a new link to the source of the star is $(2n\delta + 1)u$ – the new agent gets utility u from the direct link to the center and $n\delta u$ from all the indirect links to the original n agents, and the original n agents all get utility δu from the indirect link to the additional agent in the network.

Assume that the cost of adding such a link is c. If $(2n\delta + 1)u > c$ it is socially optimal to include the new agent in the existing network. However, if $c > u$ and the new agent has to cover all the costs of establishing the link to the center alone, he will not join the network voluntarily resulting in a socially inefficient size of the network. To ensure network efficiency it may therefore be necessary to reallocate costs and/or benefits in the network. We shall examine how allocation rules influence network formation and efficiency.

5.2 Modeling Networks as Graphs

Let $N \subset \mathbf{N} = \{1, 2, \ldots\}$ be a set of agents where $|N| = n$. A network (or graph) g is a list of unordered pairs of agents $i, j \in N$. Let g^N be the set of all pairs of agents in N and denote by $G = \{g | g \subset g^N\}$ the set of all possible graphs on N. In particular, let $g_{|S} = \{ij | ij \in g, i \in S, j \in S\}$ be the subgraph between agents (or nodes) in $S \subset N$. Moreover, for notational convenience we write $g + ij$ $(g - ij)$ for the graph g adding (subtracting) the link between i and j. In some graphs we say that there is a *source* (or root) denoted by agent 0. Let $N^0 = N \cup 0$.

Two agents i and j are *connected* in g if there is a path $i_1 i_2, i_2 i_3, \ldots, i_{h-1} i_h$ such that $i_k i_{k+1} \in g$ for $1 \leq k \leq h - 1$ where $i = i_1$ and $j = i_h$. A graph g is said to be *connected* if i and j are connected in g for all $i, j \in N$. The graph g^N is said to be *complete*. A path is called a *cycle* if it starts and ends with the same agent, e.g., if $i_1 i_2, i_2 i_3, \ldots, i_{h-1} i_h, i_h i_1$.

Let $H(g) = \{i | \exists j : ij \in g\}$. The graph $g' \subset g$ is a *component* of g, if for all $i \in H(g')$ and $j \in H(g')$, $i \neq j$, there exists a path in g' connecting i and j, and for any $i \in H(g')$ and $j \in H(g)$, $ij \in g$ implies that $ij \in g'$.

Examples of graphs with a source, that will often be referred to, are: a *chain* where the graph is a connected sequential path $0i_1, i_1 i_2, \ldots, i_{n-1} i_n$; a *star* where all agents are connected to the source via their own connection $0i_1, 0i_2, \ldots, 0i_n$, and a *tree* where the graph is a path from the source with no cycles. See Fig. 5.1.

5.3 Minimum Cost Spanning Trees

A classical example of an economic situation that may be modeled by a graph is when a group of agents want to be connected to a common supplier (or source) and these connections are costly – for example as in the cases of district heating, cable-TV, computer networks using a common server, chain stores using a common warehouse, etc. In such cases there are no obvious network externalities and consequently the two main problems are (1) to find

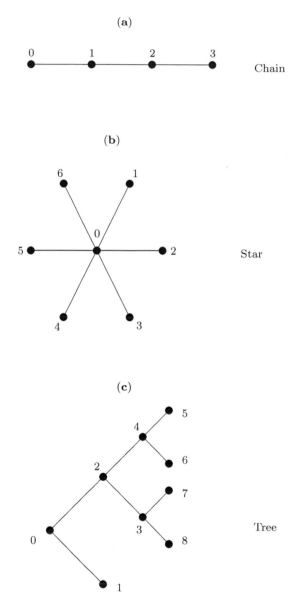

Fig. 5.1 Networks in the shape of a chain, a star and a tree

the cheapest way to connect all interested agents, and (2) to allocate total
network costs among the agents in the network.

Consider a complete graph g^{N^0} over N^0. For each link $ij \in g^{N^0}$, let $k_{ij} > 0$
be a positive cost associated with the link ij. Note, that there is $\frac{n(n+1)}{2}$ unordered pairs of agents in N^0 and hence as many link costs to be determined.
Since links are unordered $k_{ij} = k_{ji}$. Letting $k_{ii} = 0$ for all $i \in N^0$, these link
costs define a $(n+1) \times (n+1)$ cost matrix K associated with the graph g^{N^0}.
We may think of such costs as the costs of establishing the link, maintenance
costs or indirect costs such as congestion, etc.

A *spanning tree* T_{N^0} is a tree where all agents N are connected to the source
$\{0\}$ either directly or indirectly. There are $(n+1)^{n-1}$ such spanning trees. A
minimum cost spanning tree T_{N^0} is a spanning tree where the total link cost
$\sum_{ij \in T_{N^0}} k_{ij}$ is minimized over all possible spanning trees. In other words, a
minimum cost spanning tree indicates how all agents can be connected to
the source in the least costly way. Note, that there may be more than one
minimum cost spanning tree for a given complete graph. Since the graph of
T_{N^0} does not contain cycles there is a unique path connecting a given agent
i to the source.

Remark 5.1. Algorithms for finding minimum cost spanning trees in a given
graph with cost matrix K are provided in Kruskal (1956) and Prim (1957).
Using the Kruskal algorithm, links are ordered according to non-decreasing
costs and considered one by one; a link is rejected if generates a cycle with
those already accepted, otherwise it is accepted and added. There will be n
such steps in the algorithm. Using the Prim algorithm a link is established
with lowest cost either directly to the source or to the subset of agents already
linked to the source, directly or indirectly. In this way, select an agent with
the lowest link cost to the source; then among the remaining agents select an
agent with the lowest link cost either to the source or to the agent already
connected to the source, etc. Again there will be n such steps in the algorithm.
$\triangle$

For a given set of agents N and a given link cost matrix K the total
link cost of the associated minimum cost spanning tree(s) is $\sum_{ij \in T_{N^0}} k_{ij}$.
This (total) cost can be allocated among the agents using several different
approaches, for example, those considered in Claus and Kleitman (1973).

Clearly, we may use standard rules such as "sharing the total cost equally
among all agents" or "sharing the total cost in proportion to stand-alone
costs" (that is, the costs of connecting each individual agent to the source)
or "marginal costs" (that is the difference between the costs of connecting
agents N and agents $N \setminus i$ to the source for each i). Basically, these rule have
been treated in Chap. 2 and do not take the specific structure of the graph
T_{N^0} into account.

Taking the specific structure of the minimum cost spanning tree into consideration we can further use the incremental or the serial principle (see
Chap. 2) directly, as discussed in Sect. 5.3.1.

However, since a realisation of the efficient solution in terms of a minimum cost spanning tree graph requires that this solution is sustained by the associated cost allocation, it seems quite natural to utilize the framework of Chap. 3, as suggested in Bird (1976). A complete graph g^{N^0}, with its associated link cost matrix K, can be represented as a cost allocation problem (N, c^T) where N is the set of agents and c^T is a cost function defined by

$$c^T(S) = \sum_{ij \in T_{S^0}} k_{ij},$$

for all $S \subseteq N$, related to minimum cost spanning trees $\{T_{S^0}\}_{S \subseteq N}$ of the (sub)graphs $g_{|S^0}$. Note, that even though there may be more than one minimum cost spanning tree related to a given subgraph, the cost function c^T is uniquely determined for a given complete graph g^{N^0} and its associated link cost matrix.

Given a (minimum cost spanning tree) cost allocation problem (N, c^T), the various cost allocation rules discussed in Chap. 3 can all be applied. In particular, core selection rules become important since satisfying the standalone cost principle seems crucial for sustaining the solution indicated by the minimum cost spanning tree.

Example 5.1. Consider the special case where the minimum cost spanning tree is a chain (as in the airport problem mentioned in Chap. 3), i.e.,

$$T_{N^0} = \{0i_1, i_1 i_2, \ldots, i_{n-1} i_n\}.$$

The related cost allocation problem has a simple structure where, for all $S \subseteq N$, we have

$$c^T(S) = \sum_{j=1}^{j^*(S)} k_{j-1j} = k_{0j^*(S)},$$

with $j^*(S) = \max\{j | i_{j-1} i_j \in T_{S^0}\}$. Since, for any $S, H \subseteq N$, that $c^T(S \cap H) \leq \min\{c^T(S), c^T(H)\}$ and $c^T(S \cup H) = \max\{c^T(S), c^T(H)\}$ the induced cost allocation problem (N, c^T) is concave. Hence, the core is non-empty: for instance, in 3-agent chains the core is the convex hull of cost allocations

$$(0, 0, k_{0,3}), \ (0, k_{0,2}, k_{2,3}),$$

$$(k_{0,1}, 0, k_{1,2} + k_{2,3}) \text{ and } (k_{0,1}, k_{1,2}, k_{2,3}).$$

Note that the incremental cost vector $(k_{0,1}, k_{1,2}, k_{2,3})$ is an extreme point in the core.

Generally, such standard fixed tree networks where all agents are linked to the source in some predefined tree structure (e.g., as the chain mentioned above), represent a special case of the minimum cost spanning tree model.

It can be shown that the associated cost allocation problem (N, c^T) is concave and hence allocations always exists for which the stand-alone cost principle is satisfied. Characterizations of the core as well as weighted versions of the Lorenz-allocation and the Shapley value related to standard fixed tree networks can be found in Koster et al. (2001). △

Denote by $\mathcal{M}$ the set of all cost allocation problems (N, c^T) arising from minimum cost spanning trees of g^{N^0} (varying the link cost matrix K). As indicated by Example 5.1 cost allocation problems $(N, c^T) \in \mathcal{M}$ have non-empty core as it shall presently be demonstrated.

5.3.1 Cost Allocation for Specific Spanning Trees

Following the spirit of the *incremental principle*, a straightforward way to allocate costs in a specific minimum cost spanning tree T_{N^0} is to charge each agent $i \in N$ the cost of the link incident upon i on the path from the source to i in the graph T_{N^0}, as proposed in Bird (1976). Let

$$0i_1, i_1 i_2, \ldots, i_{h-1} i_h$$

be the (unique) path in T_{N^0} that connects agent i_h to the source making the cost share of agent i_h given by the Bird-allocation

$$x_{i_h}^B(T_{N^0}) = k_{i_{h-1} i_h}. \tag{5.1}$$

Because there may be several minimum cost spanning trees for the same complete graph g^{N^0}, and consequently several different Bird-allocations related to the same link cost matrix K (and cost allocation problem (N, c^T)), this type of cost allocation does not constitute a cost allocation rule (selecting a unique allocation for a given link cost matrix and thereby cost allocation problem) as demonstrated by the following example.

Example 5.2. Consider spanning trees T_{N^0} for a complete graph g^{N^0} with $N^0 = \{0, a, b, c\}$ and associated link costs given by $\{k_{0a} = 2, k_{0b} = 5, k_{0c} = 2, k_{ab} = 1, k_{bc} = 2, k_{ac} = 5\}$. In this case there are three minimum cost spanning trees $T = \{0a, ab, bc\}$, $T' = \{0c, cb, ba\}$ and $T'' = \{0a, 0c, ab\}$ each with a total link cost of 5. The related cost allocation problem (N, c^T) is given by

$$c^T(a) = 2, \ c^T(b) = 5, \ c^T(c) = 2,$$
$$c^T(a, b) = 3, \ c^T(a, c) = c^T(b, c) = 4,$$
$$c^T(a, b, c) = 5.$$

Note that (N, c^T) is balanced but *not* concave. Now, using the Bird-allocation with respect to T and T'' we get cost shares $x^B(T) = x^B(T'') = (2, 1, 2)$ while the Bird-allocation with respect to T' is given by $x^B(T') = (1, 2, 2)$. Incidently, the core of (N, c^T) is the convex hull of the two extreme points as given by the Bird-allocations.   △

It turns out that all Bird-allocations are core allocations:

Proposition 5.1 (Bird 1976; Granot and Huberman 1981). *Let $(N, c^T) \in \mathcal{M}$ be a (minimum cost spanning tree) cost allocation problem then the related Bird-allocation(s) x^B satisfy the stand-alone cost principle, i.e., $x^B \in core(N, c^T)$.*

Proof. Let x^B be a Bird-allocation related to (N, c^T) and consider an arbitrary coalition $S \subseteq N$. Construct a spanning tree T_{N^0} as T_{S^0} adding the links from all $i \in N \setminus S$ to members in S as defined by T_{N^0}. Thus,

$$\sum_{ij \in T_{N^0}} k_{ij} = c^T(S) + \sum_{i \in N \setminus S} x_i^B \geq \sum_{ij \in T_{N^0}} k_{ij} = c^T(N)$$

$$\Rightarrow \quad c^T(S) \geq \sum_{i \in S} x_i^B.$$

□

Consequently the core of a (minimum cost spanning tree) allocation problem is always non-empty. Note, that we may define a Bird cost allocation rule as a convex combination of all Bird-allocations related to a given link cost matrix. By Proposition 5.1, this rule is a core-selection since the core is a convex set.

Following the spirit of the *serial principle*, a straightforward way to allocate costs in a specific minimum cost spanning tree T_{N^0} is to charge each agent $i \in N$ an equal share (among "active" agents in the particular tree involving i) of all link costs prior to i on the particular path connecting i to the source (called "Allocation by Actual Cost" in Claus and Kleitman 1973 and the "Equal Link Split Downstream" rule in Herzog et al. 1997).

This is simple if T_{N^0} is a chain. Letting

$$0i_1, i_1 i_2, \dots, i_{h-1} i_h$$

be the path that connects agent i_h to the source, the cost share associated with the serial principle of agent i_h is given by

$$x_{i_h}^S(T_{N^0}) = \sum_{j=0}^{h-1} \frac{1}{n-j} k_{i_j i_{j+1}}. \tag{5.2}$$

In the general case where agent i_h is part of a tree we need to keep track of the number of agents "downstream" in the tree from every node that is passed on the path from the source to i_h. Let $d(i_z)$ denote the number of agents (nodes) "downstream" in the (sub)tree with source i_z. Then, letting $0i_1, i_1i_2, \ldots, i_{h-1}i_h$ be the path that connects agent i_h to the source, the cost share associated with the serial principle of agent i_h is given by

$$x_{i_h}^S(T_{N^0}) = \sum_{j=0}^{h-1} \frac{1}{d(i_j)} k_{i_j i_{j+1}}. \tag{5.3}$$

Because there may be several minimum cost spanning trees for the same graph T_{N^0}, there may also be several different serial allocations related to the same link cost matrix K (and cost allocation problem (N, c^T)) as demonstrated by the example below.

Example 5.2 (continued). Recall the situation in Example 5.2 with a graph g^{N^0} where $N^0 = \{0, a, b, c\}$ and the associated link costs are given by $\{k_{0a} = 2, k_{0b} = 5, k_{0c} = 2, k_{ab} = 1, k_{bc} = 2, k_{ac} = 5\}$. In this case there are three minimum cost spanning trees $T = \{0a, ab, bc\}$, $T' = \{0c, cb, ba\}$ and $T'' = \{0a, 0c, ab\}$ each with a total link cost of 5. Consider first (the chain) T: Using the serial principle results in the following cost shares,

$x_a^S(T) = 1/3 k_{0a} = 0.67,$

$x_b^S(T) = 1/3 k_{0a} + 1/2 k_{ab} = 0.67 + 0.5 = 1.17,$

$x_c^S(T) = 1/3 k_{0a} + 1/2 k_{ab} + k_{bc} = 0.67 + 0.5 + 2 = 3.17.$

Likewise, considering (the chain) T' we get,

$x_a^S(T) = 1/3 k_{0c} + 1/2 k_{cb} + k_{ba} = 0.67 + 1 + 1 = 2.67,$

$x_b^S(T) = 1/3 k_{0c} + 1/2 k_{cb} = 0.67 + 1 = 1.67,$

$x_c^S(T) = 1/3 k_{0c} = 0.67.$

Finally, considering (the tree) T'' we get,

$x_a^S(T) = 1/2 k_{0a} = 1,$

$x_b^S(T) = 1/2 k_{0a} + k_{ab} = 1 + 1 = 2,$

$x_c^S(T) = k_{0c} = 2.$

Note, that contrary to the Bird-allocations, two of the serial allocations, $x^S(T) = (0.67, 1.17, 3.17)$ and $x^S(T') = (2.67, 1.67, 0.67)$, do not satisfy the stand-alone cost principle since $x_c^S(T) > c^T(c)$ and $x_b^S(T) + x_c^S(T) > c^T(b, c)$ as well as $x_a^S(T') > c^{T'}(a)$ and $x_a^S(T') + x_b^S(T') > c^{T'}(a, b)$. $\qquad \triangle$

As demonstrated by the example above, using the serial principle with respect to minimum cost spanning trees related to arbitrary connected graphs does not necessarily result in core allocations of the related cost allocation problem. However, notice that if we consider a standard fixed tree network (and not a complete graph as above), i.e., if $g = T_{N^0}$, then using the serial allocation, cost shares do not exceed the stand alone cost for any coalition and consequently $x^S(T_{N^0}) \in \text{core}(N, c^T)$.

5.3.2 Characteristics of Cost Allocation Rules

As mentioned, it seems natural to consider cost sharing in a minimum cost spanning tree as a cost allocation problem $(N, c^T) \in \mathcal{M}$, which is uniquely determined by the link cost matrix K. Hence, the cost allocation rules of Chap. 3 all become relevant as candidates for solutions to the allocation problem and further selection of specific rules must rely on the desirability of the characteristics of these rules under given circumstances. Even though there are axiomatic characterizations of the individual rules in Chap. 3 this section will provide further characteristics, which are associated more closely with the specific structure of the spanning tree graphs.

Fix N^0 and let $\mathcal{K}(N^0)$ denote the set of possible link cost matrices. Since, for every link cost matrix $K \in \mathcal{K}(N^0)$, there is a uniquely determined cost allocation problem $(N, c^T) \in \mathcal{M}$ (and for simplicity of notation) we shall consider cost sharing rules ϕ as functions of the link cost matrix K – and not, as in Chap. 3, as functions of the associated cost allocation problem (N, c^T). Hence, let $\phi : \mathcal{K}(N^0) \rightarrow \mathbf{R}^n$, where

$$\sum_{i \in N} \phi_i(K) = \sum_{ij \in T_{N^0}} k_{ij}.$$

When there are no externalities, it can be argued that no agent should subsidize other agents in case the cheapest way to connect all agents to the source is via individual connections (corresponding to the case where the minimum cost spanning tree is a star and $c^T(S) = \sum_{i \in S} c^T(i) = \sum_{i \in S} k_{0i}$ for all $S \subseteq N$). Formally:

- *No Cross Subsidization:* If the minimum cost spanning tree, T_{N^0}, is star then $\phi_i(K) = k_{0i}$ for all $i \in N$.

Notice, that the four allocation rules treated in Chap. 3 all satisfy No Cross Subsidization as do the Bird and Serial allocations.

Moreover, when we consider minimum cost spanning trees that consists of "separate" trees (each connected to the source) the same line of argument would suggest that changing the link cost between any two agents associated with the same tree should not alter that cost shares of agents associated with other trees. To be more precise we need some additional definitions.

A link ij is called *relevant* if $k_{ij} \leq \max\{k_{0i}, k_{0j}\}$. A path from i to j is called relevant if every link on the path is relevant. Hence, for a given link cost matrix K, agents can be partitioned into groups $N = \{N_1, \ldots, N_p\}$ where members of a given group are connected by some relevant path while there are no relevant paths between members of different groups:

- *Group Independence:* Suppose that some partitioning

$$N = \{N_1, \ldots, N_p\}$$

occurs for cost matrix K. Consider another cost matrix K' where $k'_{nm} = k_{nm}$ for all $\{n, m\} \neq \{i, j\}$ where $i, j \in N_l$. Then $\phi_k(K) = \phi_k(K')$ for all $k \in N_t$, and for all $t \neq l$.

Matrices K and K' are identical except (perhaps) for the link cost k_{ij}, and note that when the link cost k_{ij}, for $i, j \in N_l$, changes then perhaps the group N_l is further partitioned, but the remaining groups are unchanged. In terms of the allocation problem the change in link cost may give rise to changes in the cost of coalitions $S \supseteq \{i, j\}$.

Considering the agents $i, j \in N$ for which the link cost is changed, it can also be argued that these agents ought to be affected in the same way, i.e., either they gain or lose the same amount. Formally:

- *Equal Treatment:* Consider two link cost matrices K and K' where $k'_{nm} = k_{nm}$ for all $\{n, m\} \neq \{i, j\}$. Then $\phi_i(K') - \phi_i(K) = \phi_j(K') - \phi_j(K)$.

In fact, these three conditions uniquely characterizes the Shapley value ϕ^{Sh}.

Theorem 5.1. (Kar 2002). *A cost allocation rule ϕ satisfies No Cross Subsidization, Group Independence and Equal Treatment if and only if it is the Shapley value ϕ^{Sh}.*

Proof. (sketch): Following the argument in Kar (2002) we demonstrate that there is a unique rule, which satisfies all three conditions and this will be done by induction on the number of relevant links.

If there are no relevant links the minimum cost spanning tree is a star and by No Cross Subsidization there is a unique solution $\phi_i = k_{0i}$ for all i. Assume that there is a unique solution to all matrices K with at most $(k-1)$ relevant links and consider a matrix K^k with k relevant links.

By contradiction, assume that there exists a solution $\gamma(K^k) \neq \phi(K^k)$. Moreover, assume that going from link cost matrix K^{k-1} to matrix K^k only the link $\{n, m\}$ is made relevant with $n, m \in N_t$ of the related partition with respect to K^k.

By Group Independence $\phi_i(K^k) = \gamma_i(K^k)$ for all $i \in N_l$ where $l \neq t$. For a relevant link in N_t we have by Equal Treatment and the induction hypothesis that

$$\phi_m(K^k) - \phi_n(K^k) = \phi_m(K^{k-1}) - \phi_n(K^{k-1}) = \gamma_m(K^{k-1}) - \gamma_n(K^{k-1})$$
$$= \gamma_m(K^k) - \gamma_n(K^k).$$

Now, since there are relevant links between all agents in N_t we have that

$$\phi_i(K^k) - \gamma_i(K^k) = \phi_j(K^k) - \gamma_j(K^k) \text{ for any } i, j \in N_t.$$

Since $\sum_{i \in N}(\phi_i(K^k) - \gamma_i(K^k)) = 0$ and $\phi_i(K^k) = \gamma_i(K^k)$ for all $i \in N_l$ where $l \neq t$ we get that $\sum_{i \in N_t}(\phi_i(K^k) - \gamma_i(K^k)) = 0$, and since

$$\phi_i(K^k) - \gamma_i(K^k) = \phi_j(K^k) - \gamma_j(K^k) \text{ for any } i, j \in N_t,$$

we have in particular that $\phi_i(K^k) = \gamma_i(K^k)$ for all $i \in N_t$ and consequently that $\phi(K^k) = \gamma(K^k)$, providing the contradiction. It can further be shown that the Shapley value satisfies all three conditions.   □

Remark 5.2. Somewhat related characterizations of the Shapley value are found in Myerson (1977) and Jackson and Wolinsky (1996) in the general context of network games.   △

Another important property satisfied by the Shapley value is monotonicity with respect to changes in the cost structure, as discussed in Chap. 3 (Sect. 3.5). In the present model, monotonicity can be formulated as follows:

- *Cost Monotonicity:* Consider two link cost matrices K and K' where $k_{ij} > k'_{ij}$ for $i, j \in N^0$ and $k'_{nm} = k_{nm}$ for all $\{n, m\} \neq \{i, j\}$. Then $\phi_m(K) \geq \phi_m(K')$ for all $m \in N \cap \{i, j\}$.

As such Cost Monotonicity states that when the link cost between any two nodes in N^0 increases so does the cost share of the agents involved.

Example 5.3. Consider first a network with two agents $N = \{a, b\}$ and link costs given by $k_{0a} = 3$, $k_{0b} = 2$ and $k_{ab} = 1$. Clearly, the minimum cost spanning tree is given by $T = \{0b, ba\}$ with a total link cost of 3. Since there is a unique minimum cost spanning tree in this case there is a unique Bird allocation, i.e., $x^B(T) = (1, 2)$. Now, assume that the link cost k_{0b} increases to 4. Now, the unique minimum cost spanning tree becomes $T' = \{0a, ab\}$ with a total link cost of 4. The unique Bird allocation is given by $x^B(T') = (3, 1)$. Hence, although the link cost k_{0b} increases, agent b is now paying less and consequently the Bird allocation violates Cost Monotonicity.

Allocating costs according to the serial principle (using (5.3)) also violates Cost Monotonicity: Consider a network with five agents $N = \{a, b, c, d, e\}$ and link costs given by $k_{0a} = k_{ab} = k_{0c} = 2$, $k_{cd} = k_{de} = 0$, $k_{eb} = 2.1$ and

$k_{.,.} = \infty$ otherwise. Consequently there is a unique minimum cost spanning tree $T = \{0a, ab, 0c, cd, de\}$ with total link costs 6. Now, according to the serial principle these costs are allocated as $x^S(T) = (1, 3, 0.67, 0.67, 0.67)$. Assume, then that the link cost k_{ab} is increased to ∞. This changes the minimum cost spanning tree, which now becomes

$$T' = \{0a, 0c, cd, de, eb\}$$

with total link cost 6.1. According to the serial principle these costs are allocated as $x^S(T') = (2, 2.6, 0.5, 0.5, 0.5)$ violating Cost Monotonicity for agent b. $\triangle$

Even though the Shapley value satisfies a series of desirable properties it may violate the stand-alone cost principle as discussed in Chap. 3 – also in case of minimum cost spanning trees. In the general case of balanced cost allocation problems there is a trade-off between satisfying the stand-alone cost principle and satisfying Cost Monotonicity as shown in Theorem 3.2. However, since the minimum cost spanning tree allocation problems constitute a strict subset of the balanced allocation problems it is actually possible to find allocation rules that comply with both properties as shown in Dutta and Kar (2004).

For simplicity we restrict attention to the domain of minimum cost spanning tree allocations problems where there is a unique minimum cost spanning tree and no two links have the same link cost (for generalizations, see Dutta and Kar). On this domain we use the following algorithm to define an allocation rule ϕ^{DK}:

Let $A^0 = \{0\}$, $g^0 = \emptyset$ and $t^0 = 0$.

Step 1. Choose the pair $a^1 b^1 = \operatorname{argmin}_{ij \in A^0 \times A^0_c} k_{ij}$, where $A_c = N^0 \setminus A$.

Define $t^1 = \max\{t^0, k_{a^1 b^1}\}$, $A^1 = A^0 \cup \{b^1\}$ and $g^1 = g^0 \cup \{a^1, b^1\}$.

Step h. Choose the pair $a^h b^h = \operatorname{argmin}_{ij \in A^{h-1} \times A^{h-1}_c} k_{ij}$, and define $t^h = \max\{t^{h-1}, k_{a^h b^h}\}$, $A^h = A^{h-1} \cup \{b^h\}$ and $g^h = g^{h-1} \cup \{a^h, b^h\}$ and let $\phi^{DK}_{b^{h-1}} = \min\{t^{h-1}, k_{a^h b^h}\}$.

The algorithm stops at step n with $\phi^{DK}_{b^n} = t^n$.

In Dutta and Kar (2004) it is proved that ϕ^{DK}, as defined above, satisfies Cost Monotonicity as well as the stand-alone cost principle.

Example 5.4. Consider the simple case with three agents where T_{N^0} is a chain, i.e., $T_{N^0} = \{0a, ab, bc\}$. Using the algorithm to determine ϕ^{DK} we get:

Step 1. $a^1 b^1 = 0a$ making $t^1 = k_{0a}$, $A^1 = \{0, a\}$ and $g^1 = \{0a\}$.
Step 2. $a^2 b^2 = ab$ making $t^2 = \max\{k_{0a}, k_{ab}\}$, $A^2 = \{0, a, b\}$, $g^2 = \{0a, ab\}$ and $\phi^{DK}_a = \phi^{DK}_{b^1} = \min\{k_{0a}, k_{ab}\}$.

Step 3. $a^3b^3 = bc$ making $t^3 = \max\{k_{0a}, k_{ab}, k_{bc}\}$, $A^3 = \{0, a, b, c\}$, $g^3 = \{0a, ab, bc\}$ and $\phi_b^{DK} = \phi_{b^2}^{DK} = \min\{\max\{k_{0a}, k_{ab}\}, k_{bc}\}$, and $\phi_c^{DK} = \phi_{b^3}^{DK} = \max\{k_{0a}, k_{ab}, k_{bc}\}$.

In the present case, this rule clearly satisfies the stand-alone cost principle and differs from the Bird allocation (e.g., when $k_{ab} < k_{0a}$). △

Although the allocation rule ϕ^{DK} may seem a bit arbitrary at first sight, Dutta and Kar further demonstrate that this allocation rule can be characterized by a consistency property of the Hart–Mas-Colell type (like the Shapley value, see Sect. 3.6.3) and a weak monotonicity property, which loosely speaking states that no agent is willing to pay more in order to include an agent in the network that will have no follower in the associated minimum cost spanning tree graph.

Remark 5.3. Population Monotonicity is another monotonicity property discussed in Chap. 3, Sect. 3.5. This property is *not* satisfied by Bird allocations. However, as demonstrated in Norde et al. (2004), there exists population monotonic allocation rules for minimum cost spanning tree allocation problems and they provide a specific algorithm to find such a rule. See also Bergantinos and Vidal-Puga (2007). △

Remark 5.4. Other approaches to the definition of allocation rules for minimum cost spanning trees can be taken. For instance, a minimum cost spanning tree problem is called *irreducible* if reducing any link cost reduces the total cost of connecting all agents to the source: Following Bird (1976) let (N, K) be the original problem then its irreducible form $(N, \tilde{K})$ is defined as $\tilde{k}_{ij} = k_{ij}$ for all links $ij \in T_{N^0}$ and for $ij \notin T_{N^0}$ let $\tilde{k}_{ij} = \max k_{zl}$ among the links $zl \in T_{N^0}$ forming a cycle when adding the link ij to T_{N^0}. In Bergantinos and Vidal-Puga (2007) it is suggested to use the Shapley value of the irreducible form when allocating costs of the original minimum cost spanning tree problem. For problems on irreducible form the Shapley value coincides with the average of all incremental (Bird) allocations. It is demonstrated that such a rule satisfies a series of relevant properties including being cost and population monotonic and since it can be shown that the cost allocation problem $(N, \tilde{c}^T)$ associated with the irreducible form $(N, \tilde{K})$ of (N, K) is concave then the Shapley value on $(N, \tilde{K})$ is also a core selection (satisfying the Stand-alone Test). To get an idea of the approach consider the Example 5.5.

In Hougaard et al. (2008) it is noted that allocating costs using the Shapley value on the allocation problems' irreducible form has an alternative interpretation: Pick an unbiased random ordering π of the agents, and construct a spanning tree $\mathcal{T}_\pi$ as follows. Start by connecting the first agent to the source and charging him the corresponding cost; connect next the second agent to either the source or the first agent, whichever is cheaper, and charge him that cost; ...; charge to the t-th agent the cost of the cheapest link to one of its predecessors or the source; and so on (in fact, this is similar to the Prim algorithm, with the crucial difference that in the latter, the t-th agent is not selected at random: instead it is the cheapest way to connect with the $t-1$ first agents and the source). Formally, let Π_N be the set of all orders of N. Given $\pi \in \Pi_N$, let $\mathcal{P}(i, \pi)$ denote the union of the source and the set of agents prior to agent i in the order π, i.e., $\mathcal{P}(i, \pi) = \{0\} \cup \{j \in N | \pi(j) < \pi(i)\}$. Now, for each agent $i \in N$, cost shares are found as

$$\frac{1}{n!} \sum_{\pi \in \Pi_N} \min_{j \in \mathcal{P}(i,\pi)} \{\tilde{k}_{ij}\}.$$

Incidently, note that this way of computing the cost share only relies on information concerning agent i's own link costs (and not the cost of links between other agents). Thus, such a rule can be viewed as a decentralized way to share costs in the sense that every agent can compute their own cost share without knowledge of the other agents link costs. In Hougaard et al. (2008) this gives rise to the definition of a so-called decentralized canonical pricing rule generalized to arbitrary cost matrices (and not just those on irreducible form). It is called a pricing rule since outside the domain of irreducible cost matrices it may violate budget-balance by resulting in a surplus charge. $\triangle$

Example 5.5. Let $N = \{1, 2\}$ and let link cost matrix K associated with the graph g^{N_0} be given by the link costs $k_{01} = k_{02} = 10$ and $k_{12} = 2$. Clearly, the cost structure is symmetric and there are two minimum cost spanning trees given by $T = \{(0, 1), (1, 2)\}$ and $T' = \{(0, 2), (2, 1)\}$ respectively with a total cost of 12. Bird allocations are given by $x^B(T) = (10, 2)$ and $x^B(T') = (2, 10)$ while using the serial rule gives $x^S(T) = (5, 7)$ and $x^S(T') = (7, 5)$. The four rules of Chap. 3 related to the cost allocation problem (N, c^T) all coincide and result in the allocation $x^{Sh} = x^{Nuc} = x^L = x^\tau = (6, 6)$. It seems difficult to argue for other solutions than the equal split $(6, 6)$, which indeed is also the result of using the average of both the incremental and serial principle (the Bird and serial allocations).

Now, assume that the link cost matrix is changed to K' where $k'_{02} = k_{02} + x$, $x > 0$ and $k'_{ij} = k_{ij}$ for $\{i, j\} \neq \{0, 2\}$. In this case, there is only one minimum cost spanning tree $T = \{(0, 1), (1, 2)\}$ with Bird and serial allocation as $x^B(T) = (10, 2)$ and $x^S(T) = (5, 7)$ respectively, while $x^{Sh} = x^{Nuc} = x^L = x^\tau = (6 - x/2, 6 + x/2)$. Hence allocations relating directly to the specific minimum cost spanning tree are unchanged, while the allocation rules related to the cost allocation problem (N, c^T) all change according to the size of x (in particular note that the cost share of agent 1 is negative for $x > 12$). On the one hand, it can be argued that since the minimum cost spanning tree has not been changed neither should the resulting allocation (as when using, e.g., the Bird allocation or average hereof). On the other hand, it can also be argued that since the underlying cost structure of the problem has changed so should the resulting allocation of costs (as when using, e.g., the Shapley value).

Clearly, the problem associated with link cost matrix K is the irreducible form of the problems associated with link cost matrix K'. Hence, using an allocation rule on the former, which is defined as the average of Bird allocations related to the irreducible form yields the allocation $(6, 6)$ for any value of $x > 0$, as suggested in Bergantinos and Vidal-Puga (2007). An argument in favor of such an allocation could be that agent 2, for whom cost are increased as x increases, should not pay less (when $x > 0$) than in the irreducible form (where $x = 0$). It can be shown in general that the average of Bird allocations related to the irreducible form coincides with the Shapley value of the allocation problem associated with the irreducible form.

Arguments against such a way to allocate costs are presented in Bogomolnaia and Moulin (2008): Consider for example a case with ten agents where $k_{0i} = 10$ for all i; $k_{ij} = 1$ for all $i, j \geq 2$ and $k_{1i} = 0$ for all $i \geq 2$. Hence, any minimum cost spanning tree will form a star with agent 1 in the middle and some arbitrary agent connected to the source. Note, that the presence of agent 1 reduces the total cost for the remaining agents from 18 to 10 so it seems natural that agent 1 should be charged less than the other agents, yet using the Shapley value on the irreducible form, the total cost of 10 will be split equally among all ten agents. $\triangle$

5.4 Demand-Based Cost Allocation

Often the formation of networks is closely connected with the presence of externalities, for instance, in case of telecommunication networks. Here, it is no longer obvious that No Cross Subsidization ought to be satisfied since agents benefit from the number of other agents in the network (at least by the number of agents with whom they actually communicate). Thus, the "no externality" assumption underlying the minimum cost spanning tree model is limiting the scope of relevant allocation rules.

Typically, we have no knowledge of the individual agents preferences but the amount of communication (traffic) between them is an available proxy. This proxy can be used to influence the way that connection costs are going to be shared between the agents in the network. Due to the externalities involved it may be in the interest of some agents to share the connection costs of other agents and it is not obvious how this cost sharing must take place.

The same problem is encountered when pricing the traffic itself. For example, think of the Internet: loosely speaking, the relevant agents here consist of two types; consumers and websites. It can be argued that the consumer has to pay for traffic between consumer and website since it is the consumer who requests the traffic and benefits from the information that is obtained from the website. However, it can also be argued that the website has to pay for the traffic since the website is the actual sender of the traffic and benefits from the agent's attention to the site.

Following Henriet and Moulin (1996), this section will present a framework for sharing connection costs based on actual traffic and demonstrate that allocation rules, which combine the idea that agents pay their own connection costs with the idea that agents pay for their communication parters connection cost, can be characterized by a set of intuitively relevant properties.

Assume that agents $N = \{1, \ldots, n\}$ are connected to a source (a central switching machine) in some kind of network, and that only the costs of connecting the agents to the network (in terms of local wires, switching cards, etc.) are relevant, i.e., there are no costs connected with traffic in the network. Let the individual costs of connection be denoted c_i, $i = 1, \ldots, n$ and let $c = (c_1, \ldots, c_n)$ be the cost profile of the network. It is easiest to imagine the network as a star, but c_i can be seen as the costs of connecting i to any kind of existing network. The amount of traffic between two agents i and j in the network is denoted $x_{ij} \geq 0$ and may represent, e.g., number of hours of communication between i and j per month (typically available from the network operator). Let X denote the $n \times n$ traffic matrix where by construction $x_{ij} = x_{ji}$ and $x_{ii} = 0$. Assume that all agents communicate with at least one of the other agents. The pair (c, X) will be called a traffic-based cost allocation problem.

Given a traffic-based cost allocation problem (c, X) a (traffic-based) cost allocation rule ϕ assigns (non-negative) cost shares $\phi_i(c, X)$ to every agent $i = 1, \ldots, n$, under budget-balance, i.e., where $\sum_{i=1}^n \phi_i(c, X) = \sum_{i=1}^n c_i$.

Ignoring the externalities involved a straightforward rule would assign to each agent i his individual cost of connection c_i (as indeed would all rules treated in Sect. 5.3, considering a star-shaped minimum cost spanning tree). Denote by

$$\phi_i^{PC}(c, X) = c_i \qquad (5.4)$$

for all $i = 1, \ldots, n$, the Private Cost rule.

An equally straightforward approach, which takes the amount of traffic in to consideration is to share the total network cost $C = \sum_{i=1}^n c_i$ in proportion to traffic. Denote by

$$\phi_i^{DP}(c, X) = \frac{\sum_j x_{ij}}{\sum_i \sum_j x_{ij}} C \qquad (5.5)$$

for all $i = 1, \ldots, n$, the Demand Proportional rule.

However, the opposite extreme to the Private Cost rule is a rule that allows for full traffic based cross-subsidization between agents in the sense that agent i pays a weighted sum of the connection costs of the agents with whom i communicates and where the weights are determined in proportion to the amount of traffic. Denote by

$$\phi_i^{EC}(c, X) = \sum_j \frac{x_{ij}}{\sum_i x_{ij}} c_j \qquad (5.6)$$

for all $i = 1, \ldots, n$, the External Cost rule.

Note, that using the External Cost rule, cross-subsidization may be significant from agents with low connecting costs (e.g., agents located in urban areas) to agents with high connecting costs (e.g., agents located in rural areas).

Example 5.6. Consider the 3-agent case and assume that agents 1 and 2 have relatively low connection costs ($c_1 = c_2 = 1$) whereas agent 3 has relatively high connection costs ($c_3 = 10$). Assume furthermore that agents 1 and 2 almost never communicate with agent 3 ($x_{13} = x_{23} = 1$) whereas the traffic is significant between themselves ($x_{12} = x_{21} = 20$). Now, using the External cost rule, agents 1 and 2 are forced to share the high connection cost of agent 3, even though the externalities from having agent 3 included in the network are negligible ($\phi_1^{EC}(c, X) = \phi_2^{EC}(c, X) = 5.95$). Agent 3, on the other hand, joins the network almost for free ($\phi_3^{EC}(c, X) = 0.095$). $\triangle$

Thus, it seems that some kind of combination between the Private Cost rule and the External Cost rule could be more appropriate. In fact, as demonstrated in Henriet and Moulin (1996), any convex combination of these two rules can be characterized by the following conditions.

First, in order to sustain the network structure and avoid "double cabling" it must not be beneficial for any coalition to form their own private network (within the network structure) to provide traffic between themselves. In particular:

- *Sustainability:* Consider two traffic matrices X and X' where $x_{ij} \neq x'_{ij}$ and $x_{nm} = x'_{nm}$ otherwise. Then for all coalitions $S \supseteq \{i, j\}$,

$$\sum_{l \in S} \phi_l(c, X) - \sum_{l \in S} \phi_l(c, X') \leq c_i + c_j.$$

Example 5.7. Consider the example above where $c_1 = c_2 = 1$ and $c_3 = 10$ with traffic matrix $x_{12} = x_{21} = 20$, $x_{13} = x_{31} = x_{23} = x_{32} = 1$. Using the Demand Proportional rule to the share total costs $C = 12$, we get cost shares,

$$\phi_1^{DP}(c, X) = \phi_2^{DP}(c, X) = \frac{21}{44}12 = 5.73, \quad \phi_3^{DP}(c, X) = \frac{2}{44}12 = 0.54.$$

Clearly, agents 1 and 2 may find this situation unfair so assume that they form their own network at costs $c_1 + c_2 = 2$ to provide for their own traffic and join the network with agent 3, but now with traffic $x'_{12} = x'_{21} = 0$. Using ϕ^{DP} with respect to the new traffic matrix X' we now get,

$$\phi_1^{DP}(c, X) = \phi_2^{DP}(c, X) = \frac{1}{4}12 = 3, \quad \phi_3^{DP}(c, X) = \frac{2}{4}12 = 6.$$

Thus, the coalition consisting of agents 1 and 2 has gained $11.46 - 6 = 5.46$ by forming their own network, which is more than the cost of their own connection $c_1 + c_2 = 2$. Consequently the Demand Proportional rule does *not* satisfy Sustainability.

Now, considering the External Cost rule, this manipulation by agent 1 and 2 would only lead to a cost saving of 1.90, which is smaller then the cost of connection (which is 2) so it does not pay to form their own network.   △

It is obvious that the Private Cost rule satisfies Sustainability in general. So consider the External Cost rule: By changing x_{ij} with $\Delta > 0$ all agents except for i and j will be better off, and since the total net change in costs is zero, i and j will be worse off. The question therefore is whether i and j can decrease x_{ij} ($\Delta < 0$) and thereby push more costs than $c_i + c_j$ to the complement. Now, the total cost change of the complement is

$$(\frac{x^i_{N\setminus\{i,j\}}}{x^i_N} - \frac{x^i_{N\setminus\{i,j\}}}{\Delta + x^i_N})c_i + (\frac{x^j_{N\setminus\{i,j\}}}{x^j_N} - \frac{x^j_{N\setminus\{i,j\}}}{\Delta + x^j_N})c_j,$$

(where $x^s_S = \sum_{k \in S} x_{sk}$), which is smaller than $c_i + c_j$ for $\Delta < 0$ and consequently the External Cost rule satisfies Sustainability in general.

In the same spirit as Sustainability it can be argued that it should not be profitable to a coalition containing agents i and j to form their own connection (at costs $c_i + c_j$) and transfer traffic between i and a third agent k outside the coalition via j (which is possible in a communications network even without j's consent):

- *No Transit:* Consider a given traffic matrix X and let X' be constructed from X by transferring an amount of traffic $\gamma \geq 0$ from $\{i, k\}$ via j, i.e., $x'_{ik} = x_{ik} - \gamma$, $x'_{ij} = x_{ij} + \gamma$ and $x'_{jk} = x_{jk} + \gamma$. Then for all $S \supseteq \{i, j\}$ and $k \notin S$,
$$\sum_{l \in S} \phi_l(c, X) - \sum_{l \in S} \phi_l(c, X') \leq c_i + c_j.$$

No Transit is satisfied by both the Private Cost and the External Cost rule, but not the Demand Proportional rule.

Furthermore, we have standard requirements of Additivity in cost and Unit Invariance in the measurement of traffic (satisfied by all three rules, ϕ^{PC}, ϕ^{EC} and ϕ^{DP}):

- *Additivity:* Consider two different cost profiles c and c', then for all traffic matrices X,
$$\phi(c + c', X) = \phi(c, X) + \phi(c', X).$$

- *Unit Invariance:* For all $\alpha > 0$ and all problems (c, X),
$$\phi(c, \alpha X) = \phi(c, X).$$

It can be shown that any rule satisfying the above four requirements must be a combination of the Private Cost and the External Cost rule. Formally,

Theorem 5.2 (Henriet and Moulin 1996). *Let* $|N| \geq 4$. *A traffic-based cost allocation rule* ϕ *satisfies Sustainability, No Transit, Additivity and Unit Invariance if and only if, for each* $j \in N$ *that there is a number,* $\lambda_j \in [0,1]$, *such that*

$$\phi_i(c, X) = (1 - \lambda_i)c_i + \sum_{k \neq i} \lambda_k \frac{x_{ik}}{\sum_i x_{ik}} c_k,$$

for all $i \in N$.

A standard result from the theory of functional equations can be used to show that Additivity implies linearity of the allocation rule (i.e., $\phi_i(c, X) = \sum_{j \in N} \alpha_j^i(X)c_j$ where $\alpha_j^i \geq 0$ and $\sum_{i \in N} \alpha_j^i(X) = 1$). Now, Sustainability and No Transit is used to give further structure on the weights α_j^i. For the complete proof, see Henriet and Moulin.

5.5 Efficient Network Structure

Now assume more generally that the particular way in which a relationship between a given set of agents is structured influences the value of that relationship. For example, in case the structure itself influences the magnitude of the network externality or matters for the profitability and power of the group. So each potential network has a value and a natural question becomes how this value is going to be allocated among the agents in the group, in particular taking into account that the allocation rule itself may influence the structure of the network since it influences the agents incentives to form links with other agents.

Although the literature on this topic is relatively new it is already quite substantial. Jackson (2008) offers a recent survey. A central theme is the tension between stability and efficiency of networks, as briefly considered in example (3) of the Introduction.

5.5.1 The Model

Fix a set $N = \{1, \ldots, n\}$ of agents. For any graph $g \in G$, let the value of g be given by a function $v : G \to \mathbf{R}$ (with $v = 0$ for the completely disconnected graph). Let V denote the set of all such value functions. The value may, for instance, be thought of as the total amount of traffic (communication) in the network or as any kind of total surplus (or cost) obtained by connecting the agents as indicated by the particular structure of the graph.

Let $Z(g)$ be the set of components of g. A value function is said to be *component additive* if $v(g) = \sum_{g' \in Z(g)} v(g')$. Note, that when v is component additive there are no externalities between components in the network.

A graph $g \in G$ is said to be *strongly efficient* if it has maximal value, i.e., if $v(g) \geq v(g')$ for all $g' \in G$. Note, that when value is transferable between agents this is equivalent to Pareto-optimality.

To allocate the value v among the individual agents in N we define a *value allocation rule* $\psi : G \times V \to \mathbf{R}^n$ where

$$\sum_{i \in N} \psi_i(g, v) = v(g).$$

Consider a permutation $\pi \in \Pi$. Let $g^\pi = \{ij | i = \pi(k), j = \pi(l), \ kl \in g\}$ and let $v^\pi(g^\pi) = v(g)$. A value allocation rule ψ is called *anonymous* if, for any permutation $\pi \in \Pi$ that $\psi_{\pi(i)}(g^\pi, v^\pi) = \psi_i(g, v)$ for all $i \in N$.

Moreover, the rule ψ is said to be *component balanced* if $\sum_{i \in H(g')} \psi_i(g, v) = v(g')$ for every g and $g' \in Z(g)$ and component additive value function v. In other words, if a rule is component balanced, the value of any component (for which there is no connection to the other agents in N) can only the shared between agents of the component and not with any outsiders. Hence, no component has the incentive block the network structure and form their own separate network knowing that they can then share a larger value. Although, at first glance this seems quite reasonable, we shall see in Theorem 5.3, that it turns out to play a significant role in the tension between efficiency and stability.

A graph is said to be pairwise stable if no two agents in the network both want to add a link and if no two agents outside the network can agree on adding their link to the network. Formally, the graph g is *pairwise stable* if:

1. For all $ij \in g$, $\psi_i(g, v) \geq \psi_i(g - ij, v)$ and $\psi_j(g, v) \geq \psi_j(g - ij, v)$.
2. For all $ij \notin g$, if $\psi_i(g, v) < \psi_i(g + ij, v)$ then $\psi_j(g, v) > \psi_j(g + ij, v)$.

Note, that this notion of stability only considers deviations one link at a time and only by 2-agent coalitions as illustrated by the example below.

Example 5.8. Let $N = \{1, 2, 3, 4, 5\}$ and consider the graph $g = \{12, 13, 23\} \subset g^N$. In order to check whether g is pairwise stable for some allocation rule ϕ we first have to check whether both agent 1 and 2 are weakly better off in g than in the graph $g - \{1, 2\} = \{13, 23\}$. We then have to check whether both agents 1 and 3 are weakly better off in g than in the graph $g - \{1, 3\} = \{12, 23\}$, and we then have to check whether both agents 2 and 3 are weakly better off in g than in the graph $g - \{2, 3\} = \{12, 13\}$. If this is the case, we finally have to check whether adding a link between agents 4 and 5 (i.e., considering the graph $g + \{4, 5\} = \{12, 13, 23, 45\}$) makes one of these agents strictly worse off whenever the other agent is strictly better off compared to g. If this is also the case we then conclude that g is pairwise stable.   △

Finally, note that although this model closely resembles the model from cooperative game theory (like the model in Chap. 3) then it is in some sense a richer model: In a cooperative game there is a value associated with each coalition of agents in N while in the present model there may be many different values associated with the same coalition of agents depending on the particular network that they are forming.

5.5.2 Stability and Efficiency

In the presence of various forms of network externalities it is easy to imagine situations where efficient networks are not necessarily (pairwise) stable but it turns out that it is, in fact, impossible to find an anonymous and component balanced allocation rule that ensures efficiency and stability.

Theorem 5.3 (Jackson and Wolinsky 1996). *Let $|N| \geq 3$. There does not exist an anonymous and component balanced allocation rule ψ such that for each value function v at least one strongly efficient graph is pairwise stable.*

Proof. Following the argument in Jackson and Wolinsky we consider the 3-agent case $N = \{i, j, k\}$, where v is given such that for all i, j, k, $v(ij) = v(ij, jk, ik) = 1$ and $v(ij, jk) = 1 + \epsilon$. Consequently networks of the form $g = \{ij, jk\}$ are strongly efficient. By anonymity and component balance we get that, $\psi_i(\{ij\}, v) = 0.5$ and $\psi_i(\{ij, jk, ik\}, v) = \psi_k(\{ij, jk, ik\}, v) = 0.33$. Now, pairwise stability of the strongly efficient graph requires that $\psi_j(\{ij, jk\}, v) \geq \psi_j(\{ij\}, v) = 0.5$ implying that

$$\psi_i(\{ij, jk\}, v) = \psi_k(\{ij, jk\}, v) \leq 0.25 + 0.5\epsilon.$$

But this contradicts pairwise stability since (for sufficiently small ϵ) i and k would both gain from forming a link (obtaining 0.33). For the cases $n > 3$, assign $v(g) = 0$ to any g involving agents other than i, j and k. □

There are many anonymous and component balanced allocation rules, for instance, the Shapley (Myerson) value with respect to (g, v). Moreover, as demonstrated in Jackson and Wolinsky, it is easy to find anonymous and component balanced allocation rules for which there always exists a pairwise stable graph. Hence, the tension between stability and efficiency is real in the general case. However, efficiency and stability can be reconciled for certain classes of value functions or if conditions on the allocation rule are relaxed. Consider the following example.

Example 5.9. Consider 3-agent problems $N = \{i, j, k\}$, and let $v_{ij} > 0$ be the value of the link ij (with $v_{ii} = 0$). Now, define the value function v as the simple sum of link values in g', i.e.,

$$\tilde{v}(g') = \sum_{ij \in g'} v_{ij}.$$

Clearly, only the full graph $g = \{ij, jk, ik\}$ is strongly efficient. Considering the Shapley (Myerson) value, which is anonymous and component balanced, we get the allocation,

$$\psi_i^{Sh}(g, \tilde{v}) = 0.5(v_{ij} + v_{ik})$$

$$\psi_j^{Sh}(g, \tilde{v}) = 0.5(v_{ij} + v_{jk})$$

$$\psi_k^{Sh}(g, \tilde{v}) = 0.5(v_{ik} + v_{jk})$$

To check whether g is pairwise stable we have to check whether ij are better off in $g' = \{ik, jk\}$ than in g, whether ik is better off in $g'' = \{ij, jk\}$ than in g and whether jk is better off in $g''' = \{ij, ik\}$ than in g. Since, $\tilde{v}_{ij} = 0$ in g', $\tilde{v}_{ik} = 0$ in g'' and $\tilde{v}_{jk} = 0$ in g''' it is clear that no pair is better off when using the Shapley (Myerson) value. In case of value function $\tilde{v}$ we therefore have an example of an allocation rule (the Shapley (Myerson) value) for which the strongly efficient graph g is pairwise stable. $\triangle$

Dutta and Mutuswami (1997) reconsider the tension between efficiency and stability. They suggest to adopt an implementation approach and define a notion of *strong stability* as networks that are formed in a strong Nash equilibrium of an associated network formation game defined as follows:

For each agent i the strategy set S_i consists of the set of agents j with whom i wants to form a link.

Each strategy vector $s \in \Pi_{i \in N} S_i$ gives rise to a unique network $g(s)$ where a link between i and j forms if and only if both agents want to form this link.

The pay-offs to each agent (given s) are given by the allocation rule ψ with respect to the network $g(s)$.

Comparing with the notion of pairwise stability; if a network g is strongly stable then it is also pairwise stable since pairwise stability can be seen as restricting deviating coalitions to 2-agent coalitions and a deviation can consist of severing just one existing link or forming one additional link.

Now, arguing that we should only care for anonymity for networks which are strongly stable (as these are results of the network formation game) the following result is obtained.

Theorem 5.4 (Dutta and Mutuswami 1997). *Let $|N| \geq 3$. There exists a component balanced allocation rule ψ, which is anonymous on the set of strongly stable networks such that for every value function v (assigning strictly positive values to all networks that are not totally disconnected) the set of strongly stable networks is non-empty and contained in the set of strongly efficient graphs.*

For details of the proof see Dutta and Mutuswami (1997) who construct an allocation rule (satisfying the relevant properties) that induces a strongly stable network. Moreover, it is demonstrated that a network cannot be strongly efficient unless it is strongly stable.

5.5.3 Allocation Rules Respecting Network Structure

Although many of the allocation rules that has been analysed so far easily extends to the present framework as, for example, the Shapley (Myerson) value used in Example 5.9, the richness of the network model (with values related to all different graphs) seems to call for rules, which take the specific underlying network structures into account. It can be demonstrated that the Shapley (Myerson) value has problems in this respect.

Example 5.10. Consider, as in Jackson (2005), two 3-agent problems (g, v) and $(g, \bar{v})$ where $v(\{12\}) = v(\{23\}) = v(\{12, 23\}) = 1$ and $v(g) = 0$ otherwise, while $\bar{v}(g) = 1$ for all non-empty graphs. As it appears, agent 2 plays a crucial role in the problem (g, v) being the only person with whom agent 1 and 3 are able to generate any value, while agent 2 plays no particular role in the problem $(g, \bar{v})$ where all agents are symmetric. Hence, it seems that a suitable allocation rules should treat these two problems differently. However, using the Shapley (Myerson) value, e.g., with respect to the graph $\{12, 23\}$, we get that

$$\psi^{Sh}(\{12, 23\}, v) = \psi^{Sh}(\{12, 23\}, \bar{v}) = (\frac{1}{6}, \frac{2}{3}, \frac{1}{6}).$$

Notice that compared to the cooperative game model used in Chap. 3, the (grand) coalition $\{1, 2, 3\}$ can be represented by four different network structures connecting the three agents, and consequently four different values, in the present model.   △

As suggested in Jackson (2005), one way to extend the allocation rules of Chap. 3 to the present network model ensuring a certain degree of flexibility with respect to the specific network structure, could be to represent the worth (or cost) of each coalition as the worth of the best (cheapest) network they are able to form. In many ways this seems a rather natural choice since coalitions should have strong incentives to form efficient networks.

Let $v^{Mono}(g) = \max_{g' \subset g} v(g')$ be the monotonic cover of v. Then for any allocation rule ϕ of Chap. 3 (like the Shapley value, the Nucleolus, etc.) we can define its related network flexible extension as

$$\psi^{\phi}(g, v) = \frac{v(g)}{v^{Mono}(g^N)} \phi(v^{Mono}). \tag{5.7}$$

Notice that $v(g)/v^{Mono}(g^N) = 1$ if g is efficient. Hence, for efficient networks the network flexible rule is just the chosen allocation rule ϕ used with respect to the monotonic cover of v. Moreover, for inefficient networks the allocation is simply a rescaled version of the allocation for the efficient network. Clearly, this part of the definition is somewhat *ad hoc* and could be made differently. Proportionality does not seem to be the unique natural way to extend allocation rules to inefficient networks.

Example 5.10 (continued). If, for example, ϕ is the Shapley value the network flexible allocation rule $\psi^{\phi^{Sh}}$ clearly differs from the Shapley (Myerson) value used in Example 5.10. Consider the value functions v and $\bar{v}$ of Example 5.10 again. Using the network flexible allocation rule with respect to the Shapley value we get,

$$\psi^{\phi^{Sh}}(\{12, 23\}, v) = (\frac{1}{6}, \frac{2}{3}, \frac{1}{6})$$

and

$$\psi^{\phi^{Sh}}(\{12, 23\}, \bar{v}) = (\frac{1}{3}, \frac{1}{3}, \frac{1}{3})$$

in contrast to the direct use of the Shapley (Myerson) value yielding the same result in both cases. $\triangle$

5.6 Comments

There are several ways to extend the minimum costs spanning tree model. For example, there may be several agents for each node in the network as in Herzog et al. (1997) or some nodes may be public like in the general Steiner tree model. Steiner trees are not unusual in practice. Imagine, for example, that the supplier (the source) build a "back-bone" network to which agents have individual connections like in the case of cable-TV or the Internet. The back-bone is the public part of the network with public nodes, which several agents utilize before "reaching" their individual connections. Such Steiner trees are generally more difficult to handle in terms of allocating costs. For example, it can be shown that there does not exist a cost allocation rule satisfying the Stand-alone Test, see Megiddo (1978).

But, there may also be uncertainty about link costs. For instance, in telecommunication networks routing delays on links (interpreted as link costs) are uncertain as they depend on the traffic in the network. Hence, such link costs are typically represented by intervals instead of real numbers as in the original MCST-model. Handling interval costs becomes somewhat complicated since its no longer straightforward to define the efficient (or cost minimizing) spanning tree. One way to redefine an optimality criterion is to use the notion of relative robustness: A relatively robust spanning tree is a spanning tree where the total cost minimizes the maximum deviation from the cost minimizing spanning tree over all realisations of link costs (where each realisation form a "traditional" MCST with link costs as real numbers chosen from the cost intervals for each link), see, e.g., Montemanni (2006). Another approach to modeling uncertain link costs is found in Suijs (2003). Here link costs are considered as consisting of two parts; construction and maintenance costs. While the first part can be argued to be deterministic the latter part is typically random and will be closely connected to the networks reliability. Using the framework of stochastic cooperative games, mentioned in Sect. 3.7, agents are assumed to be expected utility maximizers with constant absolute risk aversion and a two-stage Bird allocation rule is introduced to allocate the random costs. Loosely speaking, the first stage allocates the random cost as usual following the Bird rule. In the second stage agents can then redistribute these costs since Pareto improvements may be obtained from reshuffling the risks involved through mutual insurance. It turns out that such opportunities to insure risks results in (two-stage Bird) allocations that satisfies the stand-alone cost principle.

As mentioned above, Hougaard et al. (2008) introduce the notion of a decentralized pricing rule, which can be seen as an upper bound on agents payment based solely on the agents' own connection costs. A particular rule, called the canonical pricing rule, is introduced and characterized as the smallest among those which improves on the stand-alone bound and are either superadditive or piecewise-linear in connection costs.

Finally, we have only considered models where the set of agents is given and connections only differ in terms of costs or communication, but typically in practical situations (like in the case of the Internet) connections may differ in type (capacity) and the set of users (agents) is constantly changing. The point is that the presence of network externalities may influence the optimal structure of the network and this may again influence the way that costs should be allocated, but this issue seems to remain an open problem since few (if any) studies have been concerned with this.

5.7 Summary

This chapter has considered three different network scenarios: The first concerns a group of users who connects to a common supplier in the least costly way. There are no externalities in the network so the problem can be represented solely by the associated link costs. A relevant cost allocation rule therefore only takes these link costs into account. The second scenario concerns the case where there are network externalities and a proxy for these are given by a "communication" matrix. Meanwhile, the cost structure is made as simple as possible by assuming that every agent is characterized by an individual connection cost to the entire network as such. Total costs in the network (i.e., the sum of individual connection costs) are then allocated by a rule that takes the profile of individual connection costs and/or the "communication" matrix into account. Finally, the third scenario concerns general networks related to a given group of agents where the network itself has a value depending on the particular way that agents are connected. Common for all three scenarios is that the set of agents is exogenously determined and costs (or values) are certain.

In the first scenario (concerning the minimum cost spanning tree model) several allocation rules were studied and it seems that most of the well-known allocation rules have their strengths and weaknesses. Recently it has been suggested to use the Shapley value on the irreducible form of the allocation problem since such a rule satisfies a number of desirable properties, but a serious drawback of this rule seems to be the rigidity towards changes in the stand-alone costs of agents.

In the second scenario (concerning the demand-based allocation model) it was shown that a natural family of allocation rules consists of combinations of the two extreme solutions, i.e., the Private Cost rule (where each agent pays his own connection cost – thereby ignoring the externalities involved) and the External Cost rule (where each agent pays a weighted average of all the other agents connection costs – thereby allowing for full cross-subsidization between agents).

Finally, (concerning the general model of social networks) it was shown in Sect. 5.1 (3) that it is easy to imagine situations where agents are prevented from enjoying the positive network externalities due to lack of reallocation possibilities. However, it can be demonstrated that even if we use allocation rules to make such reallocations we still can not guarantee stability and optimal size of the network at the same time for arbitrary network value functions.

References

Bird CG (1976) On cost allocation for a spanning tree: a game theoretic approach. Networks 6:335–350.

Bergantinos G, Vidal-Puga JJ (2007) A fair rule in minimum cost spanning tree problems. J Econ Theory 137:326–352.

Bogomolnaia A, Moulin H (2008) Sharing the cost of a minimal cost spanning tree: beyond the Folk solution (Manus).

Claus A, Kleitman DJ (1973) Cost allocation for a spanning tree. Networks 3:289–304.

Dutta B, Kar A (2004) Cost monotonicity, consistency and minimum cost spanning tree games. Games Econ Behav 48:223–248.

Dutta B, Mutuswami S (1997) Stable networks. J Econ Theory 76:322–344.

Granot D, Huberman G (1981) Minimum cost spanning tree games. Math Programming 21:1–18.

Henriet D, Moulin H (1996) Traffic-based cost allocation in a network. RAND J Econ 27:332–345.

Herzog S, Shenker S, Estrin D (1997) Sharing multicast costs. In McKnight, Bailey (eds) Internet economics. MIT, Cambridge, MA.

Hougaard JL, Moulin H, Østerdal LP (2008) Decentralized pricing in minimum cost spanning trees. Econ Theory, (forthcoming).

Jackson MO (2005) Allocation rules for network games. Games Econ Behav 51:128–154.

Jackson MO (2008) Social and economic networks. Princeton University Press, Princeton.

Jackson MO, Wolinsky A (1996) A strategic model of social and economic networks. J Econ Theory 71:44–74.

Kar A (2002) Axiomatization of the Shapley value on minimum cost spanning tree games. Games Econ Behav 38:265–277.

Koster M, Molina E, Sprumont Y, Tijs S (2001) Sharing the cost of a network: core and core allocations. Int J Game Theory 30:567–599.

Kruskal JB (1956) On the shortest spanning subtree of a graph and the traveling salesman problem. Proc Am Math Soc 7:48–50.

Magnanti TL, Wolsey LA (1995) Optimal trees. In: Ball et al. (eds) Handbook in OR and MS. North-Holland, Amsterdam.

Megiddo N (1978) Cost allocation for Steiner trees. Networks 8:1–6.

Montemanni R (2006) A Benders decomposition approach for the robust spanning tree problem with interval data. Eur J Oper Res 174:1479–1490.

Myerson R (1977) Graphs and cooperation in games. Math Oper Res 2:225–229.

Newman MEJ (2003) The structure and function of complex networks. Soc Ind Appl Math 45:167–256.

Norde H, Moretti S, Tijs S (2004) Minimum cost spanning tree games and population monotonic allocation schemes. Eur J Oper Res 154:84–97.

Prim RC (1957) Shortest connection networks and some generalizations. Bell Syst Tech J 36:1389–1401.

Suijs J (2003) Cost allocation in spanning network enterprises with stochastic connection costs. Games Econ Behav 42:156–171.

Index

Breinigsville, PA USA
17 May 2010
238083BV00005B/2/P